Prisoner No. 100

Prisoner No. 100

An Account of My Nights and Days
in an Indian Prison

ANJUM ZAMARUD HABIB

Translated from the original Urdu by
Sahba Husain

zubaan

ZUBAAN
an imprint of Kali for Women
128b Shahpur Jat,1st floor
New Delhi 110 049
Email: zubaan@gmail.com
Website: www.zubaanbooks.com

First published by Zubaan, 2011
Copyright © Anjum Zamarud Habib, 2011

10 9 8 7 6 5 4 3 2 1

ISBN: 978 93 85932 18 2

Zubaan is an independent feminist publishing house based in New Delhi, India, with a strong academic and general list. It was set up as an imprint of the well known feminist house Kali for Women and carries forward Kali´s tradition of publishing world quality books to high editiorial and production standards. "Zubaan" means tongue, voice, language, speech in Hindustani. Zubaan is a non-profit publisher, working in the areas of the humanities social sciences, as well as in fiction, general non-fiction, and books for young adults that celebrate difference, diversity and equality, especially for and about the children of India and South Asia under its imprint Young Zubaan.

Typeset by Jojy Philip, New Delhi, 110 015
Printed at Repro Knowledgecast Limited, Thane

Dedicated

to those prisoners who do not lose hope despite
extreme torture and humiliation;

and those who wait tirelessly for the release of their
loved ones from prison;

and to my mother, Boba, who lost her sight with the tears she
shed for me during my incarceration and who did not, sadly,
live to see this book.

And in memory of martyr Sajjad Ahmed aka Waki who was
burnt alive by Indian soldiers while in custody.

Translator's Note

SAHBA HUSAIN

The first day of April is known and celebrated as fool's day when friends and family play pranks on each other. However, when I checked my mail in the early hours of April 1st, one email caught my attention; it was from Anjum Zamarud Habib who was communicating with me after a gap of more than five years. This is what she wrote:

After a long period I am talking to you through email. You know I was falsely implicated in POTA [Prevention of Terrorism Act] and was behind bars in Tihar central jail for five long years. I was totally cut off from the outside world. My imprisonment was the result of a conspiracy. Recently I have been released and felt the need for getting back in touch with my well wishers. Wishing you peace and will contact you again.

Do reply

Regards,

Anjum Zamarud Habib

I was relieved and overjoyed at the news of her release even as I wondered if this too was a prank. I wrote back to her immediately and also contacted friends in Kashmir and learnt that it was indeed true: Anjum had been released from Tihar jail in December 2007. She had completed the five year jail term of rigorous imprisonment after she was arrested on 6 February 2003 and convicted by the POTA trial court in Delhi.

I travelled to Srinagar the following week to meet her. All the while, images of her arrest – I had watched these on television some five years ago – kept running through my mind:

Anjum being paraded in front of the media, her hands held tight by policewomen on either side of her, a ring of policemen surrounding them. I remember her trying to utter a few words to assert her innocence but she was not allowed to say anything; in fact she was slapped in front of the media and her mouth was shut and gagged by a woman police sub-inspector. She looked dazed and dishevelled – I had never seen her look like that earlier. I had always known her as someone who dressed well, walked firmly and spoke her mind fearlessly. I was shell-shocked, frozen in my chair in front of the television. Wasn't it just a week earlier that we had met in my house when she told me, over a cup of tea, that she was here in Delhi to organize her travel to the US, Thailand and Pakistan for seminars that she had been invited to? She had brought with her several files that contained details of the work she had undertaken on behalf of Muslim Khawateen Markaz (MKM), the organization that she headed. She had with her documentation of the survey that she'd undertaken on the status of widows and orphans in Kashmir and several newspaper clippings relating to that. We discussed that afternoon how she and MKM could release the findings of the survey and how we could move forward in this endeavour. After reading her email, I remember how I rushed to pull out all those files that she had left behind with me to read – she'd wanted me to get back to her on how to take forward the results of the survey. I also began to reflect upon and recollect the many occasions when I had met Anjum in public meetings, protest demonstrations and seminars in Kashmir and elsewhere. She not only contributed with sharp political insights and comments but had also sung songs that were apt for the occasion and perhaps reflected her own perception as a Kashmiri who resisted 'Indian occupation of our watan'. One song that stood out with its melody and lyrics at a seminar was: '*chal udh ja re panchi ke ab yeh des hua begana*' (Fly away oh bird as this land has now become alien).

Her arrest under POTA in 2003 and her subsequent 'confession' in the trial court created a political furore in the country with direct links being made between the Pakistan High

Commission (PHC) and the separatist leadership of the Hurriyat Conference of which she was a member in her capacity as the chairperson of Muslim Khawateen Markaz. The IB (Intelligence Bureau) and the Special Cell of Delhi Police claimed that she was a 'courier' as, at the time of her arrest, she was found with cash (Rs 3 lakhs or so) that she was said to have received from the Deputy High Commissioner of Pakistan for the Hurriyat (separatists) in Jammu and Kashmir. It was also claimed that her diary contained names and contact details of some 'militant organizations'. In a dramatic development following her arrest and appearance in the trial court, the GoI asked the Deputy High Commissioner of Pakistan (Jaleel Abbas Geelani) to leave the country within 24 hours. This led the Pakistan government to retaliate and send back Indian diplomats from the Indian High Commission in Pakistan and relations between the two countries got further strained. Less than two years prior to this, the two countries had reached a near-war situation with massive troop deployment on either side of the border following the attack on the Indian Parliament in December 2001. Those arrested/convicted belonged to Kashmir. After her own arrest and conviction, much of the electronic and print media portrayed Anjum as a dangerous Kashmiri woman terrorist (aatankwadi) and a traitor (deshdrohi) to the country.

According to Anjum's elder sister Zarina Habib, Professor Abdul Ghani Bhat (who was then chairperson of the Hurriyat Conference) had promised the family that a lawyer would be appointed to represent Anjum but he later reneged on his promise. Even though his own name had appeared in the case, he did not visit the court even once. Two months later, a police team arrived in Srinagar to investigate the case and in the course of the investigation they also met and questioned him at length. His statement was carried in local newspapers the following day: he claimed that he did not know Anjum and that she was not a member of the Hurriyat! This was no less than a betrayal for Anjum's family and a serious setback for her case. Concerned that Anjum was languishing in jail in Delhi, her mother and sisters continued to visit the Hurriyat office to meet the leadership and impress upon them the urgent need to intervene in the matter and secure her release. Despite this, when a Hurriyat delegation later met the then Home Minister, LK Advani, and appealed for the release of some Kashmiri prisoners in Delhi jails, Anjum's name did not appear in their list. However, Shabbir Ahmed Dar (who was arrested along with Anjum) was released soon after due to the Hurriyat's intervention. Anjum, was however implicated in a high profile case.

This incident deeply wounded us in the family and shook our bearings. But we had to be courageous. We walked the hot, dusty streets of Delhi innumerable times, year after year, visiting the courts (court-kachehri), visiting her in jail. Her elder brother and nephew worked tirelessly for her release. The latter found employment in a private company in Delhi and used the salary mainly to visit her and for every-day legal expenses during the hearing of the case. He lived for five years in a small flat in the old city of Delhi until her release.

I've known Anjum since 2000 when I began my field work in Kashmir for a research project I had undertaken to study the impact of political conflict/violence on the everyday life of women, both within and outside their homes, and to understand the social/economic/political transformation that a prolonged conflict of this nature brought about in their lives. Also, how ordinary lives had been touched and altered by this extraordinary situation of violence, death, destruction and resistance. I first met her at a large public meeting where I introduced myself and sought time to meet again. That was the beginning of an enduring friendship.

But I had not kept up my end of the friendship. I am ashamed to say that I never once visited her when she was in prison. And, until we came together to work on this book, she carried the hurt of this absence and I its guilt. Why had I not visited her even once during her long incarceration right here in Asia's biggest jail in Delhi? Was I afraid? Of what, whom? Was it about being associated with her in the past? Was it about being afraid to confront another heartrending situation involving a Kashmiri woman that I've known and admired? Was I afraid of being implicated in the case in any manner? She had my phone numbers and email IDs in her diary that was now in the possession of the Special Cell of Delhi Police. Should I destroy the files she had left with me? Should I hide them? Why was I so afraid?

I continued to search for answers until I met Anjum in Srinagar after her release. She greeted me warmly at her sister's house where she was staying then, with a hug that was laced with silence. I searched for a smile of recognition in her vacant eyes that were beginning to moisten. I heard her feeble voice that was at once distant and hurt: why didn't you come to see me in all these five years, she asked me straight. I always considered you a friend but I must have been wrong, she said. Were you afraid, had you forgotten me? No, I protested, but yes I was afraid; not for myself but the fact that I couldn't bring myself to confront you in the physical and mental state that I had heard you were in. To be honest, I was unsure of myself; I was waiting for you I told her. We sat outside in the garden in her sister's house; she told me she could not sit on the floor anymore as her knees hurt all the time. She mentioned how difficult she had found it, at the time of her release, to lift her feet and take the first step out of the gates of Tihar jail; 'it felt like a ton of weight was bearing me down.'

She continued to speak softly, almost in whispers, ruminating – the five years in jail were much longer, a lifetime indeed where time had taken on a different dimension both spatially and temporally, both in psychological and emotional terms. It's over now she said; her confinement as well as her life. Where do I go from here, where and how do I begin again? All the work I had done thus far seems like a heap of waste, life has no meaning anymore, I am finished, she said. I remained quiet as I listened to her although I was gripped by an urgent need to talk to her, dissuade her from giving up, and ask her questions about her life behind bars. Instead, I decided to wait, afraid to hurt her again, unsure of what and how much I could say or ask or whether she was willing to share her experience at all. We moved inside when I suggested that we have a cup of tea which she prepared readily. Her smile returned slowly, lending warmth to her face and a sense of reassurance to me. Her niece had just returned from college and wanted to show me the video she had made of Anjum soon after her release, leading a local protest demonstration of women against the atrocities of the Indian Security Forces (ISF). This was her first public, political appearance; she was marching ahead with other women, holding banners, raising slogans, addressing the media and then I saw the haunting image of how she was suddenly accosted by policewomen and thrown into their waiting van and driven away. When I turned to look at her she said, 'I do not wish to waste any more time. I have returned from hell. I have to find my feet again, find meaning in a life that has been ruined. God alone knows what else is in store for me.'

Anjum's sister had earlier told me that when she was first brought home after her release, Anjum could not sleep on a mattress anymore and for weeks she preferred to sleep on the bare floor. She found it difficult to bathe and change into a fresh set of clothes; she did not sit out under the open sky but wished to stay inside the room. She found it difficult to eat what was cooked at home including her favourite dishes. She had got so accustomed to her life in jail that the family had to constantly remind her that she was a *free* person now. As if on cue, Anjum told me 'my family wants me to be happy, to smile and laugh now that I am free but I don't feel anything. I don't feel either happy or sad. I don't feel hungry. I feel numb. I feel confused. My body hurts; my back is sore and my knees are stiff.' I was terrified when she pulled her kurta down and showed me the deep scar on her chest. We fell silent for a long time as words seemed to have suddenly lost their meaning. I was at a loss, thinking of the brutalization she had suffered and endured. I wondered how she would regain the confidence and hope that had defined her very being. I felt humbled that she had now begun to share her deep trauma with me.

When we met subsequently, she did not lose much time and continued from where we had left off, or almost so.

Mujhe be-khwabi ki bimari ho gayi hai (I suffer from sleeplessness). I take sleeping pills without which I cannot fall asleep. I still feel tormented by suffocating dreams of the jail, the iron bars, the jail staff and the terrifying atmosphere there. Even after being released, I am suddenly gripped by fear at the stroke of 6 in the evening. It was at this hour that we were locked into our cells. I find it difficult to step out of the house after 6; this habit (of being locked in), it's as though it has fastened my mind with a heavy lock. I am apparently in a free world now but I am still unable to walk the street without my hand being held by someone. For five long years policewomen held my hand as I was taken from jail to the court and back to the jail. This habit (of the hand being held) has left such an imprint on my mind that it is impossible to erase it, like the many other scars.

Anjum's family had arranged for her to spend a couple of months outside Srinagar for 'counselling' but she returned earlier as she felt 'restless' and also 'afraid of the big city' she was in. It is work that will heal, she had said then. Why don't you start writing about your experience in jail, I asked her? What is there to write about she wondered but agreed to consider the idea when we discussed how this experience needed to be shared and how it might provide her the relief she was seeking. On my next visit in less than two months I was surprised that she had already written nearly 100 pages! A stack of A4 sheets, neatly handwritten in Urdu, greeted me in her study. I had come to stay the night and we sat down to read it together until the early hours of the morning. It was a moving, rich account written with simplicity of language and expression. Once she had started, it did not take her long to complete writing the book. As I finished reading the first draft, I contacted my (publisher) friend Urvashi Butalia who not only expressed keen interest in the work but also agreed to publish it.

∞

But now the question was: who would translate the Urdu manuscript into English? Although tempted, I did not consider myself for the job as I had never undertaken translation work of this nature earlier. It was Gautam Navlakha, my partner who convinced me that I should take it up as I had worked in Kashmir for so many years, I knew Anjum personally and that I would be able to bring out/retain the essence of her writing. I later learnt that both Urvashi and Anjum had taken it for granted that no one else but I would do the translation! I must thank them not only for their confidence in me but also for providing me with this rare opportunity that has meant so much to me in so many ways: it rekindled my passion for Urdu literature and brought me back in touch with the language I had grown up with, it brought me closer to my friend Anjum, her terrifying experience that she so poignantly encapsulated in her writing humbled me greatly, it was an intimate lesson on Kashmir conflict that no other book had taught me, most of all it is the indomitable spirit of the author that has deeply touched, inspired and influenced me.

It needs to be mentioned here that this book is neither in the form of a diary, nor a journal or a memoir. It does not have any particular structure with which to categorize it. According to Anjum, she 'simply wrote it as it came to her mind'. She had not maintained a diary or a scrapbook in jail but once she began to write 'everything returned to my mind, although I was aware that words would not convey the depth or intensity of my experience in jail.' She mentioned to me that she had no particular form or structure for the book and this is reflected in certain sections that are 'zig-zagular' – straddling the jail, the courtrooms, her dreams/nightmares, Kashmir, her family, her home – and the reader may herself be transported to all these domains at once. A section that begins with her recounting a dream is not necessarily developed in any particular manner but instead takes you inside the large pickle factory in the jail where many of her fellow inmates worked.

This is what is striking about the book – it provides a glimpse into the lives of different women inmates from different parts of the country and their own experience of serving the respective jail terms for the 'crimes' they did or did not commit. It is a world of women where violence stalks them closely, not only from the jail staff but from the women themselves. A world of contradictions: violence and intimacy, friendship and hostility, sharing and shunning, sympathy and longing, loneliness and learning and of course a sense of solidarity that is born out of a shared experience as prisoners are brutalized and dehumanized but refuse to surrender their minds and souls. In this world, if Anjum expected sympathy, she was rewarded with hostility, not only by some of her fellow inmates but the jail staff too. What could be the reason behind this? Her being seen as a Kashmiri woman 'terrorist', a 'traitor' to the country who therefore deserved 'special treatment' in jail. The sense/sentiment of patriotism and nationalism creeps in and confronts her unannounced despite the fact that 500 women inmates suffered and shared a similar fate of confinement and denial of basic rights and dignity. Kashmiri Muslims in Kashmir feel alienated for a particular reason and her life inside the jail was also marked by this. At times it appears as though Anjum, or any other inmate for that matter, is not even aware that her rights are being violated so easily, as in the part where she talks of the terrorist having reformed.

She also recounts her experience of facing discrimination on grounds of her religious identity. It is almost as though the jail mirrors the outside reality of alienation and discrimination that many suffer.

I am reminded of other evocative passages in the book that are a simple and lyrical narration of a complex subject such as – 'time' – how it takes on a different dimension for women within the confines of the imposing walls of the jail. Many of the women inmates who did not read or write or follow an 'English calendar' would remember the time of their arrest, or the number of visits they made to the courts, by the prevailing seasons: if it was the rainy season for one, it was spring for another, the mango season for someone and the severe winter when snow was falling for another, phagun and the marriage season are also mentioned as markers of the time of their arrest. The sound of the keys when cells are opened or locked is an indicator of the time of day or night. The eagerness with which women waited for the 'mulaqat ka parcha' (the list of prisoners to meet their families/friends) signalled the means for contact with the outside world, letters from family and friends kept their hope afloat. As Anjum has written, it is kaht-o-kitabat and mulaqat (written communication and visits) that kept the prisoners alive.

Even simple, routine aspects of daily life such as bathing, eating, changing clothes acquire an altogether different meaning inside the jail as all these become more of a luxury than a basic need. A full bucket or a half of hot water in winter months is a precious commodity that requires tough manoeuvring, including financial transactions. Falling ill is no less than a curse, particularly if it is at a time when the prisoner is locked in; she has to then resort to clapping, shouting or banging on the iron bars of the cell with metal utensils to draw the attention of the staff on duty. The reader might find the reference to Anjum's frequent illnesses or the account of her numerous visits to the court repetitive but it also provides a glimpse of the harsh reality of a prisoner's life inside the jail. The book is not only her personal account but a testament of the utter debasement of humanity as well as the steely resolve of the prisoners to see the light of day outside the walls of the prison.

Some of my friends have asked me if I believe that the author has shared *all* her experience with the reader and each time I recalled what Anjum had said even before she began to write the book: 'there are some deep wounds and a fire that rages within me that will leave my body only when I leave this world.' Well, it is a writer's discretion how much she shares, particularly when the subject is as painful as her experience of serving five years of rigorous imprisonment in jail. I do wish however that she had written a more detailed account of her interrogation in the Special Cell of Delhi Police because this is where a prisoner is most likely to be tortured prior to her/his 'confession'.

I remember the pauses and silences that marked her first few conversations with me after her release. On a few occasions, I tried to broach with her the subject of sexualized violence of women prisoners but she shook her head to convey that it did not happen. It was when I met her in Srinagar with the first draft of the translation for us to read together that she spoke about it: 'Yes, I am well aware that this happens both during interrogation and in jail but it did not happen to me,' she said. 'Also, it's not just sexual violence but intimate sexual relations between women prisoners that are an integral part of their life in jail,' she added. She sketched a particular barrack lined with cells and circled one to show that this is where 'such women' felt secure as it was not patrolled at night (being adjacent to the langar where many women worked the night shift under supervision). In this context, she also talked about the oft repeated rumour inside the jail that the water was contaminated/adulterated with certain chemicals meant to curb the sexual needs/urges of the prisoners.

Once she had finished writing, this is what she had to say,

It was not easy for me to write down the account of my experience of spending five long years in the soul searing Indian jail. Each time I picked up my pen and sat down to write the dark and terrifying images from the jail would come alive in my mind, leaving me in a state of restlessness and despair. I would remain in this state for long. Somehow, I'd try and calm my nerves and start writing again but I'd soon be struck with such mental agony as the bloodied memories would crawl back and crowd my mind. This sense remained with me throughout the period of writing this book.

For me as a first-time translator and Anjum's friend, the challenge was to capture the essence of her mood, her emotions and the atmosphere she has created in the book. To remain as close and true to her text as possible was of paramount concern for me even where certain references to her fellow inmates appeared to contain derogatory and/or racist under/overtones. But as she said, 'these are my personal views'.

The book begins with a verse from Faiz Ahmed Faiz and ends with another. I translated these and other poems/verses only after I had completed translating the main text. As a college student in Hyderabad, a hard bound copy of the collection of Faiz's poetry was my constant companion and I was dismayed now at how difficult I found it initially to translate some of these. Here, I would like to acknowledge my friend, Sohail Hashmi's help in polishing my rough translation of these verses. In the process he also read out some of Faiz's beautiful poetry to me at his house over a glass of fresh falsa juice that he had just made that morning. Needless to say, the flaws or any inconsistency in translation are mine.

Bujha Jo rozan zindan tho dil yeh samjha hai
Ke teri mang sitaron se bhar gayee hogi
Chamak uthe hain salasal tho hum ne jaana hai
Ke ab sahr tere ruq par bikhar gayee hogi

(Faiz Ahmed Faiz)

As the skylight darkened in the cell I knew
That stars must be shining in your hair
When the chains around me began to glisten I learnt
That dawn must have touched your face.

I T WAS THE LAST court date of my case and I was being taken in a caged prison van, amid tight police security to the POTA (Prevention of Terrorism Act, the act under which I had been arrested) court at Patiala House to appear before the judge. I saw her as I entered the room, sitting calmly, her mein like that of a victorious queen. She glanced at me through her glasses and began the proceedings in such a way that I felt as though my soul had suddenly left my body, and was hovering somewhere far amidst dark winds. I failed to comprehend any of the arguments or discussions that the state prosecutor and my lawyer were having; my ears did not hear and my mind was bereft of any understanding. Ultimately, Judge Ravinder Kaur pronounced her judgment, *the verdict*. I was declared a convict, charged under POTA and awarded a five year jail term with rigorous imprisonment. The courtroom fell silent. I was stunned. My eyes welled up with tears and my mouth went dry. I had suddenly lost the strength to either speak or hear. The terrifying images of the impending five years of confinement in jail began to unfold like scenes from a film in front of my eyes.

Like thousands of other humvatan, fellow nationals, I too experienced state terror and tasted death in jail; it was nothing short of a miracle that I returned from this graveyard after such a long period. But my soul is wounded, it is injured. My mind is burdened with innumerable questions: why did this happen to me? I am a free soul today but will the wounds and scars I bore in that claustrophobic, dark cell of Tihar jail ever heal? Entering the jail is like getting sucked into a deep, bottomless pit where you may as well bid farewell to life. A convict there does not know if she will ever be able to greet life again. The jail provides the worst example of dehumanization and devaluation of one's life and dignity.

It was on 5 February that I had left Srinagar for Delhi. A car from the Hurriyat office was waiting for me at Delhi airport. I went straight to the Malviya Nagar office of the Hurriyat where three other members, Shabbir Ahmed Dar, Khaleel Ahmed and Abdul Majeed Bandey, were present. We discussed the political situation in Kashmir for some time and then I sat down at the computer to check my mail. I had been invited by Alert International (a UK based independent organization that works in over 20 countries on peace building) for a four-day workshop in Bangkok for which I was making arrangements. There was a fax for me which I showed to one of my colleagues as it required certain corrections regarding my name. Since I had to go to Thai embassy in the morning to apply for a visa, I contacted the organizers through e-mail and they sent me a fax with the necessary corrections. I also had to travel to USA and Pakistan and I was therefore carrying all the travel documents along with 50 passport sized photographs and 2 passports, including the old one with which I had earlier travelled to the US, UK, Switzerland and several other countries. I thought this would help in getting an American visa again as it had become more difficult to secure a visa after 9/11.

As head of the women's organization of the Hurriyat Conference, Muslim Khawateen Markaz, the only one that worked for the social, political and human rights of women, I had undertaken documentation of the status of widows in the valley and under a programme for the welfare of war widows, I had initiated computer training for their children. In this regard, I had collected financial quotations from computer shops in Nehru Place which were also with me along with some money (cash) to buy a computer and pay the visa fee for Thailand, USA and Pakistan.

On 6 February 2003, at 10 in the morning, I set off from the Hurriyat office for Chanakypuri where all the embassies are located. Since I had a prior appointment with the Deputy High Commissioner of Pakistan for the visa, I decided to go there first. As I stepped on to the street, I was overcome by a strange sense of dread in my heart; as though an impending storm was brewing around me. However, I took a taxi and went to Shantipath for the visa application. On the way, a Gypsy jeep drew up alongside the taxi I was travelling in and signalled the driver to stop and after talking to him for a few minutes, sped away in another direction. I collected the visa form from the Pakistan High Commission and was headed for the Thai embassy. As soon as I crossed Nehru Park, my taxi was suddenly surrounded by other vehicles and I was asked to step out. The taxi was searched and a woman, who was also present among the posse of policemen, showed me her card which indicated that she was part of an IB (Intelligence Bureau) team. After the search, I heard one of the men talking to someone on his phone, 'She is not that lady' he was saying. I didn't know what the response was from the other side. After the phone call, I was searched personally and asked to step into another car. I objected strongly but just then two other cars, with loud sirens wailing, approached and an IB woman officer, sitting in a big white car, forced me into her car and took me to the Special Cell of the Delhi Police at Lodhi Road. Here, to my utter shock and disbelief, the lady officer repeated to me the entire telephonic conversation that I had with the chief of Kashmir Awareness Bureau two days ago. Hearing this, I felt the ground beneath my feet slipping away. Before I could make sense of what was happening, I was taken back to the Hurriyat office where the officials started searching, scattering and destroying office belongings indiscriminately and beating us simultaneously. They pulled out my bag from the cupboard and after throwing away my personal belongings, filled it with office papers and documents. They picked up my colleagues, the computers, books etc., and drove us back to the Special

Cell where they started interrogating us but before evening, two of my colleagues, Khaleel and Abdul Majeed Bandey, were released. When I saw Khaleel leaving, I asked him helplessly, 'You are leaving, but what about me?' He left without answering or even turning back to look at me. I did not know when the other one was released. I felt I was drowning in a deep ocean.

At the Interrogation Centre now it was only I and the other Hurriyat colleague. An intense interrogation began that continued through the night. In a moment several other officers arrived, lined us both in front of them, staring at us with utter contempt and shooting all kinds of questions at us. In the Deputy Commissioner of Police's (DCP) room, the officers used derogatory language with me and this is what one of them said to me, 'Begum Sahiba, you are a leader of Khawateen Markaz, we will strip you, take your pictures, print posters and put them up all over the country, you will not be able to ever step out again.' I began to talk helplessly to my colleague in Kashmiri which enraged the officers even more and they started hurling filthy abuse at me. It was a soul-destroying experience; I felt there was no life left in my body and I was hearing my own voice echo from a distance, my mind was blank, completely empty, I was beginning to forget everything. They were asking for my home telephone number but I could not recall it: 'Maybe they think I'm putting up an act' but I and my Allah know that my mind was truly blank. I felt their questions were pounding on me from the sky but the sound was muffled; faint, like a far-away-sound. All this appeared like a dream to me or rather a nightmare. Just then I saw Inspector Raman Lamba pulling my personal belongings out of my purse; putting my Parker pen in his pocket, 'This is a gift from you to me' he said. I wondered on what basis he was doing this. He now had my personal diary with him as well and was writing names of militant organizations in it with some figures against each. As I was watching and witnessing this deadly drama unfold, a stack of blank sheets of paper were brought to the table and I was forced to put my signature on them. I knew then that my fate was sealed.

The next morning at 10, we were taken before the POTA
court at Patiala House where Judge SN Dhingra was in the chair.
Groups of media people were jostling for space outside. I was
being led by Sub-Inspector Dhara Mishra who tightly held my
hand and when I tried to speak to the media and tell them I was
innocent, she struck me across my face and shut my mouth with
her other hand. I could not understand why she was behaving
with me in such a brutal, insulting and humiliating manner. I
kept wondering, 'why is this happening to me?'

The IB officer who had interrogated me the previous night
was walking beside me and warned me repeatedly that I should
tell the judge whatever they had instructed me to say. I still
remember his terrifying face; he was big, fair-skinned, with blue
eyes, his gaze was unnerving, as though he was ready to devour
me. As we appeared before the judge, the prosecutor placed my
diary in front of him and said 'It contains names of militant
organizations' and pointing towards me, he continued, 'she
provides financial support to them'. He then pulled out money
from my purse, wrapped it in my cloth bag and handed it over
to the judge, charging me with having received the amount from
the Deputy High Commissioner of Pakistan. All this while, I
kept pleading with the judge that these were false charges and
that I was being framed, but my voice did not seem to reach
him. Without looking at me or listening to me even once, the
judge said, 'You have received this money as a gift, an offering
(nazrana).' The police then asked the judge for a ten-day remand
for me and he readily agreed. I was led out of the courtroom by
the same lady officer, bundled into a Gypsy jeep and taken back
to the Special Cell. All hell broke loose with this police remand;
it was the beginning of many lengthy, tortuous interrogation
sessions. I had not eaten anything since the previous day and felt
weak, my mouth was parched, my lips were dry, I was offered a
cup of tea but it was too sweet to drink. I asked permission to
wash and use the toilet and two women officers accompanied
me inside the toilet; I requested them to leave so I could have
some privacy but they refused, saying that they also needed to

use the toilet. They began to search and frisk me again and all I could do was look at them helplessly. I was later given time to offer my prayers (during interrogation, whenever I took a break for namaz, they would ask me 'why do you pray five times a day?' Shortly after, a team of officers, including two women, sat down around me asking me questions that continued till late evening. At night I was lodged in the police station lockup which was stinking and filthy. There were insects crawling on the heap of black blankets in a corner, and a cement bench on the other side which was less than a foot in width; just large enough to sit on but not to sleep. It is difficult for me to find the words to describe that first night in the lockup; I was thirsty and cold but when I asked the woman police officer on duty for some water she told me to drink it from the toilet tap, I felt heartbroken and my eyes began to stream. I lay down on the floor and somehow managed to cover my legs with one of those filthy blankets but I could not bear it for more than a few minutes as insects were crawling out of it. I was taken back for interrogation in the morning and this routine continued for ten days. On the third day when I was being interrogated, an IB officer placed a few newspapers in front of me and said 'See, how famous we have made you!' I was shocked to see the headlines: 'Kashmiri woman terrorist arrested for providing financial support to terrorist organizations'. It was also mentioned in the newspapers that the government had asked the Deputy High Commissioner of Pakistan to leave India within 24 hours of my arrest and in retaliation some Indian staff at the High Commission in Pakistan were also asked to pack and return from Pakistan within the same period. I was not at all aware that my case had become so serious. 'Why are you people framing me like this?' I asked the lady officer. 'An individual has no meaning when the matter concerns two countries. You are nothing, if I get an order to kill all those sitting in front of me, I'll shoot them too,' she replied. I was terrified on hearing this but understood the underlying threat in her statement. Later that afternoon, around 2 pm, I was made to call home. My niece screamed on hearing my voice and handed the phone to my sister. In my failing voice I told her to pray for me; have faith in God. 'We are with you', she said, reassuring me that my sister Naseemjan, my brother Shafiq and Abidji (my nephew, who moved to Delhi and subsequently lived there for five years to monitor my case and visit me regularly) would be coming today by air, to meet me and arrange for a lawyer for me.

I was speaking to my sister in Kashmiri but the officers on guard asked me to switch to Hindi; I realized that our entire conversation was being recorded. I wept as I put the phone down. I was calling home for the first time in all these days; I was all alone here in this dreadful situation, with no one to turn to; I felt I was being sucked into a whirlpool.

It was on the fourth day that members of my family came to visit me. It felt as though I was coming from hell to greet them. They were there again the next day but I was allowed only three minutes to meet them from across the iron mesh. My brother had approached many Kashmiri lawyers in Delhi to take up my case which was necessary under POTA but he informed me that all of them immediately declined. After my family left, a team of officers visited me with a detailed profile of my life, from childhood until my arrest, saved in their computer. One of them addressed me 'You are well educated and come from a good family background. We regret that you are caught in such a case but if you wish to get out of it, we will do all that an educated woman like you deserves; we will provide you with an office here with all the facilities but once inside the courtroom, you will have to say what we tell you to and mention names that we give you.' I looked at them with utter disbelief and contempt and as a result they began a fresh round of interrogation that was much more severe. A lady officer said 'We will break your limbs and leave you in such a state that you will not be able to do anything in life unless you agree to cooperate with us.' As if on cue, Dhara Mishra grabbed me by my neck and struck me hard across my face. She shook me hard by my shoulders, again and again, saying 'You are a terrorist and all you Kashmiris are traitors'. This brutal and humiliating treatment continued for many days and my body was now erupting in pain.

The media had already declared me 'an enemy of the country, a terrorist who funded terrorist organizations'. One TV channel even portrayed me as a dangerous woman terrorist. Meanwhile the police arrived at my home in Islamabad (Anantnag) in Kashmir, destroyed whatever was inside, took away my belongings, drove my aged mother out and sealed the house. It was due to the local people's sustained agitation and their insistence that the house belonged to my ancestors that the seal was removed after a week.

The Delhi Bar Association refused to take up my case. After my remand on 14 February, I was sent to jail number 6 in Tihar. In the last phase of interrogation, I was photographed from different angles and made to hold up a slate with my name written on it in bold letters. Imprints of my hands and feet, soaked in black ink, were also taken on several blank sheets of paper. It was the most humiliating, soul shattering and sorrowful experiencefor me; standing barefoot in front of a policeman who was applying black ink on my palms and feet. The judge announced that I should be sent to judicial custody after ten days. When I was taken to the Patiala House lockup, there were 15 other women convicts there who had come from Tihar for their own cases. The lock-up, measuring 7' × 9' was suffocating and there was a terrible stink from a filthy toilet in one corner. I noticed as I entered the lockup that the women's eyes were fixed on me. At 5.30 in the evening we were taken in a caged prison van to Tihar; I felt that the high brown walls and iron doors were about to devour me and trap me in their maze-like interior. Inside, we were made to stand barefoot in a row until each name was called out and then we were made to sit on the floor; a procedure that greets every new prisoner/convict. We were then led further inside where, at the chakkar, the central courtyard of the jail, another head count took place in front of the jail staff before we entered ward 8, which was allotted to us. At the entrance to the ward were two women; the ward Munshi (a Munshi is from among the prisoners and supervises the maintenance of the ward. I mistook her to be a staff member of the jail) and a black habshi woman on duty at the tea vending machine.

There was a woman called Rani Thukral with me who was serving term here because she was implicated in her husband's murder. I felt apprehensive when the Munshi asked her name, but both she and the Munshi began to laugh when she gave it. But when I gave my name, they became sober and asked me if I was the same one they had heard about. I nevertheless sensed a touch of sympathy in the Munshi's voice as she led me to barrack 4. The barrack was full of women whose clothes had turned filthy and tattered; some of them were sleeping, wrapped in dirty black blankets while others were busy in conversation. Rani and I found a spot right in front of the door and were given two blankets each, one to spread and one to cover ourselves with. There were two girls from Rajasthan next to us who were picking lice from each other's hair and flicking the creatures around, Rani pulled out a packet of roti and dal from a bag and began to eat; I watched everything in a daze, overcome with feelings of helplessness and despair. She offered me a share but I refused as I could not bring myself to eat anything. After her meal she lay down, suggesting I do the same but I spent the entire night sitting in my corner until I heard the sound of keys at 5.30 in the morning when the barrack door was opened. Ward 8 has 20 tiny cells and four large barracks; and as the locks – the ginthi – are opened each morning, the head matron greets the prisoners with a loud 'Ram Ram' in response to which the prisoners have to repeat the same or else the verbal greeting turns into resounding kicks (this is to ensure that the prisoners are alive). Since I was brought to the ward at night, women who saw me in the morning kept staring at me; although I was not a stranger as the Special Cell of Delhi Police had already introduced me to the inmates by having released my pictures to the media earlier.

They had seen me on television and in the newspapers and were well aware who I was due to the propaganda regarding my case. I felt numb and could not bring myself to pick up the cup of tea, leave alone the roti that was our breakfast.

Mulaheza ward (the inspection ward where new prisoners are first brought and lodged) is the largest one in this jail; it is after three months here that prisoners are allotted other wards in accordance with their case. Ward 7 is reserved for women charged under the Dowry Act; prisoners who have been convicted are shifted to Wards 2 and 5, the latter also serving at the night langar or kitchen. Ward 3 is known as the child ward where mothers with small children are lodged and ward 4 is for women involved in the flesh trade, ward 6 is for women arrested under illegal narcotics/drugs trade (NDPS ward) and amidst all this, there is ward I that is reserved for meditation.

Rani, who was with me the previous night, had already done one jail term earlier. She gave me some tea in a steel tumbler, just when the Munshi came to get a few women from the cell to clean the ward. She asked me if I'd prefer to pay money or clean the ward. I had no money at all and I was wondering what to do when she asked me if anyone was coming to visit me – these visits were known as mulaqat; hearing this I immediately agreed to undertake the cleaning as I had been eagerly awaiting mulaqat. The ward was so large and the bathroom so filthy, and an added responsibility was to bring the big food drums from the langar – just the thought of this made me feel burdened. (It is a jail rule that every new convict has to clean the ward along with the toilet and to run any other errands for the ward).

Munshi was aware that I had a mulaqat due that day and by the grace of God, she picked up a few other women for cleaning duty. Once this was done, we were taken for a class where we were made to sit in a row and learn Hindi – this was mandatory. The class would last for two hours; from 11am to 1pm after which some of us were sent to the langar accompanied by the Munshi's assistant, known as 'mate'. Here, each woman is given a steel plate and tumbler in which the food is served from the big drums containing rice, dal and vegetable curry. I took my plate and joined the queue and waited for my turn. I lost my appetite when I saw the quality of food; the roti and rice were half cooked and the dal, watery. I found it hard to believe that other women were eating without any hesitation whereas I was not even able to swallow a morsel. The food was served until 11.30 and by 12 noon we were locked in once again. The barrack was so noisy, women fighting amongst themselves and each one pushing to use the toilet – these things were enough to drive me crazy; I was overwhelmed with a deep exhaustion that seemed to have suddenly descended upon me. The next day, Sunday, the ward had to be cleaned and this time I had no escape as there was no mulaqat scheduled for me. I was handed a big broom and thus began, informally, my rigorous imprisonment. My clothes were drenched by the time I finished washing the floor, doors and windows of the ward. It was winter, I did not have another set of clothes and I couldn't even ask anyone for it. I wanted to have a bath but there was no hot water available. Next evening, Fatima, a fellow inmate, sent a prayer mat, soap, toothpaste and toothbrush for me through another woman prisoner. Munshi, out of the kindness of her heart, sent me to cell 11 where three other women shared the space. Compared to the barrack, the cell is quieter and I came to know later that I was shifted here on the jail superintendant's (SI) instructions. When I entered the cell I found that the Munshi had sent a clean sheet for me; I lay down once the ginthi had been closed but began to wonder where I was. It occurred to me that I was a victim of some conspiracy. I was restless, desolate and helpless; there was nothing I could do other than cry my heart out. I could barely sleep and started praying in the middle of the night. At 5.30, I heard the keys turning in the lock and the cell door open. The brief time that it takes for the key to turn and the door to open is the worst in terms of waiting; the heart begins to pound as the mind registers the sound of the keys.

I had been searching for a paper and pen so that I could write a detailed note for the judge regarding the drama and conspiracy being enacted against me but there was nothing. Since I was not allowed to step out of the ward I couldn't even go to the canteen (where I could get the paper), a woman police constable was always with me, like a shadow.

There was a woman prisoner in cell 15 who had already done more than two months under Section 420 (financial fraud). She would sometimes bring hot water from the Medical Investigative Room (MIR). One day she brought the mushaqati, (a fellow woman prisoner serving term under rigorous imprisonment due to which she is given certain additional tasks along with rigorous ones) from her cell and told her, 'Anjum Baji comes from a cold region; she is also suffering from backache. Please give her some hot water to bathe.' All this was done in secrecy since I was under close vigil. I heard her account but without any hope. Early next morning, when we were being taken towards the deorhi, the main gate at the entrance leading to Jail 6 for the court date, another inmate hinted to me that hot water had been arranged for me. I asked the matron if I could go to the MIR and she sent me with her mate. As soon as I entered, I rushed to the toilet for a bath. I poured water cautiously to avoid the sound escaping the bathroom, I was afraid that someone might hear and sure enough, someone did; 'Who is inside, why are you bathing without permission?' shouted the voice. I was numb with fear but had already finished bathing and quickly put on the same dirty clothes and ran out towards the deorhi. I wished I had a clean set of clothes to change into instead of the one in which I had cleaned the ward and toilet.

Monday, 17 February was my visitation day, mulaqat. Civil rights activists Tapan Bose and Rita Manchanda came to visit me along with my nephew Abidji. Tapan had brought the wakalatnama, the power of attorney, with him but my nephew advised me not to sign it as the Hurriyat was going to arrange a lawyer for me (as indicated to my family in Kashmir). He said that if I arranged for one myself, my case would probably be sidelined. Tapan briefed me about Judge Dhingra saying that he was biased against Kashmiris but Rita reassured me and told me not to worry as things would work out, however long it may take. They gave me coupons worth Rs 250 and left with words of sympathy and hope. I returned to the cell, lost in deep thought but I couldn't see any clear way out of this mess I was in. I decided that whatever the circumstances, I would write a detailed account of my case and hand it over to the judge at the court hearing but it was not as easy as I imagined. I then thought I would send it through the jail superintendent and accordingly discussed it with one of my fellow women prisoners who advised me to meet her. With a strong belief that it is every prisoner's right to take all necessary steps to prove her innocence, I took permission from the head matron and went to meet the deputy jail superintendent (DS) but was asked to wait outside as she was having lunch. However, the Assistant Deputy SI saw me from her room and sent someone for me. 'What you are doing here?' she asked me brusquely and when I explained the purpose of my visit to her, she said that my application could be sent by post but for that I had to first meet the Welfare Officer (WO) as well as the visiting lawyer in the jail. I met the WO two days later as she was on leave then; her office was next to ward 8 and there were four or five other prisoners waiting outside. They began whispering amongst themselves as soon as they saw me and their eyes were full of hatred but soon it was my turn to enter the office. The WO looked at me with surprise even as I began to tell her about my application, she told me sharply that this was a jail and I should fold my hands behind me, move back and then speak from a distance. After listening to me, she said, less sternly now, that the jail lawyer would be visiting the next day and only he could act on this. I was tense and full of apprehension but also realized that there was no alternative than to be patient. The WO's duty is to attend to prisoners' problems but this did not seem to apply to me; a prisoner too. My ability to fall asleep had vanished; I kept staring at the wall and iron bars of my cell throughout the night, wondering when dawn would break and the door open, shuddering at the thought of home and family. It felt as if I'd been separated from them for centuries.

It is the Welfare Officer's duty to look after prisoner's problems but I was not included among those prisoners whose problems could get a hearing. On the WO's instructions I went to meet the jail lawyer the next day but she rejected my appeal instantly while staring down at me scornfully as though she was about to pronounce the death penalty on me. There is no respect for Kashmiri prisoners in jail; they are treated with such hatred and contempt there. I was the only Kashmiri woman in jail 6, in fact in the entire jail. I was in an alien city, amongst alien people, in a large and terrifying space. I was the only woman in all of Hindustan, a Kashmiri woman, arrested under POTA.

On February 24, I had a visitor who brought me some fruit. This was not allowed inside the jail. I stood there helpless and confused, not knowing what to say. Jail visits are such emotional scenes; initially I had imagined that one could sit across from the visitor and talk but no, once you are jailed in Tihar you lose the right to embrace someone, to shake hands or even touch your own family members who may be visiting you. I had waited all night for the visit and had even thought over and over again about what I would say but once there I forgot everything. All I did was to stare as though I was insane and I returned to the cell without having uttered a word. Just then a fellow woman inmate (in chakki 16) suddenly took up a fight with me for no apparent reason; she yelled at me calling me deshdrohi – anti-national – and atankwadi – terrorist – it really hurt me but I also became angry.

It was a long, sleepless night for me as I lay in the cell, strange thoughts crowding my mind and a sense of fear and terror filling my heart. Women in the jail were not only against me and hostile to me but also maintained a tight vigil over me, always looking for an excuse to harass me. On February 20, my sister and another relative visited me, providing a few moments of comfort for me. My memory had become weak due to constant mental stress and I had to think hard to recall all that I had wanted to say and share with my sister.

My health began to deteriorate because I was unable to get to sleep. Moreover, other women inmates were regularly shifted in and out of my cell; ten women were once shifted within a span of a fortnight. These were women convicted for drug abuse, pick-pocketing and other petty crimes and these vagrant, dirty women were deliberately brought into my cell. After judicial custody, I was to have my first court hearing on March 3 but my body was burning with high fever and pain and I couldn't stop worrying about what would happen in the court and how I would hand over my arzi, my application to the judge. It was already more than two weeks since I'd been trying to send it by post but without success. Now I had to figure out how to carry it with me to the court. On the appointed date, I woke up early, offered prayers and waited for tea. Bindu, a fellow inmate, came in with a bag containing an apple, a bottle of water and a bed sheet for me before going to fetch tea. Being transported to the courts was an ordeal for prisoners. There were announcements made from 6 in the morning with the Munshi screaming out our names and shoving each one of us into a queue to reach the prison van at the markaz. Prisoners are then filed, according to their cases, into separate vans for Patiala House court and Tis Hazari courts before being transported there.

Bindu, a Christian from South India had been serving term for the past two months under charges of financial fraud (under Section 420) in which her employer, 'the boss' had implicated her. She was from Kerala where her widowed mother now lived alone while her brother lived in Delhi with his wife. Bindu was the one who had shouldered the entire responsibility and burden of her mother's and her own survival. She had come to Delhi to seek employment in a private company after her father passed away the previous year. She had just begun working when she was arrested and brought to Tihar jail. Most of the women serving term under 420 belonged to private companies. On the court day the head matron accompanied me to the deorhi where each one of us was searched and frisked; the contents from my bag (apple and water bottle) were taken away. I had already given my arzi to another prisoner who was a foreign national as the jail staff were more lenient with them, also allowing them to carry food items and water to the court lock-up. After frisking, each one of us is called out and pushed into the waiting prison van. The van fills up very quickly, those who get in first are lucky enough to find a seat, the others have to sit on the floor or on someone's lap, or they have to stand. Even in the lock-up, only those who entered first found a spot to sit while others had to stand and wait their turn as their names were called out one by one; the woman constable would then unlock the door and escort each prisoner out. My name was called out at 11.30 and as soon as I was escorted out, a police officer came running to inform the woman constable that I was a 'high risk' prisoner and that I should wait my turn until more police force was made available to escort me. During this time Shabbir Ahmed Dar was also brought out from the male lock-up and two of us were then cordoned off by a posse of police officials. Later, two women constables seized my hand and dragged me to Judge Dhingra's room. He was by then busy with another case and asked us to wait. Just then I saw my sister and two other relatives enter the room. My sister was carrying a pair of slippers for me to replace the bathroom slippers I had been wearing; the judge was staring at her sternly and in this forbidding atmosphere, she could not hand the packet to me. When I requested the lady constable to let her do so, she shouted at my sister with contempt 'Don't you understand that she is a high risk prisoner? Do not even attempt to come near her or touch her. Is your sister a princess, if you are so concerned then ask the judge for permission.' My sister glanced around the room helplessly but did not have the courage to ask the judge. As my name was called out I was led to the dock (kachehri); my fingers were hurting badly as the constable had gripped my hand really hard but the worst thing was that the officer who came for my case asked the judge for a further remand of 28 days to which the judge agreed readily. I gathered courage and appealed to him to allow me to say a few words. The judge looked at me and said, 'Yes Anjum, say what you have to.' I quickly passed on my arzi to him and said 'Sir, I have not committed any such crime for which the officials of Delhi Police Special Cell and the IB have dragged me here. I do not even have a lawyer. SI Raman Lamba put the names of several militant organizations in my diary and put it before you the next day, alleging that I provided financial support to these organizations.' The judge nodded and said 'I will provide a lawyer for you. I do not believe their (police/IB) words. We still need evidence. You will get an opportunity to speak. Raman Lamba will also be brought before you.' The policewoman had started escorting me out of the court room, pushing and nudging me all along. My sister and others followed us out but they were not allowed to approach me, not even near the lock-up where I was pushed inside again. My name was announced once more after half an hour and this time I was taken out for the 'visit' (mulaqat). There was a large hall outside that resembled a cage where prisoners stood on one side of the mesh and visitors and lawyers on the other; each of us rushed to meet those who had come to see us since we were allotted only five minutes each, restless and anxious to say whatever we had to. My sister informed me about the lawyer they had appointed for me, she took out some money to give me as we were talking but the police officers shouted at her as prisoners were not allowed to carry any cash. I apologized on her behalf and said that she perhaps did not know that only 'coupon currency' is allowed inside the jail. Our five minutes were over and I found myself back in the lock-up.

The following day on March 4 nearly all the newspapers carried an account of my experience before the judge. Two women prisoners brought copies of a Hindi and Urdu newspaper and read out the news report to me. Later, I was alone in the cell for what seemed like many hours as my fellow prisoner Ganga, who spent most nights weeping in the cell, was released in the night. She was a dejected soul as her husband's family had burnt and killed her 13-year old daughter after his death. Asha, who shared the cell with me, was shifted to another barrack while two new 'convicts' charged under the Illicit Liquor Act were brought into the cell. I did not step out the entire day as I was feeling unwell and mentally disturbed. On March 6, my sister came to visit me again and brought an amulet and a copy of a particular Quranic verse for me as I had told her about the sense of fear that had gripped me lately. After meeting her I went to the MIR which was over-crowded but when my turn came, I met a lady doctor who appeared to be full of contempt for me and asked me rudely why I had come to see her, refusing to even conduct a simple physical check-up as though I was an untouchable. I felt very upset because of her insulting behaviour.

So much time had passed, and yet, even after so many days I found it difficult to believe that I was in jail, my heart and mind refused to surrender or accept the fact. I could not fathom what was happening to me or where I had landed, strange thoughts buzzed around in my mind; how did I land up here, why had my life taken such an ugly turn? It was not only difficult but impossible for me to cloak my feelings with any words as none seemed to capture the essence of my feelings or experience of being jailed. A woman from chakki 16, serving her term for fraud, was now appointed as the new helper (ward mate) to the Munshi (a Munshi is changed every month but since we did not yet have a new one, she was given the responsibility of the ward). I knew from the first day that this woman held a grudge against me as she found different ways to harass me. She put up a group of women against me, calling me a terrorist and mocking me, passing strange comments all the time.

Fortunately, Bindu and Jasbeer were sympathetic and helped me cope with her hostility, telling me that these women were jealous of my strong personality. I felt nervous each time this group of women performed puja. They would repeatedly bang their heads while singing bhajans and kirtans, and at other times they would shout and abuse each other. I found it increasingly difficult to retain my mental, psychological balance with all this violence around me

I failed to sleep most nights and would keep trying to convince myself during the day that I was indeed in jail. It was as though my mind had been fastened with heavy locks, with no space or strength to think or reason. The other women would go to the barrack and watch television but I, a high risk prisoner, was not allowed to do so, with the result that I often found myself alone in the cell. One day, I picked up a broken piece of a mirror and looked at myself for the first time; my dry, sunken face did not seem to belong to me, I was disturbed and kept staring at the mirror till I was lost in deep thought; am I alive or a wandering corpse? But I heard my mother's voice from a distance: her voice left me shaken, palpitations convulsed my body, I felt as if my heart was in my mouth...

Beena was an uncivilized, unfriendly woman who troubled me all the time. One day she began to shout that Kashmiris are treacherous (ghaddar) people. To this the head matron promptly added, 'just as you Kashmiris are fair skinned, you are equally malicious, and you have black hearts! You people support Pakistan. If it were in our control, we would hang you to death. You are mean, wicked and anti-national.' As she yelled, she came menacingly close to me and continued to abuse me. I couldn't even complain to the only policewoman there as she seemed to support all the abuse being hurled at me. But I gathered enough courage and said, 'You too are a prisoner like me and should not talk like this to another.' She was now enraged and yelled louder, until her voice pierced my heart with its violent intonations, it echoed in the large ward attracting the welfare officer's attention. Just as I asked her why these women were abusing me, the Munshi raised her hand to hit me but I managed to stop her; it was clear to me now that she hated me and I was alarmed, to see that all the other women too wanted that I get into a fist-fight with them and get into deep trouble. I had sensed from the beginning that these women were hostile to me and looking for ways to corner me but I had tried to be patient and ignore them. Their hearts were full of poison for Muslims, particularly Kashmiri Muslims. They had managed to alienate all other Muslim prisoners from me and prevented them from talking to me or meeting me but Fatima, a foreign national who operated the tea vending machine would greet me warmly as she was not afraid of these women. She whispered to me the next morning at the machine that 'we', the Muslim women, were with me and that the Munshi had been shifted after the matter was reported to the Deputy Superintendant (DS).

It had been a month since I landed in jail but it felt like a lifetime. During this time, I found that where Kashmiri prisoners were concerned, there was an all-round hostility reserved for them; the judge, the jail inmates and even the environment was hostile to them. It is difficult to maintain one's mental equilibrium in such an atmosphere, the outside world, or even its memory recedes and blurs inside the jail where one's life shrinks into its narrow, dark confines.

On March 18 a woman prisoner in ward 4 tried to commit suicide by hanging herself but escaped narrowly as the rope she used snapped. There was major commotion as all other women inmates were made to run to their cells, and at the sound of the siren; everything came to a halt. Each time the siren goes off in such emergency situations, it sends ripples of fear and insecurity amongst the inmates. There are also women in advanced stages of cancer who land in jail with strange and terrifying cases of crimes against them. It is only through films and literature that one learns about such cases but here in jail we get to experience it firsthand. We tend to believe that such cases have nothing to do with reality; that they are fictional but the reality is so ugly that I wonder if it is ever possible to capture it in words. Here, each woman has a heart rending story to tell.

On the tenth day of Muharram, two Muslim inmates came to the ward to offer sharbat. I learnt through them that the word had been spread in the entire jail that the Munshi had misbehaved with me the previous day due to which she was transferred to ward 8. This ward is known to be a source of 'income' and would therefore suit the Munshi well. Here, many of the new detainees who come are released and the coupons in their possession are then passed on to the Munshi to be converted into rupees. Being a large ward, coupons are collected for cleaning it from which also the Munshi takes a 'commission'. Other 'goods' that she lays claim to, include sets of clothes that well-to-do women prisoners leave behind on their release, on occasion she may also ask these women to call for clothes and money from their homes which she will then keep for herself. The other source of 'income' consists of a charge of Rs 500-700 that the Munshi demands at the time of transferring a prisoner from the barrack to the cell as the barrack is noisy and overcrowded with women, and there's a lot of theft and pilferage. The cell, in comparison, is quieter and the chances of theft are minimal.

On 21 March, I stepped out of the cell after offering ablutions and prayers although it was on rare occasions that I was allowed to step out. Lack of fresh air and sunshine had begun to cause many health problems for me; my knees were stiff and several black and red moles had begun to break out on my body, my left arm had a constant sensation of pain, perhaps due to a heart condition; I prayed that I would be released soon. I felt terribly stressed due to the dire conditions in the jail.

It was my court date on 31 March; my sister and nephew were already there when I was brought in. I was produced before

the judge at 12 noon and my lawyers placed my wakalatnama
before him. The proceedings were so long drawn out that I had
hardly any time left to speak to my sister who then visited me on
April 3. She had brought a few sets of clothes, some fruit and
also gave me a few coupons instead of money. She appeared
very weak in health today but reassured me saying 'Have faith in
God, we are trying our very best, the rest is in His hands.' I was
still not in a mental state to have any meaningful conversation
with her; I remained anxious about the little, rationed time that
was available to us. Added to it was the rush and noise of other
women prisoners in the surrounding windows combined with
the Munshi's repeated call 'time's up'. All this disturbed me
immensely. I could not talk freely as the policewoman would
make sure to circle around me, keeping a close watch over me.
I returned to the cell with a feeling of dejection and defeat. My
nephew had brought some non-vegetarian food for me because
of which the police constable at the deorhi had got angry and
threatened him that future visits would be discontinued, also
that he should leave the container outside as non-vegetarian
food was not allowed inside the jail. I apologized to her on my
nephew's behalf and assured her that this would not happen
again since my family members were now better aware of jail
rules; I was so worried that she may actually not allow them
to meet me in future. There are only two things that keep a
prisoner alive inside the jail: mulaqat and khat-o-kitabat (visits
and written communication). The hope of meeting one's family
is the only ray of light that helps the prisoner go through the
dark and treacherous days and nights; I am thankful to God
that my family visited me frequently as well as for the regular
communication between us.

And in all the long months that I served my jail term, I waited
and hoped that perhaps my comrades and well-wishers from the
Hurriyat would visit me, but I was disappointed to find that they
had, in a way, abandoned me although I was an active member
and associate of Hurriyat. I personally believe that perhaps they
did not wish to encourage a woman's leadership role or maybe

they simply lacked the basic courtesy to enquire after me or look into whether or not I needed legal assistance. Could it be just a coincidence that they made every possible effort to get our male colleague released but left me to rot in jail?

I was aware that I was a political prisoner and I believed that the inmates I shared the cell with would also be of a political background but I was distressed to learn that I was sharing space with women who were common criminals. I was caught among them like a fly who is trapped in a spider's web,. Every time the shrill wail of the emergency siren would sound, all activity would come to an abrupt end.

There was a meditation programme scheduled for ten days in April, and women from different wards were being transferred to ward 1. I too was transferred to Ward 1 at 7 in the evening although I had declined to go since I was suffering from acute backache and also because it interfered with the timing for namaz which I offered five times a day. When I said I wouldn't go, the Munshi left but returned shortly afterwards to tell me that the jail SI wanted to see me at the chakkar. She opened the lock to my cell and led me out. It was for the first time in two months that I stepped out of the ward in the evening and got a chance to see the sky and the stars above but I was surprised to see that women inmates from wards 5, 6 and 7 were still out in the open at this hour. The jail is so large but my movement was restricted only to ward 8. At the chakkar I saw that the SI and other jail staff were sitting there. The SI said to me, 'You must quickly pick up your belongings and move to ward 1, and you will be allowed to offer your prayers there as well as have time to rest.' I tried to reason with her but this time she said brusquely 'You have already been transferred and there is no need to say anything more.' She then turned to the head matron and told her to issue the transfer slip to me. I returned to my cell to pick up my bag accompanied by the Munshi who then took me to ward 1 and told the other Munshi there that she should accommodate me here. I was put in cell 3 which already had three other inmates.

Vipasana is a ten-day programme during which any speech or talk is forbidden for prisoners, we are made to sit quietly in a large hall with our eyes shut. The timing stretched through the entire day; from 4-6.30 am, 8-11 am, 1-5 pm and then from 6-7pm followed by a discourse from 7.15-8.30/9 pm. In these ten days, any other prayer or worship is not allowed. The next morning the SI came to the ward and spoke to the Vipasana teacher about me and assured me that I would be able to offer namaz as well as get some rest. Thus began the ten-day course. The ward was relatively peaceful without any sound and fury or quarrels amongst the inmates. This programme was initiated by Kiran Bedi through S N Goenka's organization. It was conducted once in three months and was mandatory for inmates of ward 1 which was known as a VIP ward. This is probably why the ward was clean and there were no quarrels over food and we did not have to wait in long queues. Outsiders or visitors from any NGO were first brought to this ward. Women here appeared to be tidier and busy in their allotted activities and work, they were different from other women inmates in the jail. Initially, after being transferred here I felt anxious as though this had been done to me as a punishment, but gradually I began to see the difference in atmosphere from ward 8. Soon after I arrived in the ward, the cleaning operation began in which all the inmates had to participate, including myself.

My court date was 23 May. This was the date on which the challan – the Prosecution's case file containing the chargesheet as well as all other documents pertaining to the case – was handed over in court. Later, on 26 May my sister and brother visited me with a photostat copy of the challan and told me that my elder brother wanted to appoint a lawyer for my case but I immediately declined the offer as I did not wish to seek any more help from him. (My elder brother and I shared a cordial relationship but not a close one. He did not approve of my

politics or my political participation in Tehreek. He was highly
placed in government service which is one of the reasons that
I maintained a certain distance from him. I did not want him to
get into any trouble because of my political engagement as that
was entirely my own choice.)

On June 2 I was back in the court where a junior Kashmiri
woman lawyer had been sent; she submitted my arzi to the
judge with an appeal that since the challan was written in Hindi
which I could not read or understand, it should be translated
into English.

Inside the jail, my life was in ruins and my health was
deteriorating by the day. The very meaning of my existence had
changed. I was being treated so harshly and prevented from
talking to anyone. Whenever I tried to do so, the other inmates
would be advised by the jail staff to stay away from me. This
was how I was alienated from others and became lonely; a tool
in their hands to experiment with new ways and strategies of
inflicting mental torture on me. I was under strict surveillance
and not allowed to go outside the ward. With me in the ward
were Surekha and Gurdeep; the former a Christian from South
India who was arrested for her involvement in drug trafficking
and the narcotics trade and the latter an athlete serving her term
in a murder case. Gurdeep and I woke up every morning at 4
and while I would offer namaz, she would do her puja path,
Surekha usually woke up late. The cell was unlocked at 6 and
water was available for only half an hour after that. We would
both fill and store water for the day and would also bathe. It
was Gurdeep's job to prepare mulaqat slips and so she would
leave for the deorhi by 8 am. The SI being a Punjabi, favoured
and trusted all Punjabi prisoners who were therefore able to get
work inside the jail more easily whereas someone like me was
looked upon with suspicion. Because they did not trust me, I
am not given any work despite the fact that there is a dearth of
educated prisoners in jail. In fact I had appealed to AS Neetu
madam, in-charge of our ward, to give me some work so that
I could also stay busy like the others. I'd been ill for several

days but when Neetu madam saw me in the ward she asked me to go and attend the class outside, I had no strength as I was running a high fever; so she relented and sent me to MIR where I consulted a doctor and returned with medicines. Even before I entered the ward the AS asked me what the doctor had said. I told her I was suffering from acute stress and hypertension due to which I had fever and other physical symptoms as the doctor told me; she advised me to take up some work/activities but when I mentioned this to AS, she dismissed it saying she'd consider the matter later.

On completion of the Vipasana programme, one of the newspapers carried a story, sent by the SI, about me under the title, 'The Terrorist has Reformed'. I had earlier been asked, as were the other inmates, to write down my thoughts regarding the programme. The SI, aware of the benefits of improving the conditions in the jail, was engaging in some form of propaganda regarding this. By sending my story to the newspaper she wanted to establish that I was indeed a terrorist who had undergone a positive change through the Vipasana programme. Since the story was published in Hindi, a jail inmate read it out to me and I was perturbed that every aspect of my life in jail got linked to my being a 'terrorist'. The next time the same programme was being conducted, I complained to the concerned staff that reports such as the one published about me could jeopardize my trial and my case but my plea was ignored. This is the jail authorities' concern I was told.

June 18, Monday, was a terrible day for me as I longed for my family and my home. Spending dreamless nights in the cell with soaring summer temperatures (48 C) and having boiling hot water run from the taps was truly a taste of life in hell. That we managed to survive day upon day like this was nothing short of a miracle. My niece visited me one day, promising that she'd return a few days later, but when she did not, I began to worry as I had not even heard from home for many days. Every time I closed my eyes my deceased elder sister would appear, like an apparition, weeping and looking at me from a distance, leaving me even more miserable. My nephew from Islamabad came to visit me the next day and cried as he said that he could not live in Islamabad any more as he felt the pain of my absence there. He also said that there were too many problems at home following my arrest. I felt there was no respite; on the one hand I was dealing with various problems in the jail and on the other, my family's hardship left me full of worry and anxiety. I had not yet established contact with my lawyer and this also weighed on my mind; if I had got bail I would have represented my own case as I did not want to bother my family any more but I did not realize that I was thinking ahead of time.

The woman lawyer in Delhi that my family had earlier hired did not seem to be too interested in my case and I began to wonder if we should have another lawyer in her place. She had told my family that she was busy until the end of the year and would be able to scrutinize and take up the case only then. In this sense, till now I truly did not have a lawyer to represent me/my case. When my nephew visited me in mid-July I asked him if he had any news but he did not have any information, I felt dejected that perhaps no lawyer would now want to take up my case but a week later he visited again to take my thumb impression on the wakalatnama. Finally, after consulting Iftikhar Geelani (a Kashmiri journalist who was arrested and spent nine months in Tihar) the well known lawyer VK Ohri, who had represented him earlier, was appointed for me.

I hadn't been able to sleep properly for some days now – the scorching weather gave me frequent headaches, and during the day I couldn't get any rest at all because my fellow inmate was a noisy, ill tempered woman who didn't care how I felt. One morning, I tried to rest after my prayers but she kept disturbing me – I couldn't bear it and I began to cry uncontrollably. A little later, Gurdeep came to my cell and comforted me. Another inmate in the ward, Rukhsana, was sympathetic and always willing to run minor errands for me including fetching tea and filling/storing water. We sat down and had tea together while she and Gurdeep tried to lighten my mood before leaving for ward 6. After they left, I bathed, combed my hair and waited for the precious slip of paper that would enable me to go for mulaqat.

A little later I got the paper and just as I began to head towards the iron mesh that was our meeting place, I heard Boba, my mother's voice. I was surprised, wondering if my ears were playing tricks on me but there she was... I was overwhelmed by a strong wave of emotion as I stood in front of her, I could not believe that I was meeting her again as I had lost all hope of doing so during this period of confinement. My elder sister's daughter, Shabbo, had come with her but before she could even get near us, the policewoman stopped her and asked her to go back outside. She told me threateningly that the meeting would be cancelled if I even so much as asked why my niece was being told to leave. I asked my mother instead who said that the police had found a mobile phone in her purse during the frisking and checking and had therefore stopped her. My nephew wasn't allowed to enter either and now the police were asking my mother also to leave. She and I pleaded with the policewoman to allow us to speak to each other particularly since it was her first visit in all these months. Perhaps she took pity on my aged, frail mother and she told us to go ahead. We were a little distracted though because we were worried about my niece and nephew who were waiting outside with their phone confiscated by the police. Still, meeting my mother, just looking at her face, and talking with her gave me a sense of peace and contentment. My heart was less heavy, my mind less burdened; and it was as though all my sorrow and hardship had suddenly vanished. My niece had, in the meanwhile, talked to the SI madam who

allowed her to come in to meet me. She came running towards
me saying 'I was so sad that I may not get to meet you after
coming here all the way from home (Kashmir). I apologized to
the SI and told her I was not aware of the rule and requested her
to let me meet you since I had come from so far and she agreed.'
I saw that Suman madam was on AS duty here and appealed to
her to grant us a little more time for mulaqat as my mother had
travelled all this distance only to meet me. I saw from her face
that she was expecting some money in exchange for this favour
so I told my mother, 'this madam takes good care of me inside
the jail, please leave some money for her outside.' This mulaqat
turned out to be so much better than others as we managed to
buy a little extra time to talk to each other.

Meeting my mother gave me enough strength to cope with
each passing day until August 2 which was my court date. It
was also when Shabbir Ahmed Dar's bail plea was coming up in
court. I was produced in court at 10 am. A Kashmiri advocate,
Zafar Shah had come for Shabbir's bail plea and my lawyer, VK
Ohri was also present when I arrived. Zafar Shah engaged in
a long argument regarding the bail plea while my lawyer tried
to explain the meaning of jihad to the judge and after almost
two hours of arguments, the next date for hearing was fixed for
August 17.

Outside, Zafar Ahmed Shah told me 'Anjum, we have not
forgotten you; I will represent you when your bail plea comes up.'
The Hurriyat had sent him for Shabbir but had not appointed
any lawyer for me. My own lawyer, Ohri, told me that he would
send his junior lawyer Khan to meet me for a detailed discussion.
He came to visit me on August 5 and while discussing the details
of my case, he told me 'Your previous (woman) lawyer was also
competent, why did you replace her? You perhaps do not know
that Judge Dhingra will not give you bail and your case will
anyhow have to go to the High Court. If your case had reached
the High Court after remaining for 5-6 months in Dhingra's
court, the chances of your release would have been better. If
Shabbir's bail plea is accepted before yours we will apply for

your bail; it is premature to do so now as it will not benefit us.' He went on to say, 'this is the weakest case under POTA and also politically sensitive as the Indian government had asked the Deputy High Commissioner of Pakistan to leave the country within 24 hours; the government had to do this as well as find a reason to close down the Hurriyat office in Delhi and it used this case to try and carve out an excuse. This case will take time to resolve but I assure you that you will be released.'

The constant to-ing and fro-ing to jail made me fall ill frequently and one day my right eye became infected causing me great pain and unease; the doctor advised me not to step out of the cell for fear of infecting other inmates and enquired if any member of my family ever suffered from tuberculosis. She prescribed some medicines but her enquiry regarding TB left me in a state of shock and despair.

August 17 was my hearing date and I was produced in court at 10 am, Gurdeep was also with me and as soon as the Judge entered the courtroom he asked the policewoman to take me back to the lockup until after 2 pm but to let Gurdeep remain here. The policewoman clutched my hand and escorted me back to the lockup; I was later produced in court at 4.30 pm when three Kashmiri boys were also brought in as it was their hearing too. We greeted each other through hand gestures but since the judge had still not entered, we were able to exchange a few words too. One of them, Sajjad Sheikh asked me if I needed anything in jail; I told him what I needed most was prayer and good wishes. My nephew who was also present expressed concern for my health and asked me if I was taking any treatment for my infected eye; the medication had not helped and he requested Shabbir's lawyer (my lawyer was not present) to put forward an appeal in court for a pair of sunglasses for me to protect my eyes. He wrote the appeal and handed it over to me to place before the judge who had just then entered the courtroom which was full of media persons and police personnel. As our names were called out we stood in front of the judge; Dhingra's manner of looking, staring at us, was so fearful or maybe it was our own inner fear that we saw reflected in his eyes. He handed each one of us a paper listing all the charges against us under POTA. It was also written that we must know that the charges had been framed/listed by the police and that we should sign the paper in accordance with our acceptance or rejection of these charges; 'guilty' or 'not guilty'. I did not know what to do since my lawyer was not present and I looked around helplessly in a state of confusion. However, Shabbir's lawyer advised us to sign under the rejection column of 'not guilty' which we accordingly did and handed back the paper to the judge who then announced that the case proceedings would now be undertaken on a regular basis and asked the lawyer for a suitable next date which was fixed for September 1. We were asked to remain in the courtroom perhaps because our paperwork had not yet been completed or because the sentence was going to be pronounced against the Kashmiri boys; they were now being escorted inside the court. It had already been 'established' in court that these boys were Lashkar warriors/soldiers and as soon as they were produced before the judge, he read out the sentence: Ten years rigorous imprisonment (RI) for Feroze Ahmed Sheikh and five years RI each for the other two. As the sentence was read out, the courtroom reverberated with slogans of Allah-o-Akbar and Azadi! The policemen promptly led the boys out of the courtroom covering their mouths with their bare hands to prevent them from shouting more slogans. I also became very emotional and glanced at Shabbir who stood there, stunned by the spontaneity of the moment; we were looking at each other as though the judge had shown our own future to us. Since all of us were high risk prisoners, we were being escorted by a posse of police personnel who had surrounded us; people from the press/media were waiting outside with their cameras focused on the Kashmiri boys. Suddenly, my legs were giving way, refusing to walk, my body turning almost lifeless; the

boys were walking ahead of us shouting slogans as they went
and all of a sudden, I heard my voice joining theirs, I could not
resist it anymore. I heard them telling the police that 'There is a
bigger court (adalat) above us than this one. 80,000 of our youth
have become martyrs and we shall not give up until we achieve
Azadi.' When the sentence was pronounced and the slogans rent
the air, Dhingra was looking at us from above his glasses, and
he seemed to be laughing at us. Once in the lockup, I became
anxious and did not know what to do but we were soon pushed
into the waiting police van outside which proceeded to Tihar jail.
I forgot my own sorrow and hardship as I thought of the fate of
these boys until we reached Tihar and were asked to get out of
the van. I was escorted to my cell after the routine body search
but my mind was buzzing with images from the morning and I
remained spellbound for many days to come, feeling drawn to
the passion despite my attempt to restrain my thoughts.

Alka was imprisoned in ward 5 under fraud charges (420).
She and I had earlier shared a cell in ward 8. She was a nice,
interesting girl but had a tendency to talk more than the others;
she was an assistant to the Munshi in her ward and therefore
able to move freely from one ward to another. She talked to me
whenever she came to ward I. Unlike her, I was not allowed to
visit any other ward since I was under strict surveillance and
anyone who spoke to me was discouraged from doing so. The
'informer' staff in the jail would report everything to the SI
including the false charge against me that I was initiating other
inmates into proper 'terror training'.

One day the matron instructed Alka not to talk to me anymore
and said that she was warning me on behalf of the Deputy SI
as a complaint against me had already reached her. Alka came
to me the next day asking me to meet the DS madam and find
out why there was such a strict regime against me. I had already
been thinking of doing this, I too wanted to find out why there

were so many restrictions against me alone while there were at least 500 other inmates in the jail. I went to her and asked, 'madam, have the other women inmates been instructed against talking to me? Am I not allowed to talk to anyone? Whoever approaches me or talks to me is summoned by the head matron and advised, on behalf of the DS, not to speak to me.' As I spoke to her, my eyes filled up; she said all these are rumors without a grain of truth but when I told her what Alka had earlier said, she asked me to bring her over. Alka confirmed in her presence that she had indeed been instructed by the head matron not to speak to me anymore. The DS then called the matron to find out if this was true but she instantly denied it and got angry when Alka insisted that it was indeed true. I told madam I had never breached any jail rules nor misbehaved with anyone; why then was such restriction imposed upon me and why was I singled out for such mental harassment? The DS agreed with me that I had not breached any rules and that I must not believe whatever 'this girl' was telling me but I knew instinctively that Alka was telling the truth because this was not the first time that this kind of treatment was being meted out to me; we are so helpless and dependent in jail that there is nothing we can do to defend ourselves. The DS now got angry with both of us and started shouting at us since she did not like the fact that Alka had confronted her thus. Just as we were leaving, the SI from jail no 3 arrived and we were called back as madam had already complained to him against us; he asked my name as well as the case under which I was here. I was standing there barefoot, with my hands folded behind my back, like a convicted criminal, when he enquired from madam if I was a Pakistani national. When she informed him that I was from J&K he looked at me disdainfully and said 'Do not ever forget that you are in jail due to such a big and sensitive case.' All I could do was to repeat what I had already told madam regarding jail rules etc., but there was no further response from him. The jail authorities had ensured that I lived a narrow, constricted existence in jail which made me feel more insecure, also because there were a number of scoundrel, bossy type women amongst the jail staff.

I was being harassed from the day I landed in jail, but I thought that this was perhaps normal here and this is how jail authorities behaved with all inmates but I soon realized that this kind of treatment was reserved for me alone, a Kashmiri woman prisoner. I was more worried now as I sensed that a kind of hostility was being built up against me; I did not know what to do – in the absence of any friend or well-wisher, I could not even express myself properly. Was there anyone who would listen to my plea? 'God, you alone know the truth, please have mercy upon me.' I was foolish to have spoken the truth in front of the SI and would certainly have to pay a price for it. What would the jail authorities do to me? This question began to nag at me. Although the SI understood what I had told him, he did not wish to acknowledge it (any plea from an inmate to the SI is taken as a complaint). Since it was time for the lockup, we had to return to our wards but the very next day, at 6.30 pm, I was asked to reach the chakkar (coming to the chakkar is known as appearance – peshi – and an inmate is summoned there for breaking jail rules or getting into a fight with other inmates) where the SI was also present in the DSI's office with the head matron and other jail staff waiting outside. Alka had already been summoned and they were engaged in a serious conversation with her in the office while I waited outside. She came out crying as I was instructed to come in; I took off my slippers, folded my hands behind my back and entered the office. As soon as the SI saw me, he said 'You are being given a written warning that you misbehaved with the DS.' I was astonished; when had I ever done this? I said, 'Sir, I did not misbehave, I am so far away here from my family, and can I not express my difficulties to the DS? I have not committed any such mistake for which I am being given this written warning.' He responded, 'Trust me; I am not going to send you to court. I am speaking to you with respect because you are an educated woman from a decent family background. But there are some norms and rules that must be observed in jail. There are many prisoners from J&K and Pakistan in jail 3 where we often beat them up and make them do sit-ups (known as murgha banana, this is a crouched posture used as a torture technique). Here, madam is like your sister who looks after all of you.'

'I did not misbehave with her or say anything impertinent to her,' I repeated but he insisted that I put my signature on the 'ticket' (a card on which charges/complaints against a prisoner are listed) where it was written, along with other complaints, that I had been rude to madam, and had demanded, 'Who are you? I will not listen to you'. I pleaded with Sir that all this was false but there were now several policewomen around me who'd been witnesses and I was also reminded of what Sir had earlier said regarding the Kashmiri and Pakistani prisoners. I thought perhaps he had said that deliberately to issue a threat that I would meet with a similar fate. I felt utterly helpless as there was no option except to sign on the dotted line. In jail, it is not the outside authorities that matter; it is the jail authorities, the ward Munshi and older prisoners who control our lives, our fate. It was falsely written against me that I instigated other inmates against India and that some patriotic, India-loving women had objected and registered a complaint against me and that is when I am supposed to have questioned the DS's authority.

Jail is an altogether different world. Here, the norms that operate are those between master and slave and they have to be followed strictly. In jail, our very existence, our individuality, is merged into that of the 'jail community', it is no longer our own. Barefoot, with our heads bent in front of the authorities, we have to repeat 'Yes, madam, yes madam' all the time; the master-slave relation is humiliating and eats into whatever little dignity we may preserve once inside the confines of the jail.

On August 14, early in the morning, several policewomen suddenly raided my cell and scattered and destroyed whatever few belongings I had. All this was done in the name of search operations. The next day, August 15, we were forcibly taken from our cells and wards for an Independence Day programme;

it was raining heavily that morning and it was decided to conduct the programme inside the big VM hall.

I began to realize that it was the DS who was responsible for the kind of harassment that was meted out to me; she had incited other jail staff such as the welfare officer, the AS and other officials to regularly humiliate me in different ways. In Indian jails, Kashmiri prisoners' lives are hell, an experience reserved only for us. Some women inmates tried to convince me that AS madam is 'not so bad, give her some money and she will be all right to you'. I had already given her money through my mother when she last visited me but I still feared her greatly as I had recently seen how she had slapped an aged woman prisoner simply because she was not able to stand for long during a prayer session. She'd tried to support herself against a tree nearby, but she was so frail that she fell to the ground with the impact of the slap. It was mandatory for all prisoners, irrespective of age or health, to stay upright as we were made to sing '*aye malik tere bande hum*' (the song is played over microphones every morning in all the ten jails in Tihar; although sung as a prayer, for me as a prisoner it had multiple meanings). Seeing the plight of this old prisoner reminded me of my mother; can anyone tolerate a mother's humiliation, or see her insulted, in this manner?

I hardly ever stepped out of my cell for fear of further harassment as the new staff would constantly follow me, saying that the DS had given them strict instructions not to allow me outside the cell. To protect my own dignity and self respect, I preferred to stay in, but this caused me health problems including weight-gain and swelling in my knees, although this physical pain was something I could tolerate better than the mental stress.

The jail SI, Sunita Sabarwal madam, would often look into my cell as she made her rounds of the wards. One day, when she saw me she asked 'how are you?' When I told her that I would like to keep myself busy she suggested that I join the sewing centre. According to jail norms, educated prisoners are given office work or similar duties that only an educated prisoner can perform but there was no such option given to me. However, I agreed to go to the sewing centre as it was better to be involved in something than sit in the cell or face aggressive women inmates. The person in charge of the sewing centre was Kiran Pratap, a fellow inmate in my ward. This is how I began my first productive activity in jail.

The witness procedure in my case began on September 22 and I asked my lawyer to move my bail application too but he advised me that it was not an opportune time as Shabbir's bail plea had already been rejected. The judge had also been transferred and the new judge fixed November 29 as the next date, pending special powers that had not yet been conferred on him. My nephew Khalid had come to the court for me and Hurriyat advocate Ghulam Nabi Shaheen was there for Shabbir. Ghulam Nabi Shaheen assured me that he would visit me in jail but did not keep his word; it is worth remembering that he belongs to the Muslim Conference of Professor Abdul Ghani Bhat. However, my nephew who visited me said 'Please do not think of anything other than your case for now because POTA is a draconian Act and we are worried about how and when you'll be set free, there is also no one who has come forward from the Hurriyat to represent you or to offer any help.'

I shared the cell with 25-year old Rukhsana who hailed from a village in Uttar Pradesh (UP). Her story was strange, almost fictional. She had been in love with a local boy since her childhood and he had exploited her all along and then refused to marry her. Her parents then married her off to her aunt's son instead but due to her aunt's constant nagging and frequent sarcasm as well as her own husband's indifference towards her, she left home one night and boarded a train without even thinking where it would take her. At night two men approached her, took her with them and included her in their 'gang'. This was a gang of thieves who would board trains, offer biscuits laced with intoxicants to unsuspecting passengers, steal their belongings once they lost consciousness and run away. They would then travel to Nepal for a few days and return to do their usual business on the trains. This girl was unable to forget the boy, her 'first love' and claimed that once she was released, she would search him out and kill him as he had ruined her life. She took good care of me whenever I was unwell; I treated her like my daughter and loved her so. She was to be released in two months and I prayed that she would not fall into the hands of unscrupulous men yet again. Women who come out of jail do not find a place in society, they are so vulnerable to exploitation. May God protect her.

On 29 October, Afshan Guru was released from Tihar jail. She is a Sikh girl who had married Shuakat Guru. SAR Geelani, Afzal Guru and Shaukat Guru and Navjot Kaur (Afshan) had been arrested under POTA for attacking the Indian Parliament in December of 2001. Navjot was not directly involved in the attack, and her only crime seemed to be that she was married to one of the accused, Shaukat Guru. My feeling though was that despite the marriage, she had not become a Muslim at heart and this was clearly apparent when Shaukat and Afzal were sentenced but she was let off. She celebrated her own release, telling other women inmates 'I am free now but Shaukat has been given the death sentence.' I often wonder why our young men marry non-Muslim women. If an Afzal or Shaukat Guru is hanged, thousands of other young men will take their place and it is my personal belief that from now, no other Shaukat should ever marry a Navjot.

The month of Ramadan had begun. We were given roti, dal and tea for sehri (the post midnight meal at 3 am). A portion of food was also kept from the night langar -which was meant for inmates with court dates the next morning – for those observing a fast. Here in jail, many Hindu women also fasted during the month of Ramadan.

I would keep awake entire nights without a trace of sleep in my eyes, staring at the ceiling of my cell, missing my family and yearning for them. I would see each one's face in front of my eyes, weep till my tears ran dry and feel driven to wrench away the iron bars of my cell and run out. I would stare at the cell door and will it to open so that I could be released from this hell, even though temporarily.

On 29 November I received a beautiful card from my nephew on the occasion of Eid. It is a strange coincidence that what he wrote in the card is what I had been thinking about all night; how all of us in the family had always fasted together and had also celebrated Eid at home but here, this special day passed off like any other. I dreamt of my mother; she appeared as soon as I shut my eyes, worried for me and tried to get me out from here. It was 3 am when I suddenly woke up with severe palpitations, perhaps because of the dream. I couldn't fall asleep again so I did my ablutions and settled down to offer namaz. I was in no mood to attend the morning class but since it was mandatory, I sat there from 9-11 am. The winter chill was creeping in along with the significance of 8 December; this is the day I had lost my eldest sister in a road accident in Kashmir a few years ago as she was travelling home from office. That scene danced in front of my eyes the entire day, leaving me more desolate than the daily grind of the jail did. This tragic incident has left a deep and lasting imprint on our family, including her young children for whom this remains the darkest day of their lives.

We began to feel the winter chill inside the jail and we were given some black blankets along with the ones that my family brought with them on their visit here. Because of the cold, I was suffering from acute neck and back ache but the medicines did not seem to do me any good. I always worried for my family's security after they visited me and prayed that they reached home safe. Rukhsana was released on 31 December and I was really pleased to see her off. It was already a year since I landed in jail and the time has somehow gone by despite the most arduous and depressing nature of daily life here.

2004: My sister came to meet me on 15 January and expressed unhappiness over a remark I had made in my previous letter to her that 'I do not nurse any grudge or complaint.' I repeated what I had said to her adding that 'In fact I am grateful to you that you have sent your son to Delhi to look after my case and follow it up. You have been coming regularly from Kashmir to meet me from the time I was jailed; how can I then have any complaints?'

Ten days later, on 25 January, the jail staff conducted an aggressive search during which the few belongings that I had were destroyed. My clothes were pulled out of the bag and each piece was searched, inspected and thrown around in the cell, even a tiny needle was picked up and taken away. I became a spectacle in the entire ward and women started coming to see me and the state of my cell. I felt awful for being treated like an untouchable; they came to see how everything including my clothes, soap, toothpaste, toothbrush and comb were scattered on the floor as though a storm had hit the cell. The ward in-charge, head matron and two policewomen had accompanied AS Sir during the search operation. I spent the entire day quietly collecting my belongings and putting them in place.

All of us women were brought outside on 26 January for the Republic Day programme. I lay down as soon as I returned to the cell as I was racked by an overwhelming tiredness and anxiety; I had not been able to sleep a wink at night. I was gripped by a sense of deep dread, I felt as though I was about to die, that my life was ebbing. It is terrifying, and requires great courage to confront death. I actually felt that death was knocking at my door. I will appeal to the jail authorities that in the event of my death, they should hand over my body to my family members without conducting the routine post mortem. That was the sort of thing I was thinking.

My sister visited me shortly afterwards and talking to her eased my tension and anxiety a little but at night, just as I was falling asleep I felt as if someone was calling out to me. I turned over and tried to sleep again but this time it was as if someone was beside me and sticking a needle into my body, right behind my heart, which caused a stirring sensation in my heart. I was so frightened that a sharp scream escaped my lips. It woke up my fellow inmate, Teja. She rushed to me to enquire what had happened and I told her how frightened I was. I got up and took out a copy of the Quranic verse that I always carried in my purse and began to pray to God while reciting the verse frantically; may God have mercy upon me and protect me. But sleep was miles away and I spent the whole night reciting the verse repeatedly; I was now afraid to even fall asleep; what if there were more nightmares? I wanted to bathe in the morning but Teja advised me against it as it was cold and raining, I did wuzu and offered namaz. My body felt heavy and my chest was hurting, I had no strength or energy to visit the MIR although offering namaz gave me some solace.

During winter, the number of people in jail increased considerably as petty offenders and vagrants were booked and brought in but most often, these were homeless, impoverished women looking for night shelter and two square meals a day; jail was the ideal place for them during this time. Many of them were also rounded up by the police prior to January 26 as a precautionary measure.

It was Eid-ul-Zuha on 2 February but for me this special day also went by as any other ordinary one. I had not been able to write anything for sometime mainly due to ill health and mental stress.

I had a court date on 15 March and I felt hopeful that I might get bail this time. It was a similar feeling I had many times earlier in jail that I would soon be set free but fate was against me; the long duration between dates and the frequent change of presiding judge ensured that I remained confined. This was a cause for anxiety and led to demoralization of prisoners. The atmosphere in jail was becoming increasingly strict and more suffocating.

Shabbir Ahmed Dar was released on 11 May and I was given July 2 as the next date in court although the POTA Review Committee had fixed May 26 which was later postponed. On 20 May my lawyer moved my bail application but it was rejected. The Hurriyat had submitted a list of names of Kashmiri prisoners to the Government of India with a recommendation that they be released but my name was missing in the list. I lost all hope once Shabbir Dar was also released.

> *Watan ko bechne walo! Gareban kya bachaoge*
> *Uthenge jis ghari mehshar main shohda apne madfan se (Sahil)*

> When the martyrs rise from their tombs
> How will you save your raiments, oh sellers of the nation?

During one of the Vipasana programmes, a quarrel erupted in ward I as a result of which women inmates from this ward were shifted to another one while I was sent to ward 4 which was meant for prostitutes and those in the flesh trade; it was noisy and disorderly here with women using abusive language and fighting with each other. It was not a suitable ward for me and I mentioned this to the SI madam appealing to her to shift me to another one but she refused saying, 'There is a ward for high risk prisoners where I can send you.' In this ward a prisoner stays in isolation in the cell and is not allowed to come out the entire day. This new SI was indifferent to the needs of prisoners and did not allow them to speak in front of her and treated us like untouchables. 'You people are here for having committed serious crimes and wrongdoings and are therefore paying a price for that.'

On 18 June, a delegation from the Srinagar Bar Association (SBA) came to visit me for which I was summoned to the SI's

room. I left my shoes outside and when I entered and saw members of the delegation, I felt both strange, and good. They offered me a chair but I declined as prisoners are not allowed to sit on chairs; I sat on a stool nearby and we talked for about 45 minutes during which the SI served them tea. One of them offered me a cup but I had to decline again; how could I tell them that prisoners are not allowed to have tea in a cup? The SI promptly told them that tea had already been served to prisoners and they need not worry; she also insisted that they speak to me in Hindi rather than Kashmiri. I informed members of the delegation, Advocate Miyan Qayyum and Bashir Ahmed, that I was presently in ward 4 where I suffered constant mental agony. They requested the SI to consider the matter and shift me elsewhere.

A few days later, I was brought to ward 6. This ward was filled to capacity by women charged under drug trafficking, in fact it almost seemed to belong to them. The toilet was filthy and the 'living' conditions inside the ward were sub-human; I was restless and could not fall asleep at night, the moment my eyes shut I felt as though someone was shaking me violently to wake me up. My body was hurting and by the morning it had begun to swell; I lay there in the cell for more than 48 hours with no desire or energy to get up. There was a two-day holiday because of which I could not even seek any medical treatment, but on Monday I visited the doctor who prescribed medication and also advised me to get an ECG, chest X-ray and blood test done.

On 2 July, I had to spend the entire day in the Patiala House court lockup as the hearing was delayed for one reason or another; jail is better than a court lockup where it is traumatizing to spend an entire day. The impact of the mental stress and physical discomfort on a prisoner attending court for one day lasts for the next three or four days before we come back to some semblance of normalcy. The prisoners are brought out of the ward at 7 in the morning and taken to the deorhi where they are made to sit in a row after which they are pushed inside a small van; or rather, a cage, and shut in the court lockup once they reach there. Inside the lockup it's so tiny that there is no place to sit. The stench from the toilet wafts through powerfully all day, causing severe headaches and nausea. Despite the scorching summer heat, there is only one old, small fan in the lockup and as many people as possible crowd under it for some respite while others suffer silently. It's difficult to find words to describe what an ordeal this is. Some of the women prisoners are accompanied by small children who cry all day long. A whole day in the lockup – from 9 in the morning till 5.30 in the evening is like experiencing doomsday!

I was produced in court a little after 10 but neither the judge nor my nephew was there. The policeman in the courtroom asked the policewoman escorting me to take me outside until the judge arrived but she refused saying that it was very hot there and also because I was a high risk prisoner. Just as he enquired from me about my lawyer, my nephew walked in and informed me that the lawyer would soon be here, 'Advocate Salman Khurshid will be coming,' he said. He arrived within five minutes along with my elder brother Dr Mohamed Hamidulla and few other lawyers as well as my own lawyer VK Ohri, but they went off to another room as another case was being heard in the courtroom. I could not believe that my elder brother, Dr Sahib [Dr Hamidulla, but addressed by the family as 'Dr Sahib'] had also come; I felt a sense of relief on seeing him. My name was called out after some time and soon I was standing in the dock in front of the judge, the policewoman clutching my hand. When Advocate Salman Khurshid and others entered, I was able to look at my brother to my heart's content, it had been such a long time. When the court proceedings began, Salman Khurshid argued for more than an hour in favour of my bail plea and I felt that the possibility for bail was now real as there were not many opposing remarks and more importantly, he put forth his argument to his finest ability. The judge fixed July 9 for a decision in this regard after which my brother and Salman Khurshid left the courtroom but the proceedings continued as DCP LN Rao and Inspector Raman Lamba, who were appointed as important witnesses in this case, were giving their testimony. Later, the newspapers reported the details of the court proceedings and gave July 25 as the next date of hearing.

Twenty-six-year old Zohra, who was from Afghanistan, was arrested under the Drug Trafficking Act and had been serving a prison term for the past five years. Her father, Barat Ali, was still in jail – he'd been there nine years – for the same offence. She had entered the drug trade to support and sustain her family after her father's arrest. At the time of her death, she was working at the tea vending machine in ward 8 when a policewoman, Sunita, following a minor fracas, beat her in front of other women inmates from the ward. She kicked her repeatedly in her lower abdomen and when she was later taken to the MIR, she was not treated properly. She continued to bleed for a month and was not able to eat or digest any food; she writhed in pain the whole night and rang the emergency bell repeatedly – when she did this, they would come and take her to the MIR for the night and send back to the ward after giving her some medication. She pleaded with the doctors to send her to a hospital outside the jail but the Medical SI, Kakkar, refused each time on a plea that the jail SI was not giving permission. They were worried that Zohra might complain against them to the doctors if she went to another hospital. When her father came to visit her on Saturday, she was in the MIR, wrestling with the severe pain she suffered. This was to be her last night and the last time that she was meeting her father. When Barat Ali saw the shocking state his daughter was in, he pleaded with Dr Kakkar to send her to Deen Dayal hospital for proper treatment, assuring him that his daughter would not complain against any one there. At the time of his visit, Zohra was suffering from a severe headache and her father sat by her side, pressing her head gently to ease her pain. Later, at around 3 pm she was finally shifted to DD hospital but her condition had already become critical while she was still in the deorhi waiting for a van to transport her to hospital; she was half dead as she waited, and breathed her last on reaching the hospital. At around 5.30 pm Dr Kakkar visited the MIR and changed Zohra's prescriptions; it is not a usual practice for doctors to visit the MIR at this time of day but since she had already heard of Zohra's death, she had come to the MIR to keep her own record clean.

On Sunday 4 July, the news of Zohra's death spread like wildfire in the jail. All the women prisoners came out crying, and collected in the centre. Soon there was ma'tam (mourning) all around which took a turn for the worse with increasing commotion and confusion in the jail. Women were shouting slogans against the SI and were soon out of control. There was not enough jail staff as it was a holiday and the women's noise and wailing sounded almost like it was coming from an imambarah (a sacred place where Shia Muslims commemorate the martyrdom of Prophet Mohamed's grandsons). Elsewhere, the police sirens were wailing but nobody heard or paid attention to them in the noise and fury of the moment. The jail authorities called in the (fauj) army and as soon as the women saw them marching in with lathis, they went on a rampage, smashing and destroying whatever they could; the MIR and other places soon became a pile of rubble with smashed windows, TV screens and flower pots. Some four or five women were also injured but the jail authorities could not manage to control the agitating women; about five hundred of them were beating their chests and reciting marsiahs (verses sung in memory of the martyrdom of the Prophet's grandsons). Siddiqua, Fatima, Sandra, Shamima, Tahira and I were summoned to the deorhi where our statements were recorded and our testimonies were written down. Zohra had died due to the brutal beating she had received from a policewoman and then due to medical negligence when she was taken to hospital. The jail authorities' indifference was responsible for this and the women inmates were enraged, their agitation continuing for a week without stopping. The jail authorities shut down both the langars and food for us was being brought from other jails in Tihar. The women were demanding that the DG come personally to take stock of the situation but he sent other higher officials instead. All through this turmoil, I kept urging the women to continue to agitate but without misbehaving with any officer. Seeing this, an IPS officer, Vijay Kumar, handed me a mobile phone and asked me to speak to the DG personally but although I could not hear anything due to the noise around me, I kept repeating that he (the DG) should come to the jail immediately before the situation went out of control completely. The women starved and remained thirsty through the day, crying and yet tolerating the brutal lathis from the jail officials, agitating and holding demonstrations in the severe heat outside. A few women managed to reach the SI's room and smashed everything there as well while some others arrived at the deorhi's big door and started shaking it violently. While our statements were being recorded, other women were being forced back into the wards with lathis raining on them but every ward was reverberating with women's screams and cries from inside. Later at night, a shadow of death appeared to be lurking around the jail and the night was consumed by a deep, fearful silence. Weary and helpless, women were now feeling insecure which, given the turbulent situation, was understandable.

On 6 July, DG Aggarwal arrived in jail with a full battalion of armed forces. Women inmates were summoned to the hall after which the door was bolted and the hall was secured from outside on all sides. It felt like we were going to be killed inside the hall. The DG began his speech, 'You women are wild beasts and I feel ashamed to call you my sisters. This is the first such incident in our jail's history. You will certainly be punished for this. You have destroyed jail property. You should be ashamed that you behaved in this manner even though you are prisoners. I have no sympathy for you.' Then, 'If anyone of you wishes to say something, do so quickly,' he said.

I stood up and asked for the microphone from the DG but he refused to pass it on to me so I decided to speak without it. 'We thought that DG Sir would express some regret and grief and say that Zohra was my sister and I have come to share my sorrow with you. If her death has occurred due to someone's mistake or negligence, I will enquire into it and have it thoroughly investigated. If you had then shouted at us, scolded us we would have felt ashamed but unfortunately, as soon as you arrived, you addressed us as wild beasts and hurt our feelings deeply.' At the time, inside the hall, it seemed imminent that we would be fired upon and I therefore felt the urgency to say whatever I had to. I added, 'We women are not afraid of death,' upon which there was thunderous applause from all the women gathered there. I told them not to clap, reminding them that 'this was a time to mourn and reflect; today it was Zohra and tomorrow it could be any one of us because there is no guarantee of life anymore.' My utterances seemed to have annoyed the jail authorities because no one amongst the prisoners had perhaps dared to speak in this manner to officers in the past. I named some of the policewomen to the DG and said 'These policewomen harass us and often tell us that "*hum tumhein baton se nahin balke laton se apni baat manwayenge* (we will make you listen to us through kicks rather than words).' The DG asked me to shut up and forced me to sit down. However, the women felt encouraged by all that I had said and a few of them also stood up to speak. As he was leaving, the DG told us that there will be an inquiry into the incidents of rioting and those found responsible for destruction of jail property would be punished; an investigation team was thus formed and they began to write down the women's statements.

On 9 July Friday my bail plea was to be heard. All the Muslim women prisoners met outside their wards after the noon prayers to offer dua-e-maghfrat (prayer to mourn the dead, for their souls to rest in peace) for Zohra in which a few Hindu women also participated. Until the evening, I was under the impression that I would receive the much awaited slip of paper for my release but there was nothing. There *were* indeed papers but my name was not there among those to be released. The newspapers of the next day carried a report that my bail plea had once again been rejected. I had already been feeling unwell and this news made it worse for me; my fever rose, I had a viral infection and then came down with malaria for which I was treated but my health did not improve.

I was running high fever and so a few medical tests were conducted including an X-ray but my health continued to deteriorate; I had lost my appetite and felt increasingly weak. Six women, including me, were framed in the incidents following Zohra's death. I had suspected this would happen and had warned my nephew about it and had also asked him to consult my lawyer and inform him that the jail staff was harassing me but on that day I got to know that a case had already been lodged against me, along with the other women. I was anyhow feeling dejected about my own POTA case and this new one added to my anguish; God alone knew what was in store for me. I received a copy of the FIR from the Hari Nagar police station where SI Santosh had lodged the case under sections IPC 34/427/149/332/186 and 353.

17 July was scheduled for internal visits in jail. It was a Saturday and the day when close relatives from other jails came to visit women inmates in Jail 6. This was the first Saturday and the first internal meeting after Zohra's death; her father Barat Ali did not come this Saturday. There were a large number of men from the different forces who had been called in for that day's meetings as traces of the agitation following Zohra's death still hung in the air. Police were to be seen everywhere in jail – they included squads from the Tamil Nadu Special Police (TSP). Jail authorities were apprehensive of fresh bedlam but the women inmates refrained from indulging in any untoward incident as they knew that this would invite not only lathis on the visiting male relatives but bullets too. They knew that earlier, in 1990, men were fired upon in front of their women relatives and their bodies piled up, for being part of an agitation in the

jail premises. It was for this reason that women conducted themselves sensibly and with restraint but we were also aware of the big volcano simmering in our hearts. There was palpable fear everywhere, all the wards had been shut and only those women inmates were brought out for whom there was a visitor. Men prisoners who had come to visit from other jails also appeared to be full of fear yet they told the women that their heroic act following Zohra's death was commendable and that even men prisoners would not have been able to achieve what the women had done in terms of the sustained agitation. 'Men prisoners from different jails in Tihar are proud of your courage,' they said to the women. 'If a death of this nature occurred in men's jails, we would not have been able to raise our voices against it as you have done; it is a matter of pride for us and we have therefore prepared this food for you', said the men. Six of us women who were charged under various sections of IPC became quite famous in all the jails in Tihar and other prisoners also became familiar with our names.

I addressed a letter to the president of the Srinagar Bar Association in which I wrote about the incident that took place in the jail as well as the injustice that was being meted out to me and requested that the Bar raise its collective voice against it as I had begun to feel more insecure and unsafe in jail. May God protect me, Amen! In the meanwhile the jail authorities put pressure on all other women prisoners and managed to mobilize them against the six of us. Many women succumbed to their pressure tactics as jail authorities ruled and more or less owned prisoners' lives. They have the power to spoil our records and stall our bail proceedings; prisoners are therefore a helpless and powerless lot. A summon was issued against us and first, it was Siddiqua, Rehmana and Santosh's turn at the Tis Hazari court for a hearing and they were given bail on the same day. The next day, Tahira, Bobby and I were produced before the lady judge where my nephew was already present along with my lawyer. The Hari Nagar Police Inspector appealed for our remand but the judge rejected the appeal, we also got bail on the same day. However, I was worried as there were distorted news reports being published against us in the newspapers for the past few days and the jail authorities were also turning against us; their anti-Muslim attitude bothered me immensely and the restrictions imposed on us were getting harsher. Of late, the jail had been enveloped in a strange kind of silence that seemed to me like a lull before a storm. For my part, I felt a strong sense of courage within me, but also, at the same time, a deep anxiety.

> *Ai khuda ab teri firdaus par mera huq hai*
> *Tu ne is dard ke dozakh mein jalaya hai mujhe*

> Oh lord, I claim your heaven now
> You have burnt me in your hell of torment.

I had not been able to eat a single satisfactory meal in jail as the food was tasteless and sub-standard and because of this I suffered from a constant stomach ache; the rotten dal and vegetables were nauseating. The barracks had far more prisoners than could be accommodated because of which there were frequent quarrels and fights among them and chances of theft and pilferage were high; it was quite natural for prisoners to lose their mental balance in this dark, intimidating and suffocating atmosphere. Chewing tobacco and smoking cigarettes was a common practice among a large number of women prisoners. A small tobacco pouch that costs Rs 2 outside sold for four or five hundred rupees worth of coupons inside the jail and those prisoners who were involved in this 'trade' made tidy sums of money. The tobacco found its way inside with help and cooperation from the jail staff. Dr Kiran Bedi had managed to put a stop to drug trafficking inside the jail but it turned into a lucrative trade after her departure from Tihar. A few women also used 'gutka' along with tobacco and it was for the first time that I saw women using 'packet tobacco' (small pouch containing dry tobacco) as this practice is not prevalent among women in Kashmir (where cannabis is mixed and rolled in a cigarette). Bribery was another popular practice in jail. If a prisoner needed anything from outside that was against jail rules, it was possible to procure it from the jail staff by offering a bribe. Or, if a letter had to be sent out without being censored, this too was possible through bribery and for this the prisoners had to arrange currency notes; a five hundred rupee note is known as 'Gandhiji' and to get one, a prisoner needed 700 jail coupons, and women engaged in this 'trade' made a good fortune too.

Jail authorities are not free of religious prejudice. They consider Kashmiri Muslims to be terrorists. There are several religious organizations that visit the jail to meet Hindu and Christian prisoners and are allowed to organize prayers, bhajans and kirtans for them but there was never a Muslim organization that has visited or was allowed to visit.

I was being harassed often by being thrown from one ward to another; the tortuous routine of shifting became a headache for me as I had to adjust to a new ward each time; indeed, in the space of a month I had to change three wards. The new SI was a scheming woman and had already mobilized a group of women against me. The newspapers regularly reported that 'Anjum Zamarud Habib, who is a terrorist, was arrested under POTA and is serving her term in Tihar jail. She incites women inmates in the jail and has led a hunger strike inside and also indulged in destruction of property and slogan-shouting against jail authorities.' I got worried as I read these reports thinking that my family members might believe these false reports to be true. They are perhaps not aware that I have been ill-treated from the first day, with jail authorities spewing venom against me. That women reacted so strongly to Zohra's death was also being blamed on me as though I alone was responsible for it. But God knows who the guilty are although it is true that I had spoken fearlessly in front of the DG. Since Zohra was a Muslim woman, the jail authorities were trying, though unsuccessfully, to give a communal colour to this case as well as to establish that Muslims are an uncivilized people. But I thank God that this case also included names of two Hindu women inmates. The jail authorities would certainly have to account in front of God for the way young Zohra was mercilessly killed.

It was twenty days after Zohra's death that her mother came to jail to collect her belongings. Siddiqua took some of her things to the deorhi where I also joined her along with Fatima and we took the rest of Zohra's things with us. Zohra's mother was a simple woman; she burst into tears on seeing her daughter's belongings which also moved us to tears. Due to the incidents following her death, the SI had been transferred and a new one had taken her place. She called Zohra's mother to her room while we returned to our wards. I was feeling sad also because my sister had read about the case and wanted to know the facts. I sat down to write a letter to her which I did not want to send through the jail for fear that it may not even leave the jail due to the censorship procedure that each letter from a prisoner had to go through. I therefore went out of the ward in search of the matron (who, at times, took my letters out to post) to the chakkar where she told me that there was a letter for me that I could collect from the WO. I went to Anjali madam's room and asked for my letter; she told me that I must read it in front of her as it had not yet been censored. The letter was from my sister and nephew and I felt happy as a letter from the family is like half a mulaqat for a prisoner. As I began to read the letter my eyes filled up and madam then asked me to go to my cell and read it because she knew that my letters only contained news of family members and there was nothing to be censored. In any case, I received my letters only 3-4 days after they were delivered in jail as there were only a few staff members who could read Urdu and this delayed the censorship procedure. Inside my cell, I read the letter many times over and each time I read it, I felt a new wave of happiness and contentment.

It was a terribly hot day on 28 July and my body broke out in a rash and small watery pimples that itched and pained all day;

I did not know what to do and kept scratching myself like an insane person. I went to the MIR where they gave me a piece of ice to rub on my body but the effect lasted only as long as the ice cube did; I was writhing in pain and was given an injection but the pain was still unbearable.[*]

In the evening, the new SI madam summoned the six women who had earlier been charged in Zohra's case. When we reached the chakkar she told us that she wanted to introduce herself to us and that other women should also be called over; she asked our names while also introducing herself as Swatantra Pawa. By now other women inmates had also arrived and the meeting began. Deputy SI Meena spoke first and told us that the SI was a good lady and praised her a lot. She glanced at me and said 'Anjum, now you stand up and say something.' I stood up and said 'madam, if you take one step towards us, we will move ten steps towards you.' I said this because the DS had already said that while it is difficult to forget incidents from the past, it is possible to work together. 'You will have to give us your support and we will try to bring about a new dawn but first, the cases against us should be lifted, we are not wild beasts or born criminals as the DG had said but victims of circumstances. We should be treated with compassion and affection so that we are released from this constant agony.' However, the DS interpreted what I said in a different way and said that 'You will not gain anything from giving an emotional speech and inciting other women inmates,' The SI madam perhaps wanted to hear all that I had to say and gave a hint to the DS to let me continue to speak. I took advantage of this moment and said, 'Speaking the truth does not amount to incitement. First you invite me to speak and then you criticise me for doing it.' After I spoke, she asked another prisoner, Shamsia to speak but since she was seated in the front row, I could not hear what she said

[*] During a conversation with me Anjum mentioned how hellish it was to fall sick in jail; however unbearable the pain, the authorities did not treat any illness seriously except in situations of alarming health conditions when a prisoner is taken to an outside hospital. (Translator's note)

but I heard the SI say that she needed our support and that she wanted to help us; 'Are you willing to support me, Anjum?' she asked me and I nodded in agreement. Zohra's death had also shaken the jail authorities and they were trying to cool down the situation. Unlike the previous one, the new SI appeared to be a good woman and seemed to have understood the problems arising out of this situation. She also let us stand in front of her and speak which the other one had not allowed. Earlier, we had to speak to her from a distance, like untouchables.

The SI madam made a flattering remark to me, 'You are such a beautiful woman, and it appears you are well educated, we need the support of women like you.' When she heard this, the DS madam said, 'I also believe that she is a beautiful woman but she has spoiled her own beauty with her anger.' I responded by saying that this anger is a gift of my time in jail 'the pain and anguish that we suffer here is bound to reflect in our faces,' I said. The meeting was good and since I knew my mother would be visiting the next day, I gathered courage and made a request to the DS that I be given a little extra time with my mother as she was coming from Kashmir only to meet me to which she responded favourably. I woke up early and offered namaz at 5 and stepped out of the cell after getting ready. A mulaqat with one's mother is an altogether different experience but once I met her and returned to my cell, my heart was heavy and I felt pulled down by the weight of conflicting emotions; I could not sleep the whole night, staring at the ceiling and waiting for the door to open again. I kept thinking of my mother who looked so frail and anxious; she was suffering greatly at this old age because of me. What is written in my destiny, I wondered? I pray to God to open the doors of mercy for me, my mother, my sisters and brothers, for Kashmir, and for the followers of Islam. Amen!

I did not feel well today – my head was hurting and my fellow inmate, Auntyji rubbed some oil and combed my hair, and since

I had begun to lose hair in jail, I decided to apply some henna too. My mother Boba was visiting me the next day and I was grooming myself for our mulaqat. Whenever my family visited, they stayed in Delhi for an entire week to be able to meet me at least twice before returning home. Today, my mother brought with her some of the things I had asked for; looking at her I felt that the summer heat had pulled her down and when I asked her she said that the heat was indeed unbearable for her. She asked me, 'Are you also not suffering because of this severe heat?' What could I say to her except that this jail was a living hell for me but instead, I told her that I was now quite accustomed to it; I did not want her to feel worse on my account.

Swatantra Pawa, the new SI, was a good woman. She summoned women inmates to the chakkar once again on 4 August. She asked each one of us if we had any problems or worries and whether we needed anything. I did not go for the meeting as I was running a high fever and was also suffering from an allergy but Matron Nirmala came to fetch me saying that the SI had particularly asked for me. I told her that I did not even have the strength to walk there and requested that I be allowed to rest. As soon as the meeting was over, SI madam and the DS arrived at my cell and inquired after my health and said 'since Anjum could not come, we decided to come to Anjum.' They stood around in my cell, talking to me for a few minutes and left. When the women returned to the cell after the meeting, they told me that the SI was looking for me during the meeting and the DS had also asked the women about me and even while the women were still there, they had left for my ward. Madam had begun to like me from day one; thank God that there is at least one officer who is making an effort to understand me.

A few months after landing in jail, the staff begins to recognize you but their behaviour is constrained because of the jail authorities. On 15 August, madam came on a round of the wards at 10.30 in the morning and when she came to ours, I heard her asking about me: 'Where is Anjum and how is she?' I was standing outside when she caught my eye and immediately inquired after my well being and said, 'your education should benefit other inmates here, if you can teach them, you will spend your time fruitfully and it'll also help reduce your daily tension.' I wanted to tell her that I had in fact tried to do this many times earlier but no one trusted me with the responsibility. As she was leaving, she shook my hand and told me that she thought of me and remembered me even while she was at home; it warmed my heart to hear this from her. I went to the MIR after she left as I was still feeling unwell mainly because the medicines were not effective but I picked up the medicines and by the time I returned to my cell it was 12 noon and I was locked inside. Unlike every day, the lock to our cell did not open at 3 pm today as the Matron who locks us in at 12 each day had done her shift and left the keys in the Assistant SI's room. The other Matron, on the next shift, spent more than an hour searching for the keys and was unable to find them. This led to an uproar from the barracks as women waited impatiently for the doors to open. The doors were finally thrown open at 4 by which time the women in the barracks were getting restless due to the suffocating heat inside.

August 6 was a Friday. I woke up at 4.30 and after doing my ablutions, offered my morning prayers until 6 when the locks to our cell were opened. I came out and strolled for an hour as I was advised to do because my weight had increased since I landed in jail and my knees were swollen and aching. I had tea at 7 after which I bathed and put on a set of new clothes from home. I had to wash my hair as my cellmate had oiled it the previous night to ease my headache. I hadn't been able to eat properly for the last month and one day I asked Joy, a black woman inmate, for a packet of cornflakes which I ate with some milk that I had got from the canteen. I was feeling particularly weak that day, not even being able to stand up as it made me feel dizzy with my eyes blacking out. I anyhow went to attend class after which I went to the MIR to get more medicines and then I went to the sewing centre to get the clothes altered that my mother had brought for me but the teacher there told me to first remove the stitches on my own and bring them back. By then it was closing time and I was locked in the cell again.I lay down after eating a little food. The door was unlocked at 3 pm as it was a day when we are able to withdraw jail currency (coupons) from the Prisoners' Personal Account (PPA/c) for which we had to get the AS's signature from the chakkar. I withdrew coupons for Rs 250 and headed for the canteen and bought a few items of daily use. I was offering namaz at 9 pm when SI madam came on a round of the wards and stood at the door of my cell; she greeted my cellmates with a Namaste first and then a Salam to which they responded and stood up but since I was praying I did not say anything. Madam was enquiring about my health from my fellow cellmate, Aunty 'Is Anjum eating properly now? How is she?' Aunty replied that I was not being able to eat and that she had to insist on feeding me at times. Madam told her it was the other cell inmates' duty to look after me when I was ill; she waited for some more time thinking I would be finishing my prayers soon but since I had started late, I was still busy. She went away to take a round of other wards but returned to my cell later and asked after me from the door; I stood up to greet her when she said 'if your treatment is not satisfactory here, I could send you to Deen Dayal hospital but in the meantime you must try to eat well. If a family member does not eat properly, it worries me. It is my duty to take care of you all.' I thanked her standing against the iron fence of my cell, my hands folded back, nodding my head in agreement until she bid us good night and left.

It was 'internal mulaqat' today, when inmates from the different jails in Tihar meet each other, and at 12.30, SI madam and DS Sir Ved Prakash, were making a round of the wards and they came to my cell. Madam said 'Anjum, I will have to eat lunch with you today to ensure that you eat properly!' I quickly stood up, greeted her and told her that I would certainly eat and she need not worry; she looked at the fruit lying in the cell (these were leftovers from the previous mulaqat with the family) and prompted me to eat an apple while urging Aunty to look after me. The other aunty had also returned to the cell after meeting her son who was lodged in another jail in Tihar. The three of us shared some lunch after which I lay down to rest, getting up at 2 to offer namaz and then I rested again as I was feeling completely drained of energy. The door was unlocked at 3 and both the aunties got busy with their puja while I went outside to borrow a radio from Pushpa Darshan and returned to the cell with it. I was soaked in sweat as though someone had poured a bucket of water over my head. The scorching heat made me long for Kashmir's soft breeze and pleasant climate, and I felt the tears well up in my eyes.

> *Ja kar saba la naseem wadi-e-gul se*
> *Jhulus rahi hoon tarah tarah zindan mein kab se*
> *Chchu jaye gi ji uthon gi phir se*
> *Aayegi khushbu pooch lena roothe ho kab se. (Anjum)*

Oh morning breeze bring me a breath of fresh air
I have been singed in this prison in many ways
A touch of cool breeze will revive me
Why has the fragrance of my Valley forsaken me?

It was a holiday so the Matron was locking the wards and cells hurriedly; it was 9.30 pm and I was writing a letter while the other two inmates were lying down and casually talking with each other. The two of them were serving term in a dowry death case, one was Asha and the other was Maya Devi. Both of them took good care of me and ensured that I did not have to do any daily chores in the cell, including washing dishes.

On 8 August, I woke up at 5 and offered namaz before the locks opened at 6. Since my head was feeling heavy, I lay down again after namaz, had tea at 7.15 after which I massaged some oil on my swollen knees before going for a bath. I stepped out of the cell but returned soon as I began to feel dizzy. We were locked in at 12 noon and when the door opened at 3, I struggled to get up and visit the MIR where my blood pressure was checked and although the doctor suggested a few tests, Matron Nirmala urged me to return to the cell as it would soon be locked. So I came back without any medicines. At around 10 pm, the AS, Nitu madam came on a round and enquired after my health and also asked me if my mood was all right. When am I ever in a bad mood, I asked her. I had seen how other women kept the jail staff happy whereas I usually stayed aloof and did not talk to them unnecessarily because of which they perhaps had this impression that I was a moody person. Why would I want to talk to the same staff that was responsible for harassing and causing me problems? It was no use talking to them as their hearts were full of prejudice. Asha Aunty put forward a request for a small TV set but the Matron advised her to approach the ward in-charge AS who could then get it approved from the SI.

Saturday and Sunday were particularly boring days in jail, but Monday was a day for mulaqat, for which we all waited impatiently, and it compensated for the two most boring days. As usual, I woke up early and offered namaz. Today I had to go to the MIR for a whole lot of medical tests that had been recommended; the sister there first conducted a blood test and informed me that my sugar level was normal, the rest of the tests had to be done later in the morning. I returned to the cell to get ready for the mulaqat for which my nephew, Abidji had already come and was waiting for me. He had brought a beautiful, blue, embroidered suit for me from Lucknow where he had gone on some office work. As he handed it to me he said 'Insha'Allah, you will be wearing this same suit and walking out of jail soon.' Before leaving for Lucknow, he had already submitted all the required documents to the lawyer so that he could apply for bail for me in the High Court. Later, I went to Vyamshala where a camp had been set up for free eye check-up and some of the poor inmates were also given spectacles free of cost. I needed to get my eyes checked too as my eyesight had weakened over the years here. These camps are organized by different NGOs at regular intervals. There was a boy in the team of volunteers who was also there last year and, by the grace of God, he respected me. He told me that 'I went to Kashmir and Ladakh and returned after six months and this visit to Tihar is part of my (NGO) training. You belong to such a beautiful place; I am amazed that you are able to tolerate this acute summer heat here.' SI madam had also reached the camp by now and had her eyes checked after asking all other women if they had done so too. I returned to the cell where both the aunties were waiting for me to share with them a 'special' lunch from home that their family had brought for them.

I had already read the newspapers when the cell door was unlocked at 3 pm. According to news reports, Geelani Sahib had established a separate organization called 'Tehreek-e-Hurriyat Jammu Kashmir'. The splitting of the Hurriyat Conference into two factions was a painful moment for me as I was one of the founding members of the United Hurriyat. We have offered many sacrifices, and continue to do so, for the sake of our nation's independence. The All Party Hurriyat Conference (APHC) was formed to instil a sentiment of unity, loyalty, sacrifice, discipline and propriety among those on the path of our great struggle and it is the duty of any organization to maintain the dignity and purity of the struggle. We cannot measure anyone's intention or motive but some people, in the garb of the Hurriyat, were its worst enemies. Even though the Hurriyat Conference did not do anything for me while I was in jail, the fact that it had split disturbed me deeply, both as a woman political activist who valued freedom, and as a servant and well wisher of my community. I do not know the reason but whatever happened or led to the break-up is not a good sign. "*Ibadath ke liye kafi nahin tasbeeh ghuma dena, ibadath hai ye jeewan khaum ki khatir laga dena, ibadath hai watan ke vaste sar kata dena, kisi muzloom ko zalim se chhudana ibadath hai, kisi naadar ki mushkil mein kam aana ibadath hai*". (True worship is to be willing to sacrifice your life for your community and nation and to help the oppressed to rise against it, not simply to turn the prayer beads).

Tea was served at 4 but I was in a bad mood and feeling upset with what I had read about the Hurriyat. The ward mate came up to me and said that there was an old TV set in the store which I could get repaired and bring to my cell, 'You will then be able to listen to news from your watan and also watch the saas-bahu episodes, it will lighten your mood and also help you spend your time in a better way. A TV mechanic is there in the deorhi now.' A TV mechanic came on a round once in ten days with a public announcement that 'If anyone needs to get their TV or radio repaired, bring it to the deorhi at the chakkar.' Mona handed over a small black and white TV from the store to me which I sent to the deorhi with a girl from the ward as I did not have the permission to go there myself. The repair would take a day and cost around 100 rupees, said the mechanic.

My day started as usual, by the grace of God, at 5, with morning prayers. Since I had had my eyes tested earlier, a gentleman, Mr Deepak, associated with an NGO, brought a pair of glasses for me for which I was asked to come to the chakkar. I thanked him but suggested that he offer it to a poor woman inmate instead as I could get one from home but he insisted, 'You are like my elder sister and this is a small gesture from your younger brother and I would be glad if I am able to help my elder sister in this way.' After hearing this from him, I could not refuse his offer and accepted the glasses.

The day was hot; it felt as though fire was leaping from the skies and due to the severe heat, my head began to pound as soon as we were locked inside the cell by 12 noon. When the doors opened in the evening I went to the MIR and found that my blood pressure had shot up and my arm was swollen. Since the doctor was indifferent to my problems, I decided to visit the homeopath who was then in jail. She used acupuncture to ease the pain and also gave me some medicines; I found her good but very talkative, her treatment was effective but while she charged the jail staff a nominal amount for medicines, the prisoners were asked to pay much more. If a pouch of medicine cost Rs 10 for the staff, we had to pay Rs 25-50 for the same thing, it was a common practice for the staff to get free medicines for themselves in the name of the prisoners. I was often ill during the summer months. My tongue was full of blisters because of which I could not eat anything or even drink water. Asha had gone for a court hearing of her case and Maya had a mulaqat; I was all alone in the cell, turning over the pages of my life. I was reflecting and remembering my journey from the days of being a student until today; it unfolded like a story in my mind. My student life was excellent and I represented students as their president; I was an NCC (National Cadet Corps) commander and a badminton champion. I was also conferred an All Round Best Student title and was loved by all. Every teacher loved me and I was part of a large student group in the university which had a fairly good reputation in the hostel also; indeed, people always singled me out in that group. We would create a ruckus in the hostel each day and once when the food quality was poor, we created such a din that a few of the professors who lived on the premises had to rush to the hostel to control the situation. In the morning, the registrar had to come himself and he told me, 'Why don't you take the responsibility for running the mess? We'll provide you with a jeep so that you can make the necessary purchases and then it's up to you to ensure that the food quality improves.' But I refused and said, 'This is not my job, particularly when the exams are on our heads. How can I accept this responsibility when I know that this is your job, not mine?' Now, when I remember all this, I feel like laughing. The other girls agreed with whatever I said but even though I had sounded so confident, I was in fact unsure of whether to accept this responsibility or not. However, the registrar, and the other officers who had accompanied him, kept looking on and asked me to tell them how this problem could be resolved. I cannot recall what I said in response but after this incident all the professors, the Vice Chancellor and other officials got to know me by my name. My elder brother, Dr Hamidulla was an Assistant Registrar at the university then and when I came home on a Saturday and sat down for dinner with the rest of the family, he said, in front of them 'Anjum, you are becoming very popular in the university, even the VC and the Registrar now know you by name.'

I was lost in this world of nostalgia when Maya Aunty returned from her mulaqat and asked me to eat with her but I refused her offer politely as I was not feeling well and wasn't in the mood to eat. She ate by herself and lay down to rest. We were locked in again and I read the newspapers. It began to rain suddenly in the afternoon but because we were locked in we could not run out and bring in the clothes that we had hung outside to dry. When the door was unlocked finally at 3, I ran out and brought the clothes in. Later, I went to the MIR to have my blood pressure checked as the doctor had advised that I do it regularly for a week; I found that it was still a little high. Instead of returning to the cell, I decided to sit in the open until the evening prayers. Since my tongue was still full of blisters I could not even talk and although I had brought medicines and mouthwash, they gave me no relief. Suddenly, I realized that it was 6 pm and the door was about to close, so, I returned to the cell and offered some tea to Asha Aunty who had just come back from court.

On 13 August I wore the blue suit that my nephew had brought from Lucknow; I remember what he had said when he gave it to me; that I would step out of jail in the same suit – but my bail plea had been turned down again, so I thought, of what use was it now for me to store away this suit? I decided to wear it instead, for who knew when I was destined to step out of this hell? Suddenly the emergency siren rent the air and all the women started running towards their wards with policewomen chasing them with bunches of keys in their hands to lock the women in the barracks and cells. Within seconds, the locks were fastened on each door. We had to remain inside for the entire day; I was reading a newspaper and learnt that POTA was being reviewed for its repeal due to which there was relief among many families

that had been affected since its promulgation. I was the lone Kashmiri woman in all of India who had been charged and arrested under POTA. Abidji, my nephew, was quite busy with my case; he was performing his duty as a brother and son for me. I thank God that I am blessed with such wise and caring brothers and sisters, may God protect them and bless them.

August 17 was our court date for the 'jail case' (incidents following Zohra's death) and we had to sit in Tis Hazari court lockup for the entire day; a harrowing experience although this lockup is larger than the Patiala House one with a cleaner toilet and clean drinking water too. Unlike in the other lockup, we were served tea twice while we waited for our turn. Returning from the lockup to Tihar made the jail appear open and spacious! It was nerve wracking to sit in a small shut up room from 8.30 in the morning until 5-6.30 in the evening; all prisoners who'd been there returned to their cells in an exhausted and demoralized state.

Today the heavy doors closed early because of a holiday and yesterday too we were locked in for the whole day. On 15 August, all the women prisoners were asked to gather in front of the chakkar and the Munshi of each ward ensured that women formed a queue to reach there; the SI madam raised the Indian flag, took the salute and began her speech by addressing the prisoners as 'My friends' instead of the usual 'Women detainees'. She repeatedly prayed for our release during her speech after which there was a brief cultural programme with songs and a dance performance. The function ended at 11.30 when the women returned to their wards. I went to MIR in the evening where Tahira, a fellow prisoner, had been convalescing for the past few days since she had suffered a minor heart attack earlier, but she had been shifted to Deen Dayal hospital a couple of days ago. Tahira had been in jail for six years now and her case was still going on. Asha Aunty also fell ill that day and I took her with me to the MIR.

I did not step out of the cell the next day as I was exhausted after the previous day's court date. On 20 August I woke up early but with a heavy heart; I came out of the cell as soon as the door was unlocked as I was feeling restless, and could not settle down to anything. I was called to the chakkar at 4 in the evening where I learnt that two courses, in painting and henna design, were starting that day and that Pushpa Darshan had registered my name for these along with twenty other inmates. My name was called out from the chakkar where SI madam, DS and a team of NGO members who had come to teach the courses were present. I preferred painting and had my name registered accordingly. The DS asked me to take responsibility for the course but I was not willing to do so; however, it was difficult for me to refuse in the presence of SI madam. The orientation continued till 7 in the evening and the ten-day workshop was scheduled to begin from Monday. I could not sleep a wink the next day either and continued to toss and turn in bed until 4 am when I got up to pray. There was a strange sense of despair and hopelessness in my heart and I stayed on the prayer mat till 7 am. It began to rain heavily and the weather seemed to be improving but I was so deeply immersed in sorrow that I could not even enjoy this pleasant weather. I came out and prayed for my release as I watched the rain; it is said that rain brings relief and respite from problems and a prayer during the rains is often accepted. I returned to the cell and headed for a bath after which I lay down to rest for a while. The newspaper was delivered in the meantime and when my eye fell on the news of Manzoor-ul-Islam's martyrdom, it felt as though the earth had slipped away from beneath my feet. I could not read any further and remained in a daze the whole day; I wanted to sob deeply and aloud but could not even cry and I did not wish to talk to anyone. Manzoor-ul-Islam was a key mujahid of the Jammu and Kashmir Liberation Front (JKLF) from Islamabad (Anatnag) and had spent 11 years in jail; he passed away within a year of his release. I am not aware of any details leading to his martyrdom and even my family will not share these details with me simply to save me from further pain and torment. In the decade of the nineties when the Mazhamati Tehreek (separatist movement) began, I was the first girl from Islamabad to have come out openly in support of Manzoor-ul-Islam and I provided him shelter in my house on many occasions due to which our house was raided by the Security Forces frequently. I was also arrested twice in this connection. Thinking of his entire life's journey including his active participation in the Tehreek brought alive his image in front of my eyes; may God bless him in heaven and may he accept his martyrdom, Amen! I do not know what else to write about him. I felt ill next morning due to all this and stayed in bed until evening when I went to the MIR and collected some medicines.

A few days later it was mulaqat day and I got a little more news about Manzoor-ul-Islam's martyrdom. My brother-in-law, Ashraf Sahib, who worked as a programme executive with Commercial Broadcasting Service, Srinagar, had a heart attack and had to be admitted to the Intensive Care Unit in a hospital and this news added to my worries. There was talk regarding my case and when I enquired about my bail I learnt that POTA was under review and therefore it was not an opportune time to apply for bail. Abidji said 'If nothing happens in the next 10-12 days, I have all the necessary documents and I will apply for bail then.'

My next court date came after nearly two months but even on that day there were no case proceedings and the judge asked the state prosecutor to fix the date of hearing on a day-to-day basis and finish this case. When my lawyer asked for a date, the judge mentioned that the proceedings would be on a daily basis now but my lawyer appealed for the hearing to begin from September 6. The judge then checked his diary and while agreeing to the date, advised him to be present in court. When we were coming out of the court room my lawyer told me that I need not worry about the 'jail case'. My nephew had told him that daily proceedings should be avoided because this is what Dr Sahib and Salman Khurshid had suggested because POTA was under consideration for being repealed and the bail plea had already been submitted in the High Court prior to this, so no judgment should be passed from here. When the time for mulaqat ended I was brought back to the lockup. That day had been a court date for many Kashmiri boys too due to which some of their family members had come and we greeted each other with gestures. They were enquiring about the 'jail case' and the hungama that had led to it. They expressed their regret that I had been implicated in a false case. I had to remain inside the stinking lockup once again for the entire day where there was not even any space to sit down as we were 16 women there, waiting for our court date. How we spend a day in a lockup can be known and understood only by those who experience it, it is beyond any one else's imagination or comprehension.

The evidence/witness procedure began on the same day. At the time, Abdul Majeed Bandey and Habibulla (owner of Shiraz Travels) from whom I had purchased my air ticket, were supposed to testify but the former did not appear in court. In reality, I was totally unaware of the status of my case except what Abidji informed me from time to time. My family was very worried and anxious due to this case.

One day in August I woke up early but did not feel well at all; just the sight of insects in the food was enough to make me sick. Due to the severe summer heat the dal, rice and vegetables that were cooked in large quantities in the langar had insects breeding in them, including in the rotis. The prisoners complained to the authorities many times but it made no difference. In jail, even human beings are treated like insects. Inside, it's a different world where a master-slave hierarchy operates and is strictly followed. A prisoner gradually becomes an inhabitant of this world and by constantly having to follow the different rules and regulations; she ends up with a bent back due to the burden of following orders from jail authorities with her head bowed in front of them.

In summer we were given earthen pots to store water but tiny black insects would find their way in and breed in these pots, yet we had to keep the water to use for five or six people as it was not easy to find empty pots. There were lizards on the walls and small snakes crawling on the floor, we were always afraid that a lizard might fall on our heads or into the food on our plate or that a snake might coil itself in our beds. We could not sleep at night because of this and also because of the sweltering heat, although there were fans on the ceiling but these only blew hot air on us. If a fan stopped working, it meant making a hundred visits in the heat to the chakkar to have it repaired.

I joined the sewing centre and after a couple of days spent there I was able to cut a kurta design on paper. One day, shortly after this, I read in the newspaper that POTA was being removed and felt happy. I wished it would happen soon so that I could be relieved from this unbearable heat in prison.

My court date in the 'jail case' was scheduled for August 31. I found that there wasn't any money in my PP account; I sent a letter by speed-post to my mother asking her to send a money order urgently. Two poems in English, under the title 'Sister Act' had been published in the newspaper recently and I really enjoyed reading them; I therefore cut them out and sent them to my two sisters, Baji and Neelji (and I have included them at the end of this book). Later I went to the sewing centre where I cut out the churidar-kurta pattern that I planned to stitch the next day. My back was hurting badly when I returned from there, it was so hot in the cell that I rushed in for a bath and changed into a fresh set of clothes. The two aunties in the cell had a mulaqat from where they brought 'home food' and waited for me to join them for lunch. I ate with them, took a pain-killer for my back-ache and lay down to rest but there was no respite from pain even by evening when I went to the MIR and brought some more medicines. The pain was so acute that I could not even turn on my side in bed. I went back to the MIR the next morning where the doctor prescribed an injection and also advised me to lie on my back and to avoid bending forward.

The next day a team from ICRC came to visit me, the same team had come twice to meet me last year, it included Maximi

Ekani Abraham and Micheala Dinnere. I was at first asked to come to the chakkar to meet them but apparently they said they preferred to see me in the cell and had got permission to do so. As soon as they entered, one of them asked me, 'Are you able to live here with three other women inmates?' They were surprised to see that there was hardly any light in the cell and also that there was a toilet in one corner of this tiny cell. They enquired if I had any problem but I said 'no' because I knew that they would not be able to redress it. They told me that they had not received the letter I had sent them regarding the false charges against me in Zohra's case but that they did receive a copy of the one I had submitted to the Srinagar Bar Association. They surveyed the cell while asking me a few more questions and left after a short while. Later I ate my lunch and medicines and lay down as I was feeling weak in my body and also sleepy because of the injection I had taken in the morning.

Many NGOs would visit the jail to help and advise women prisoners but more in name than in deed. Women representatives of Vidya Jyothi and Jagrathi Sansthan would come and enrol women prisoners by initiating a discourse on behalf of their guru 'Maharaj-ji'. Apart from this, they organized different programmes in which women participated with interest; music lessons, henna design and application, and a unit for making herbal face packs was also run and managed by them. Pravachan, a religious discourse programme, was conducted almost every day since a majority of prisoners were Hindu women and they participated in this event willingly but there were others who did not want to attend but were forced to do so. After a week of Pravachan, new women were given 'gyan' or knowledge/enlightenment for one day and they too would become followers and devotees of Maharaj-ji, the teacher and guru. These women then wore the Maharaj's locket around their necks and instead of the usual greeting of 'Namaste'; they would say 'Jai

Maharaj-ji' to each other. I was also asked to come for Pravachan many times but I refused. One day, Sangamitra Bharati who was the leading devotee, came to my cell and took me to Vyamshala to listen to Pravachan. I was aware that all this was done on instructions from SI madam. There, they started preaching about Islam and eulogizing it while at the same time pointing out that they did not come here to preach any one religion but to give a lesson in humanism; there were many Muslim brothers and sisters in the organization, they said. Preparations began for launching a big programme and soon there were teachers for classes in music, yoga and painting.

Despite medication, my backache had not gone away. Since the medicines did not improve my condition, the medical SI decided to send me to a psychiatrist and thus began the routine of giving me sleep inducing drugs. Each day before lock up time, the Matron would come accompanied by a sister with the drugs and ensure that the packet was opened in her presence. I began to sleep better but my ability to think as well as my memory were affected. I had now become addicted to these drugs which were sold in 'black' in jail but I was not aware that they could lead to a state of mental numbness.

Prisoners in the jail were a worried and anxious lot; each one had a different story and each story hurt. They would keep staring at the imposing iron bars and wonder when the locks would open and when we'd gain freedom. Prisoners were tired of silently obeying the jail authorities and this was reflected in the fact that there were cases of attempted suicides nearly every week, of which one or two would be 'successful' in taking their lives, thereby ending the horror of their imprisonment.

It was on the first day of my inspection that drugs were administered to me, when after Zohra's death DG Aggarwal came and could not tolerate seeing other women prisoners agitating with me against her death. I had stopped talking to anyone. Zohra's death seemed to have fanned the simmering volcano inside me. I have experienced and suffered many oppressive situations but I cannot tolerate others being oppressed in front of my eyes. This incident (Zohra's death) had shaken me to the core of my being, and it made me forget my own sorrow.

The jail authorities saw my enthusiasm and my strong feelings against oppression and tyranny. Indeed, as DG Aggarwal had himself said, 'this is the first time in the history of this jail that a collective voice has been raised against injustice.' It was to silence this voice and suppress the sentiment for humanity which is considered a big crime in jail that these psychotropic drugs were being given to me. It was after I began to take these drugs that I became quite anti-social, I did not want to talk to anyone, I preferred to be alone. Fear/terror took hold of me; earlier I used to wait impatiently for an entire week for mulaqat but now I did not even want to go for it as my feet dragged, my speech slurred and I was confused about whether I could say anything or communicate meaningfully with anyone.

⚬⚬⚬

At some point madam SI had appointed me to look after the jail library. I would go to the chakkar at 9.30, collect the keys and open the library. A few women would come and borrow books. The library did not have much to offer, there was a collection of small story books in Hindi as well as some Hindu religious books. For non-Indian prisoners, their respective embassies sent books for them which the women would return to the library after reading them, these books were in good quantity. Delhi Public library had donated some books and there were others in Urdu from National Council for Promotion of Urdu Languge.

On 14 September I was taken to Patiala House for both my POTA and 'jail case' hearings. I was produced before the judge at 11.30. Abidji was waiting outside. The courtroom was relatively empty today unlike other times when it was filled to capacity. I was produced before the judge as soon as I entered the courtroom and the proceedings began but since my lawyer had not yet reached, the judge asked me 'Madam, where is your lawyer?' Abidji went to look for him and bring him but by the time he came, LN Rao (DCP Special Cell, Delhi Police, Lodhi Road) had completed his statement, My lawyer Ohri Sahib entered the courtroom along with his junior who carried an arzi in his hand on which he took my signature and then submitted it to the judge with a plea that there be no proceedings in this case as POTA was under consideration with the Review Committee of the government. The judge examined the arzi and said, 'This lady has been in jail for the past two years and I want to wrap up this case as soon as possible.' He then addressed my lawyer and said, 'I receive a lot of letters saying that "Anjum Zamarud should not be released. She should not be given bail".' My lawyer responded, 'Sir, there is politics going on in jail also and there are many groups here too.' The judge cut him short and said, in a much louder voice, 'It is not from the jail but from Srinagar that these letters come stating that she should not be released.' My lawyer replied, 'She is a political leader and there must be those against her. This happens in politics.' When I heard what the judge said, I felt hurt and wounded, wondering who these people were, men or women, who wanted to continue to see me behind bars. Who would benefit from my remaining confined in jail? My eyes filled up as these questions surfaced in my mind. When I got back to the lockup my mind remained preoccupied with all these questions: I kept wondering why all this was happening to me, and who the secret enemy was who did not want me out of jail. I have never wished ill of anyone, why then should people wish ill of me? May God unmask this person and this mystery. I felt dejected that here I was, tolerating all this hardship for the sake of my community, and look what was happening to me. This is not about any power politics, not about any one's private property, not even about any state conspiracy; it is about the movement for Azadi and what counts in it is the difficulty and hardship of sacrifice, jail terms and interrogation sessions. Then, who is this person without a conscience who harbours this kind of hatred in his/her heart against me? I felt really heartbroken that such a dirty conspiracy was being hatched against those offering sacrifices for the sake of their community. There are such monsters within our own community who negate the very value of sacrifice. I pray to God that this hidden enemy, this wolf is punished and the enemy of the movement for Azadi ceases to exist. Oh God, save me from the curse of this enemy. Protect me, give me strength and enlighten me with inner faith. Oh the merciful, have mercy upon me, oh the generous One, be generous to me, Amen!

I met Abidji for only five minutes and mentioned what I had heard in the courtroom; he also felt worried and began to wonder. In truth, a political conspiracy was being hatched against me from much earlier. But I decided that I had left my problems in God's care; He alone has the power to do something and change the course of any situation. Still, I was not so dejected even on the day I was arrested as I was on the day I heard from the judge that he had received these letters from Kashmir, from Srinagar asking him that I not be released or given bail.

Na zalim bhediyon ka khauf hai na ke caseon ka darr
Qafas behtar nazar aata hai mujh ko apne maskin se

I do not fear the tyrants or the number of cases against me
This prison appears to be a better abode than my own dwelling
(Sahil Maqbool)

I was taken from Patiala court to Tees Hazari court where 18 September was given as the next date of hearing. I was produced twice as Rehmana Yousuf had been produced earlier with regard to her own case. She was arrested under the Lal Qila (Red Fort) shoot-out case and these days, the witness procedure was taking place in her case. Her only 'crime' was that she had married a Pakistani national and was arrested soon after marriage. A father and son (Nazir Ahmed Qasid) duo from Kashmir (Konipura) were the co-accused in this case.

My head felt heavy when I woke up early in the morning the next day. I hadn't slept till well past 1 am, I'd been deep in thought about what had happened in court. I kept wondering who the people were who had written against me to the judge.

And I kept asking myself: where will all my thinking lead except to add to my tension and woes? There were already enough things for me to worry about in jail without my adding to them. So I decided to leave things to God, and instead, I went to the library at 10, issued a few books and returned to the cell at 12 noon. I stayed in bed more or less all day and by evening my eyes were swollen and my face was beginning to swell too. I was still grappling with yesterday's hurt and agony.

I received a letter from my mother in the evening. It was the best thing that could have happened on a depressing day like this. If Boba's prayers are with me, I know that the entire universe and God too is with me. I saw that the letter had been posted in Kashmir over ten days ago, but it came at the right time to me. I took this as a message from God that things would be all right. I was not dejected anymore but I remained anxious.

On the next mulaqat day Baji and Khalid had come to meet me. They were going to the shrine at Ajmer Sharif the next day to pray for me and pledge a vow on my behalf. Baji told me about a special namaz and advised me to offer it to empower myself over 'the enemy', she wrote down the details of how to perform this namaz on a piece of paper and also offered a talisman to me for my early release from prison. Baji was telling me that we should change my lawyer; everyone was in favour of appointing Ram Jethmalani instead, but his fee was known to be exorbitant and I told her that it would be impossible to arrange for such a large amount. Baji's reply that she was ready to sell her house and car to raise the required sum of money brought tears to my eyes. We heard that on 17 September 2004 a meeting was called to revoke POTA, presided over by the Home Minister Shivraj Patil. In the evening the radio carried the news that POTA had indeed been revoked and I felt really happy. I was also happy because Maya Aunty was being released that day. Prisoners share in each other's happiness to overcome the indifferent, drab and sorrowful atmosphere in jail. Whenever a woman was released from a ward, other women inmates would greet the news happily by clapping their hands in a gesture to welcome her release, even while remaining behind locked bars in their own cells. If the news of a release was known in advance, women from the wards would collect together and beat drums and sing songs of joy. Maya Aunty embraced me. She had tears in her eyes as she said, 'Beti, I will always remember you and think of you.' I carried her luggage till the door of the ward and from there she went to the deorhi on her own. I told her to pray for me as I had been caught in a big, serious case. She told me that she was sure I would soon be released, 'When God showers mercy, even the worst difficulties are resolved and yours too will be eased.'

The hearing in the 'jail case' was fixed for 18 September and a little before that we received the challan which included witness accounts of twenty women constables against us. When we returned from court, Siddiqua wanted to meet the Deputy SI Ved Prakash. She was fuming with anger. Six of us 'accused' women entered Sir's room and showing him the challan, demanded to know what all this was about. 'You people have made baseless allegations against us and imposed this case on us.' He said that he did not know who could have done this, he didn't think it was any of them, but that the officer at Hari Nagar had written it. We were, however, not satisfied with his explanation. Siddiqua and four other women went inside the AS's room while I decided to remain outside; I began to shout at the top of my voice 'you people have shown us your true colours by giving this false evidence against us; we do not have any faith in a policeman's uniform. Look at Siddiqua! She is a prisoner for the past ten years.' Soon, all the matrons and the AS went away towards the deorhi and the prisoners were locked in their cells. SI Sir was on duty as in-charge of ward 6 in place of SI madam who was on leave. He came on a round and stood in front of my cell; he first congratulated me on account of POTA having been revoked, I stood up and thanked him. He then said, 'Now you are going to be released from a big case and even this petty jail case will come to an end. The jail people have unnecessarily dragged you all in this case. Actually, the entire staff was worried that there will be a major fracas.' All of us prisoners had got together and demanded that SI Sir come and meet us. So that was how he'd come along with the DS, AS and the matron for a round of the wards. I kept awake the whole night; even Aunty did not sleep a wink. I offered my prayers in the morning the next day. The entire jail remained locked as the jail authorities feared that the six women, who had returned with the challan in a rage a day earlier, might inform the other inmates and thereby mobilize them for a showdown with the authorities again. For this reason, the army had already been called in and stationed at the deorhi to meet any challenge from the women inmates. There were severe restrictions imposed on me and my ward remained locked the entire time but some of the habshi women created such a ruckus at being locked in that they had to be brought out. In any case the staff did not exercise much control over them. Just before noon, the SI came on a round with the other staff and had the women brought out from their wards and cells. He said, 'It was on my instructions that the jail remained locked today because the six women were given a challan in the jail case yesterday in which the staff has testified against them although I am aware that these women are innocent and in fact, the names of those who had actually indulged in destruction are missing. The women were angry yesterday and we feared that this would lead to a hungama again. But you people have maintained peace and I wish to thank the six women as well as all of you for cooperating with the jail authorities.' He left after having said this; it was around noon due to which the locks were fastened yet again. The doors opened at 3 pm but as it was a holiday, we were locked in earlier. So basically we remained under lock and key the entire day and night.

I woke up early, and after completing my prayers stepped out at 6 when the door was unlocked. Tea was served at 7 after which I took a bath and left for the library. At 12, I visited the doctor as I had begun to have various symptoms due to hormonal imbalance caused by consuming jail medicines for so long. Asha Aunty who shared the cell with me also came to fetch some medicines. Today it was her mulaqat but she was crying a lot and when I asked her the reason she said, 'my daughter had come to visit me today. Her children are going to be sitting for their exams and she told me that it would perhaps be difficult for her to visit me until their exams were over. I told her that she must certainly be with her children and not visit me as such visits always leave her feeling disturbed.' The pathos in her voice moved me to tears. She went back to the cell and I returned to the library as I had to fill forms for those women inmates who were appearing for their exams through IGNOU (Indira Gandhi National Open University). The AS, Raman Madam was in charge of this but since she did not even know her alphabets, she made me do all her work but I managed it with interest as it had to do with reading and writing.

When I went to the cell at 1 o'clock aunty was waiting for me for lunch with food that her daughter had brought from home. After Maya aunty left, a girl called Anita took her place in our cell. She was from Assam and had been arrested under the Illegal Arms Act. She was actually a Muslim woman but her boyfriend was a Hindu. They had come to Delhi for some work and according to Anita, when they were returning from Delhi by train, there were some soldiers travelling in the same compartment and when they were getting off the train, they accidentally picked up one of the soldiers' bags as it was identical with theirs. Later, there was a raid on their hotel room and it was found that their bag contained an Army ID card, a uniform, a belt etc. An army officer acknowledged that this could be due to a genuine mistake but by then, the arrests had been made.

In the next mulaqat Baji and Khalidji came to meet me. They had returned from Ajmer Sharif the previous day and had brought a white chaddar (a sheet that is laid on the shrine by a devotee) for me while offering one at the shrine for my well-being and early release. Khalid went to meet Anjali madam. Two days prior to their visit to Ajmer Sharif, he had wanted to deposit Rs 2000 in my name but at that time Anjali madam had said that there was already some money in my account and therefore there was no need to deposit more. My sister told her that they were returning home and may not be able to visit for many days due to Ramadan and Eid but Anjali madam refused to accept their plea. I had started telling my family members not to visit me frequently as it was a long and tedious journey for them; it was also beginning to affect Baji's health and this time I saw that she had her foot in a bandage. She came again after two months; each time someone came for mulaqat it filled me with happiness but I was also beginning to worry for them. For prisoners, mulaqat was the only means to stay alive.

I read in the newspaper that POTA had been revoked but it was not going to benefit those who had already been arrested under this Act and that their cases would continue as before. The news left me cold and anxious.

Many Muslim women were brought into jail who had been arrested under charges of prostitution and vagrancy. Almost all of them were from war zones. They belonged to those Muslim majority states in Russia that had seceded, such as Azerbaijan, Chechnya, Uzbekistan and Tajikistan. I was astonished when I saw them and could not believe that they had left their own countries and come to India, only to indulge in prostitution. There was increasing impoverishment in these countries due to the deteriorating situation caused by war and these women had perhaps taken to this profession out of compulsion. It had a strange impact on me as I thought to myself that even we were fighting a war and, God forbid, we also do not end up in a similar situation as these women. I pray to God that our nation achieves freedom with respect and dignity. I was even more astonished later when I saw two young Kashmiri women arrested and brought here on similar charges of prostitution. When I saw them working in the field, they recognized me. I went to the matron in charge of the ward and requested her that they should not be made to do this work after which I visited the

canteen and bought a few things of daily use that I handed over
to them. I told them, 'Today I am meeting Kashmiri women
here for the first time but I am not at all happy about it. Had you
come here due to ladai-jhagda or any other case, I would have
proudly proclaimed that you are Kashmiri but you have been
brought under such a shameful case that I am not even able to
mention it.' Both of them were associated with the Valley; they
hugged me and wept inconsolably.

They had sad stories to tell. One girl gave her name as
Zahida. Her father had died while she was still a child. The
family lived in dire poverty and, she yearned for even the most
basic necessities of life. She happened to meet a girl from
Srinagar during a wedding there who brought her to Delhi with
a promise of finding her a job. Instead, she struck a deal with a
a Sikh man and sold the young woman away into prostitution.
Zahida went home after many months but her mother, seeing
the bodily changes in her daughter, beat her up and threw her
out of the house and she was forced to return to Delhi and
come back into the 'profession'. The other girl gave her name as
Ruby and her story was that her father had begun to force her to
have sex with him after her mother's death. She was working in
a carpet manufacturing unit but somehow she too got dragged
into the net of prostitution.

September 30 was Shab-e-Barat (an auspicious occasion when
prayers are offered through the night). May God accept my
prayers and release me from this prison, Amen!

I had a court appearance for my 'jail case' in early October.
Abidji came with the lawyer and congratulated me because
he had managed to put in the papers at the High Court for
my bail. November 30 was fixed for the next hearing. Abidji
said, 'Insha'Allah the case will be over soon and you will be
acquitted.' Everyone was congratulating Doctor Sahib (my elder
brother) including Advocate Salman Khurshid who said that he

I was produced there and then taken back to the lock-up. Abidji had been waiting since 10 in the morning but I was produced only by 12 noon. He had brought a Ramadan calendar for me with details of sehri and iftar timings; he gave it to me along with whatever news he had from home. I requested him to bring a jacket and a blanket for me on his next visit. He wished me for Ramadan and expressed hope that this would be my last one in jail. He handed me a copy of the Approval sheet that he had received after submitting my bail application in the High Court; Insha'Allah the release would take place on 30 November.

I offered namaz after returning from mulaqat and lay down for a while as there was enough space in the lockup on that day to do so. At 5, we were made to stand in a queue and get into the waiting prison van which took us back to Tihar; a musical programme had been organized in the jail on that day but was nearly over by the time we came back. I went to my ward, had tea, changed my clothes and offered namaz. I spoke with aunty for some time, I later switched on the radio that I had borrowed from the matron; I listened to Kashmiri news on the radio every day but on that day I was disappointed as there was no signal.

The langar that provided for sehri had not yet received the required rations so we were given only an apple and roti each. A few days earlier, Muslim women prisoners had submitted an appeal to the SI with a request that certain food items be made available in the canteen during Ramadan. The langar finally got the rations and we were therefore given the usual serving of roti, vegetable and tea for sehri; the roti was soft and vegetables quite good, but the tea was cold. Hindu women in jail also fasted; some of them had the night langar duty and by the time they carried the tea from there, it had turned cold. Had the round of serving tea begun from my ward, I would perhaps have got a hot cup but then I'd have had to drink it much earlier than the sehri time. The food (chai, roti, dal) was packed in little polythene bags and given to us through the space between the iron bars.

On the sixth day of Ramadan, Abidji came for mulaqat and brought the jacket and blanket that I had asked for. He told me that three panels had been established for the review of POTA cases and rather than the courts, these panels would scrutinize the cases and also decide about which prisoners were to be released and which not.

A couple of days later when I came out of my cell at around 9 in the morning, a habshi woman prisoner called me and introduced me to a few other women who were sitting with her. I was seeing these women for the first time as they had been brought in the previous night. I later learnt that these Pakistani women had been arrested under the 'false/counterfeit currency' Act. I greeted them and the 'old' prisoners who were also sitting there. All of them belonged to ward 8. Elizabeth asked me to come and sit with them; I heard the Pakistani women narrating their stories to the other two women while claiming their innocence and bemoaning the state of helplessness they found themselves in. I addressed them and said that everybody is a distressed person here; why are you sharing your worries with them? As we talked, they showed me their hands that were still covered in black ink that is applied when a new prisoner arrives; their palms extended in front of me, they told me to look at the terrible state they were in and that they had not even been able to wash their hands since yesterday. For humanity's sake, I told them to come to my cell and wash up as I knew that they did not have soap etc., but as soon as they entered my cell, Munshi Babita from ward 8 followed them and said 'Anjum Baji, these women are new convicts and I have been searching for them.' Saying this, she took them away with her; new convicts are not allowed to go to any other ward and secondly, the wards/cells for them are locked much earlier but most importantly, these were Pakistani women. I told Babita that since they did not have soap etc., she should get some for them. When I came out of the cell after they left, I saw a 6-foot tall, big-built habshi woman prisoner, Sandra, standing there and abusing me loudly. I asked her why she was doing that but she responded by shouting louder, alleging that I had advised and prevented the Pakistani women from speaking to the habshi women. I said, 'I did not say or do any such thing as I did not even know these women. Since many women prisoners mistake me to be a Pakistani, Elizabeth had called me to say that some women have come from 'my' country and that I should meet them. We did not even talk about anything as the ward Munshi came and took them away before they could even wash up.' Not convinced, she went ahead where a few matrons were sitting; she complained to them and made all kinds of false allegations against me. Elizabeth was also glaring at me with anger; I told her that Sandra is under some misunderstanding regarding me and that I had not said or done anything wrong to her but she continued to abuse me. I told her that I was observing a fast and she should not abuse me just as I had not abused her but she took long strides towards me and suddenly pushed me hard, my legs buckled under and I fell down on my back. Elizabeth grabbed me by the collar and began to tear at my clothes. She scratched me and dug her sharp nails into my chest which began to bleed instantly, she then pulled me by my hair but I could not do anything. The beating continued even as the matron and some of the women tried to free me from her clutches but she would not let go of my hair. However, they managed finally to pick me up but I was in such a helpless and pitiable state. Standing there, I couldn't stop crying, my hair was completely dishevelled and my clothes were torn to shreds. Whenever this scene comes to my mind, it traumatises me as much today as it did then. I was still crying when some of my jail comrades came and brought me back to the cell. I kept crying; Elizabeth had torn a chunk of hair from my scalp and my head was now shorn of it. The AS madam came from the chakkar and expressed anguish on seeing the state I was in and tried to console me with a few kind words. I told her about the entire incident but I was aware of how helpless the jail staff also felt in relation to these habshi prisoners.

She told me that she would make a phone call to the SI madam; just then women from ward 6 arrived at my cell and were shocked to see my bleeding chest and torn clothes and hair but tried to console me by saying that I was a brave and innocent woman. Since I was beaten so mercilessly in front of everyone and my clothes torn, I felt humiliated and ashamed; I was wondering why this had happened to me. During this time, SI madam came to my cell, asked for a chair and after asking other women to leave; she sat down and asked me what had happened. I kept crying; madam told me I was a brave woman and that I should be strong in dealing with this situation. I told her everything as clearly as I could, that these uncivilized black women had beaten me up so mercilessly for no fault of mine. She saw my wounds and asked me to go with her to the MIR where she had these examined by the Senior Medical officer (SMO) who also administered an injection and gave some medicines. Madam told the AS Jyothi madam to issue a punishment against these women at the earliest. I returned to the cell but my wounds were raw and hurting and my head was exploding with pain; I could not control my tears and continued to cry for a long time. At 1 pm, madam SI called Sandra and Elizabeth to her office and an hour later, she also called me there and took our individual statements. I told her everything truthfully but Sandra gave a false statement and Elizabeth lied too. She had brought her own torn shirt and alleged that I had torn it whereas everyone, including madam, knew that I had not even raised my hand or abused her. Madam heard everything and asked us to compromise as she did not want any such quarrels in the jail; but she failed to understand my feelings. She consoled me, saying 'See, you are going to leave soon' and then added 'you are involved in a big case and I do not wish that your name be dragged into any other case, the women involved in this fight are Pakistani and if your name gets associated with theirs, it will not be good for you. I want you all to come to an understanding with each other and, if you have any respect for me you'll do as I say.' In deference to madam, I did compromise with the two women but my heart was weeping tears of blood. I had to pretend to hug these women but how could the anger and resentment be forgotten so soon when my wounds were still bleeding? Anyway, I returned to the cell and shed more tears over my own helplessness. The next day, when I was reading a newspaper outside, a woman inmate came and sat by me and started talking to me when Sandra also arrived and told her to go away; she then turned to me and said that I should leave from here as this place was actually meant for the tea vendor. When I refused to move, she was outraged and started abusing and threatening to beat me up again. AS Renuka and a matron were also present there but they did not make any attempt to stop Sandra from behaving with me in this manner. She was now threatening that she would send my dead body to my house; the situation was becoming serious and unwieldy again. I regret the jail staff's attitude; I knew that even if Sandra had made an attempt on my life, I could not expect any support or sympathy from them. However, soon after this, the doors were closed and we remained locked for the entire day. In the evening, Deputy SI, Meena madam (Internal In-charge) went to Sandra's ward and spoke unabashedly in her favour. Meena madam had recently been promoted to the rank of an Inspector; she was appointed here by the DG following the incidents after Zohra's death. She knew the old prisoners well and was also aware of the politics inside the jail; she knew the ways in which prisoners could be used, threatened and controlled but she was not a capable officer. To maintain her authority and dominance in jail, she had surrounded herself with a few rogue women as even the jail staff and prisoners were afraid of Sandra; she had the ability to easily mobilize all the habshi women around her which made it difficult for the staff to exercise any control over them. Sandra was also favoured as she was a source of lucrative income for the staff; she would smuggle tobacco inside the jail for the staff and was also responsible for running the canteen at the time. Elizabeth was totally uncivilized and readily got involved in any altercation between prisoners, including physical fights. The jail staff was helpless in front of these aggressive habshi and foreign women. In the past few days alone, Elizabeth had beaten at least four women prisoners but the jail authorities chose to turn a blind eye and refused to take any action against her.

The women prisoners dreaded the beating as many of these habshi women were known to be suffering from HIVAIDS. I was confused as to whether I should put an arzi in court or write to the DG regarding the beating I had been subjected to. Madam SI did not do any justice to me by forgiving these women who now felt free to strut around.They would taunt me that they had beaten me in public, torn my clothes and yet madam had said nothing to them. I felt deeply hurt and dishonoured. I began to lose sleep again. On Monday morning, I went to the senior madam's office, registered my name outside and entered her room, Meena madam and AS Renuka were also there. I told madam that keeping her advice in mind, I had remained patient but these women had again begun to harass me and to be rude. The previous day they had picked a quarrel with me. And despite this Meena madam had gone to their ward, smiling and clapping, so it was not surprising that they were encouraged by this. I also mentioned that these women were being nurtured under her tutelage, she had her own favoured group of women in jail but I was not one among them. Madam said, 'Anjum, you are very dear to us, and we feel like you are one of our own, you come from a good, educated family – that is apparent from your face; we are all with you and I want to tell you that you must never feel alone here.' In the meantime, Meena madam was trying to interrupt and say that I was a victim of misunderstanding, but I did not pay any attention to her except to say that I was talking to her boss and not to her. SI madam was not only sympathetic to me but also supported me, and tried to calm and comfort me. That helped me a lot. Before returning to my cell, I went to the MIR and collected some medicines. There, I inadvertently bumped into Fatima; another habshi woman, I was so preoccupied I didn't even notice and I picked up the medicines and returned to the cell just in time and then I took some time for my prayers.

Half an hour later, madam left her office for a round of the wards; she first went to Sandra's ward where Fatima and my jail comrade shared the same barrack. Sandra and Fatima were conspiring among themselves against me; they were plotting that they would beat me up because Fatima had told her I'd pushed her in the MIR. They were shouting at my friend and threatening her with violence and and then they issued a warning that they would burn down the entire jail along with the terrorist Anjum.

My friend was trying to appease them by saying that I did not push Fatima deliberately and that it was unintentional on my part but they refused to believe her because they just wanted to make life difficult for me. The SI madam happened to hear all this; so she confronted them and said she had now understood who was behind all the trouble. Sandra was stunned when she saw her standing in front of her; she promptly got to her feet and began to apologize to madam and promised that she would not cause any further trouble and that there would be no occasion for a complaint against her. Madam told her in response that she did not want her to stay here anymore and would seek a transfer for her; Sandra started crying but madam said that she was giving her a week's grace-time and that if she got into another fight during this period, then she would have to face the consequences. Sandra interrupted her, pleading for forgiveness and repeating that she would never do such a thing again. I learnt about all this much later; Madam came to our ward around 2 pm when I had just finished my afternoon prayer. I was alone in the cell; aunty had gone to the barrack to watch TV and Anita was at the crèche where she had her duty. Madam stood at the door of my cell and enquired after me but I did not say anything in response as I had nothing to say; I simply kept standing inside. She then said a few things such as 'You should keep a low profile. I have pulled up Meena and told her that she must stop scheming against you. I am aware that she has been promoted from the post of police constable to an inspector because of which she has started thinking too much of herself. You are from a good family but have spoilt your own life. What is there in politics? I pray that you get released from here soon. There is more restriction on you in jail because of the serious nature of your case but I do wish that you get some respite. I am trying to ensure that you do not suffer any more and that your name is not dragged in small, petty cases.' She spoke in this vein for nearly an hour and, after she left, I lay down to rest. At 3.30, I took out the clothes that Elizabeth had torn off my body and sat down to sew and mend them but even before I had put the thread in the needle, Sandra rushed into my cell and began to apologize to me but I remained silent. She said that when she was willing to forget all that had happened; I too should make a similar effort. In the meantime, aunty had returned and asked Sandra why she had done this to me. Is she not your sister, she asked her. Sandra replied in broken Hindi that she was enraged then but felt ashamed now for having done wrong. She helped me to my feet, hugged me and said 'the jail has remained locked because of us; the women are suffering due to this. Let us both go to madam and request her that the women should be unlocked from their cells and that we will not fight anymore.' We went there and Sandra informed madam that she and I had patched up and that she did not harbour any ill will against me anymore. Madam did not respond except to say that the cells would be opened once Meena madam came and with this assurance, we returned to the cell. But seeing us together was not acceptable to those women who wanted us to carry on fighting. In some ways this fight was good because at least now I knew who my enemies were. When I got a chance to talk to Sandra I told her that some of the prisoners were making use of her and taking advantage of our fights; Sandra replied 'we are both educated and we have to give a fitting reply to these illiterate women I will not be fooled by them anymore.'

After iftar, as I was coming out of the cell, I heard Sandra screaming loudly and, within seconds, all the habshi women had collected outside her cell and started marching towards Meena madam's office but they quickly came back when they saw the senior Madam also sitting there. Meena madam had transferred Sandra from ward 5 to Ward 1 because of which she was shouting and screaming. The entire staff had now gathered. Meena madam was saved due to the presence of senior madam; otherwise Sandra would have beaten her up. She tore her own clothes and all the other habshi women joined in her wailing. During this time, the senior madam arrived and reprimanded Meena madam in front of everyone and demanded to know why she had transferred Sandra when she had already promised that she would behave herself. Sandra was also angry because Meena had not allowed her into her office earlier on the pretext that she was busy with some urgent work whereas she was busy gossiping with one of her hangers-on, Sadhana. Sandra mentioned this to senior madam who instructed Meena not to undertake any transfer of prisoners without her permission; this is how Sandra's transfer was immediately deferred and the commotion controlled. I was watching all this from my ward; I did not step out at all. Thank God, my patience paid off and those who Meena madam had tried to incite against me were now themselves against her.

On 26 October, I went to Anjali madam to withdraw some money. I found two sealed envelopes there on her table; one letter was from Shabbo, Qudsia and Sehr and the other one was from Neelji. Anjali madam asked me to sit down while asking the other women to leave the room. She started talking to me. 'You are upset and feeling lonely these days due to all that has been happening with you. You must totally stop thinking in an intellectual manner here. One is forced to talk to other prisoners here as there is no choice, but forget your own ego and intellect. This is a terrible place where speaking correctly is also considered wrong. You are fighting for a cause and try to take these small difficulties as part of this larger cause. Do not take these petty words and deeds here so seriously. Your health is deteriorating; think of yourself first before considering anything else. Do

not, by any means, think about why this is happening with you. There is no place for this 'why' here. If you put too much stress on 'why', you will suffer even more. When an elephant walks, the dogs in the lane always bark but the elephant finds its way and continues to walk ahead with pride, without paying any attention to the barking dogs. I understand your difficulties and worries; you are a sensitive person and that is why you tend to feel much more. Please do not think that anyone is after your honour because women here do not even know what honour means or who an honourable person is. Therefore, it does not pay to worry about these things.' I kept listening to her quietly, picked up my letters and coupons and went to the canteen to buy some milk for iftar. I returned to my cell and sat down to read the letters.

The faces of my dear, loved ones appear before me and cause me much anguish...

> *Dar-e-qafs pe andheron ki mohur lagthi hai*
> *Tho Faiz dil mein sitarey utarne lagte hain (Faiz)*

> When darkness seals the prison door
> Stars begin to light up my heart

The pain of spending lonely days in jail, away from one's sisters and brothers, well-wishers, and from one's own country can only be understood by one who actually undergoes this experience. To imagine this scenario for someone who breathes in open air is not only difficult but impossible. Jail is the kind of world where its hardships and difficulties can either weaken a person or make her stronger. If you have trust in God, you can tell yourself that each difficulty, each hardship is sent to try us, as if it were a test. And it becomes easier to deal with them.

The restrictions that were imposed upon me, along with the attitude of the jail authorities towards me showed how deeply they were prejudiced about me. But I trusted in God and therefore was able to cope with these problems; each time I was tested but it did not break my will. I was getting physically weaker as I was being hammered day and night with such humiliations and sometimes I felt it would be really difficult to maintain my mental balance, but somehow I managed.

29 October was the scheduled date for the jail case; I slept for almost the entire day there in the lockup until the next date was given for 23 November. When I returned from there I did wuzu (ablution), offered namaz and went back to sleep. I did not speak to any one throughout the day; in any case I hardly spoke to the women inmates or the staff anymore, particularly since that fight with Sandra. At night, after iftar, I sat down to reply to the letters I had earlier received. While writing letters, I felt as though I was partially home and partly here in jail; I would be in such a complex mental state, lost in memories that it took hours to write a single letter.

On 4 November, three women were released from our ward, and the entire ward celebrated. Whenever women were released from a particular ward, it began to be known as the 'lucky' ward. If a ward did not have a single release for a prolonged period, women would start offering puja path and string lemons and green chillies and hang them at the entrance door.

One of the wards that I was presently lodged in was known as the 'bahu' (daughter-in-law) ward as the women here were arrested under 'dowry death' charges; some of them were here for either burning their bahus or hanging them to death, but a few women were also innocent.

Dowry death cases were quite complex; whether the daughter-in-law was killed in an accident or committed suicide because she was in love with someone else, her natal family invariably accused her in-laws and implicated them in these cases. There are many complications in such cases where, at times, an entire family is arrested; if a sister is married in another town or city, even she does not escape being implicated in the case or arrested. In many cases, the woman gives a dying declaration which may go either in her in-laws' favour or against them. Even if the declaration is in their favour, the family members are made to taste Tihar jail's life and if the declaration is against them, then God alone can protect them.

The aunty who shared the cell with me had also been arrested in a dowry death case, but I believed her to be innocent. As she said, she got her only son married in a grand manner, her husband was blind and within a few weeks, her daughter-in-law got burnt in an accident at home. She gave a dying declaration in favour of her in-laws. However, her natal family registered a 'dowry death' case against them. Aunty and her son were both in jail due to this case and she was grateful that her daughters had not been implicated. Aunty was always busy in puja path. Anita, my other cell mate, was moved from the cell to a barrack and a woman named Urmila took her place. She was arrested in a case of theft; she was a dirty woman from a slum, I gave her soap and told her to bathe and change. This was not the first instance when such dirty women were lodged in my cell; every night such new convicts were brought into ward 8 from mulaheza and kept there.

On the 23rd day of Ramadan I had a body massage done with oil. My face had turned so dry and there were dark circles under my eyes. During Ramadan, the body gets drier due to dehydration and, in any case, my skin texture had become progressively dry in jail as there wasn't any skin cream available here; I had got a bottle of Maxim Moisturizer from outside which I used sparingly as it was not easy to get anything from outside.

I was not able to sleep for a minute the entire night. It was as though I was reading a script from my own life. My youth had vanished within the blink of an eye. I am a spectator, watching the journey of my own youth moving rapidly from one shore to another and then, vanishing without a trace. I dozed off for a while but remained awake from midnight until morning; staring at the four walls of the cell and its iron grill. At 3.45 am, women arrived to distribute sehri (the same dal, roti and chai) and I ate half a roti with some dal. Of late I did not feel like eating anything. I kept busy in my prayers until 6 in the morning after which I lay down to sleep but could not. I got up as the cell had to be cleaned today; I called Urmila and asked her to clean the fan with a towel. We washed the utensils and the cell too after which I left for the library. I returned at 12.30; I had carried a newspaper from there which I read for an hour and later offered my prayers and went to sleep. I dreamt of my deceased father, Tatthji. I was sitting in my room accompanied by my brother Shafiq, my uncle and my mother. The electricity voltage begins to fluctuate and my brother runs upstairs to fetch a transformer, there's one in the living room too but my father refuses to adjust it; I tell my brother that he should do it as he knows best about it. During this time, Thatthji comes but his body is not fully clothed; his chest is burnt as a result of a spark from Shafiq's transformer, I get disturbed seeing him in this condition and suddenly I was jolted out of sleep. My heart was hammering; I started praying for my father Thatthji's wellbeing and asked that he be kept in heaven (Amen). May my sister also find peace in heaven; I prayed that all those members of my family who have departed from this world, may they reside in heaven and, when I too bid farewell to this world, may God forgive me for my sins and find me place in heaven. Amen.

Today SI madam returned to jail after many days as one of her close relatives had passed away. I went to her office to offer my condolences but she was busy; I waited for some time and returned after leaving a written message of condolence for her.

On ThursdayAbidji came to visit me. I had fallen asleep after sehri, thinking that no one would come to see me but I got up and got ready when I learnt in the morning that my name was there in the mulaqat list. He gave me news of the family and I asked if they had received the Eid cards I had sent for them. Here in jail, the only greeting cards that are available are the ones that are made by prisoners and if we wanted to get cards from outside, we had to submit an application to the WO and the payment had to be made through a prisoner's PP account. It was mostly foreign i.e. habshi Christian prisoners who got their cards from outside while some Muslim women prisoners also did so on the occasion of Eid, but most got them from inside. Hindu festivals were celebrated in a much better way with different kinds of foods being made available in the canteen.

Similarly, foreign women prisoners celebrated Christmas in a big way. I have to say with regret though that Muslim festivals were not celebrated in a similar fashion.

Abidji and I exchanged Eid greetings; he prayed for this to be my last Eid in jail. Last evening I was summoned to the deorhi where a letter from the POTA Review Committee was handed over to me. It said that 23 November had been fixed for the last hearing in my case. When I received this letter I was wondering how to reach it to Abidji as I did not know then that I would meet him at mulaqat, I thank God that he came to see me otherwise I would have been worried. I handed the letter to him. He had deposited Rs 10.000 for my bail in the 'jail case' but I had not yet heard anything about it from the jail authorities. However, Abidji was confident that I would get bail on 30 November. No one knows better than me how I counted the days, waiting anxiously for this moment. Abidji was hopeful that if the POTA Review Committee came to a conclusion prior to this date, it would be much better for me. God knew what would happen. On shab-e-qadr (auspicious night during Ramadan) and the last Friday I prayed to Allah to accept my prayers on this auspicious day.

While in jail, I heard the news of the Palestinian chairman, Yasser Arafat passing away. Seventy-five year old Arafat was being treated in a military hospital in Paris where he breathed his last. He had spent his entire life in the struggle for Palestinian freedom and he remained under house arrest for many years.

It is the last day of Ramadan. It will be Eid tomorrow; this will be my fourth Eid in confinement. I was at the Lodhi Colony Special Cell during the first one. God willing, this Eid will be a harbinger of my release, may it shower happiness on my brothers, sisters and other loved relatives. May this Eid usher Azadi, progress and prosperity for my community, and mercy for the followers of Islam. May this Eid be an occasion for the release of young Kashmiri prisoners from jail as well as for all the Muslim women who are confined here. Amen.

The new moon was sighted on 14 November. The Shahi Imam had declared that Eid will be observed on the next day but in Kashmir, it was already celebrated today.

My heart is restless these days; the gap of several months between hearing dates means prolonged periods of suffocation within the four walls of this cell. I also worry about my future. Despite the punishing nature of life here, I have tried to keep myself busy in some work or the other. However, Kashmir's memory has never left me; I was yearning to return to the same mohalla, its lanes and by-lanes where I grew up and lived. I often sat and reminisced for hours until I began to imagine that I was a free being, sitting in my own house, but then the grim reality of finding oneself behind these cold iron bars was enough to shake me out of this illusion.

It was 9.30 at night on 19 November, the junior matron stood at the door, asking after my health and well being. Then she said, 'Baji, you have become very well known of late.' She then asked me to come to the door as she had 'something urgent' she wanted to discuss with me. I went out and she said, 'I have just been told by Ashwini madam (DS of jail 4) that Meena madam has sent a written complaint to the SI and DG against her, alleging that she (Ashwini) had gone to meet Anjum, a woman terrorist from jail 6, on the pretext of visiting the beauty parlour. Ashwini madam asked me to make sure that this news reaches you. I must say that I find it odd that Meena madam should drag your name into any problem that she may have with Ashwini madam.' I told her that I had visited the beauty parlour on 13 November and met Ashwini madam as I came out, but there were many other women prisoners too with whom she had exchanged a few words as she did with me. I had to rush to the cell as it was time for the doors to close and I did not want to be late. I know that there is some misunderstanding between the two women but since Meena madam also did not like me, she found an excuse to somehow drag my name into this. I was worried that the jail staff might implicate me in another false case. Meena madam did not like the fact that SI madam was sympathetic to me and also supportive.

It is a norm in jail that any prisoner, who worked with the senior madam (SI) or was close to her, was considered her special informer. The staff also believed that the SI was regularly informed about cases of bribery and other violations. Maybe this happens, but I know that I always only spoke to her regarding my own work.

23 November was the date for the jail case as well as the hearing in my POTA case under the Review Committee (RC). I waited impatiently for Abidji in court, hoping that he would come with some good news for me. I was going insane with anxiety, not able to sit down or eat a single morsel of food. I offered namaz but found no relief. Strange thoughts crowded my mind. However, at 5.30 I was put in the prison van and returned to Tihar jail. I had no idea what had happened and now, I began to wait impatiently for mulaqat.

Two days later, Tasleem, a family friend with whom Baji stayed in Delhi, came for mulaqat. My head had been hurting for the past three days, and I was really anxious about the decision of the Review Committee. I learnt that Advocate Salman Khurshid had argued for more than an hour in front of the Committee but the judge had not come to any decision as the state prosecutor was absent; the next date was therefore fixed for 4 December. I suddenly felt as though my arms and legs had broken; as if there was no life in my body. The repeated postponement of dates was wearing me out. How much more can a person bear this burden? My sister, Baji, had also been very worried and anxious – more so than me in fact, especially because my nephew, who was in court, did not respond to her repeated calls. She had not eaten anything for two days, I was told. I returned to the cell after mulaqat and realized that my body was burning with fever.

On 29 November I was produced in court at 11.30. There was Engineer Farooq Ahmed Khan from Islamabad along with other local Kashmiri boys in the men's lock-up; we exchanged greetings. I met Abidji as I climbed the first step leading to the court. He informed me that 11 January 2005 was given as the next date; the policewoman quickly went and returned with the date. Abidji walked by my side up to the lock-up, reassuring me all along that Insha'Allah, I would get bail the next day and be released by the POTA Review Committee. I happened to meet the Kashmiri boys again on my way back when one of them said 'We are proud of you. You are our dear sister. Those who have been released from jail [arrested along with Anjum] have sold their conscience, have bowed their heads.' I gave the boys my blessings and replied that I bowed my head only and only in front of Allah to which they replied 'You are the honour of our community and may God always protect your honour.' Abidji told me that Usha Mehra of the POTA Review Committee was a good judge and it was on her judgment that both Afshan Guru and SAR Geelani had been released earlier. Then mulaqat time was over and I was brought back to the lock-up.

I did wuzu and namaz and lay down to rest; there was a little more space in the lock-up today as we were only seven women. The bus arrived at 4.45 pm and we were sent back to Tihar. It was 9 pm and I was thinking that the next date was so far and the judge had not yet been given the legal brief.

I kept waiting, both on 30 November and 1 December, for the release papers. They came, but my name was not on them. I was so worried. But eventually, that day also passed.

There were many instances in jail when I believed that I would be released soon but the courts have their own complicated system: either the judge is absent, or the state prosecutor does not appear or there is a lawyers' strike. And the prisoner waits and waits. In jail, you can do some things to ease the stress and I decided to join painting classes. I thought how ironical it was – my life had become so colourless, and here I was trying to compensate by splashing colour on sheets of cartridge paper.

A few days later Abidji came for mulaqat and informed me that since the judge was not present in court on the day of the hearing, another date had been fixed, 31 January 2005. The meeting was brief – a member of parliament was expected to visit the jail so we could not take long. The mulaqat failed to lighten my mental burden. I could not any longer bring myself to be enthusiastic about the mulaqat, the moment I always waited for impatiently. There was no joy in it, and I came back from it dejected and disappointed. In fact, I felt so lethargic, I did not even get up to dress properly, I just stayed in bed. I did not seem to have any control over my tears which coursed from my eyes all day. What sort of an unending torture was this, I wondered, why was I being tried in this way? So low were my energy levels that I would get exhausted just with the daily jail routine. Even in the painting classes, which provided some relief, I remained restless. Sometimes I would paint until midnight and madam AS would ask me why I kept awake so late. But what could I tell her? That sleep had vanished from my eyes? She was glad to see my paintings and said that the classes were a good way for me to 'pass the time'. I woke up early every morning but my heart was burdened with an unbearable heaviness. The weather also did not help – it had turned uncomfortably cold.

One morning, as I walked to the library after my prayers, a young girl came up to me at the chakkar and said, 'Baji, someone has come for your mulaqat.' I told her that it was not my turn today but she insisted that someone was indeed waiting for me and showed me the mulaqat sheet. I was surprised that it was true; my name was announced and I went ahead towards the jangla and saw that Farida Baji was waiting for me. Whenever she came to Tihar, she met as many women prisoners as possible as she had herself served 4 years here for the Lajpat Nagar bomb blast case in Delhi in 1996. She always brought clothes, shawls and fruit for the women. When I thanked her for her visit she said there was no need to thank her, it was her duty: 'in fact, I should have made many more visits but I could not do so due to my own worries about my case.' She had brought a suit, lots of food and some fruit for me and Rehmana. She also gave me coupons of Rs 200 which I declined at first but later accepted at her insistence. I really liked her visiting me.

The painting class was becoming more interesting each day as we were being taught new ways of using colour; painting on glass, doing watercolours, fabric painting etc. Colours are so attractive. Also, our teacher was a kind woman. Jail is a strange world where we look for joy and happiness in small, simple activities that perhaps have no meaning in the 'free' world outside. Once the painting classes were over, some of the women from here in jail 6 would be selected and taken to ward 2 for a painting competition. I knew my name would not be among them – I was a high risk prisoner so these things were not for me – but I continued to attend these classes with keen interest.

Almost all prisoners in jail become victim of depression and it is perhaps because of this that there are frequent quarrels between them. In winter, there are added problems to deal with, as the food is always cold and bland, and the rotis are either burnt or half cooked. A few old prisoners who worked at the langar ensured that the staff got tasty food with a generous helping of ghee and spices, but this was not meant for us prisoners. The langar Munshi earned enough money by selling vegetables and rotis on the side. The canteen was managed by an old prisoner, Sandra. She did not have any good food to offer and instead, she looted the prisoners by selling everything at exorbitant rates, but no one dared complain against her because of her reputation. One day, the SI madam called a meeting to find out if prisoners had any problems; many complaints were registered following which she instituted a committee to look into these. One woman inmate dared to complain about the canteen items being expensive and about the tasteless food on offer. After the meeting, all the habshi women gathered around Sandra to teach this woman a lesson for complaining against her; fortunately it was time for the doors to be locked and the woman managed to run away to her cell in time to be locked in. However, the next day, she was forced to apologize to Sandra as she was aware that she would otherwise become a victim of her rage. As a rule, there was a bid every three months for prisoners to take turns to run the canteen and, to retain control over it beyond the three months, a prisoner had to submit Rs 1100 to the jail authorities on a daily basis; the money was made during the 'internal mulaqat' on Saturdays. Now that Sandra had taken control of the canteen, she did not wish to hand it over to anyone else and even the DS, who was in-charge of the canteen, did not dare raise any objection. Sandra was thus able to run a parallel tobacco trade from inside the canteen; she 'managed' the canteen for as long as she was in jail. When she was released on parole, she left without giving any account of the income and expenditure and it is believed that she made off with Rs 10.000 and then, once outside, disappeared without a trace.

Winter was severe inside the jail and we had to sleep on cement floors. Not having permission to use curtains on the door and without any heating arrangements, I longed for the Kashmiri kangri (small cane basket with burning coal) and the firhan (long, woollen gown). It is difficult to procure hot water in jail but a few clever women somehow managed to do so. The langar Munshi secretly sold each bucket of hot water for coupons of Rs 10, to desperate prisoners. It was a similar situation in the night langar where the washerwoman prisoner managed to make a decent income by secretly selling hot water, but only to 'confidential' prisoners.

I often remained unwell in jail as the sub-standard medicines available there were not effective. I tried to make do as best as I could with these but each day would bring a new worry or problem. Abidji came one day and informed me that nothing had come of the POTA Review Committee. At this point, I lost all hope; it seemed to me that I would never be able to step out of this jail. Abidji had brought a few warm clothes and a pair of shoes for me and said that soon, Boba, Neel and her two daughters, Shaalu and Bashi would come to meet me. I was not particularly happy to hear this as it meant that they would have travelled all this way only for a twenty-minute meeting with me, and then I would spend a week worrying about whether they would get back safely. I wrote a letter and couriered it to Neelji, pleading with her not to come and also told Abidji to dissuade them from making this journey. I felt that it was not so important anymore for them to visit me – I had lost all hope and I did not want to show it in front of my family. They were worried not only about the POTA case but also the 'jail case' and suspected that the jail authorities were closing down all avenues for my release. I did not wish to see them anxious and worried. I wrote to them only about the 'good' things in jail, rather than the problems I faced. I felt that the choice to join the Tehreek had been mine, and therefore I should hold myself responsible for my situation. Since I was associated with the Hurriyat Conference, I was also ashamed that nobody from there had bothred to do anything for me so far. My family members had approached all the separatist leaders at the time of their talks with the Government of India (GoI) but they returned disappointed; I had warned them not to meet any of them but they did not want to leave any stone unturned for my release. I am of a revolutionary mind and consider politics to be a form of worship and I had entered politics with a simple desire to serve my community.

On 27 December I was on my way for the candle project (one of the many classes run in jail for women inmates where they learnt to make decorative wax candles) when I happened to glance at the mulaqat sheet at the chakkar. I was surprised to see my name there as I was not expecting anyone, hadn't Abidji come a day before with whatever I needed? I went to the jangla to see who had come. Just as I saw Neelji, the matron informed me that my mother had also come to visit me; I saw my nieces Shalu and Bashi too who came inside while my mother and Neelji waited outside with Abidji. A prisoner is allowed to meet only three people at a time. My eyes lit up when I saw them although my mother and sister appeared to have become much weaker. I asked them why they had come, when I had already sent them a letter telling them not to; but they hadn't received my letter as they had been in Jammu for the past few days. Neelji said that my nieces were missing me greatly and that Boba too was waiting impatiently to meet me; I was now so happy to meet them that all my worries disappeared. During the visit, I requested the Munshi to give me a paper and pen; I wrote an appeal to the SI that since my mother was old and ailing, we should be allowed to meet at the deorhi for her to be able to sit down. I went to the SI madam with the appeal and was glad that she agreed immediately; I met my mother in the DS's room along with my niece for twenty minutes after which they had to leave. I felt rejuvenated, almost as if I'd got a new lease of life with this mulaqat and this feeling lasted until the next one.

Working on the candle project seemed to have enhanced my respect among others and it also helped me remain busy for the whole day. It was also an opportunity to avoid meeting those prisoners who always found some excuse or the other to bother me. There was one prisoner here, Sharda Jain who had been arrested on charges of killing a Congress Party member, Atma Ram. She was a mean and wicked woman and tried to instigate other women against me on some pretext or the other. She used to work at the sewing centre and it was because of her that I'd left the centre.

I made some special candles for my family members and felt pleased with the idea of presenting these as gifts to them. I saw their faces and had an imagined conversation with them as I made each candle. A few days later, the same family members (from the previous visit) came to meet me but Neelji was initially not allowed to enter as she did not have an ID card although the matron later relented and I was able to meet her too. After mulaqat, I asked them to come to the deorhi where I had already taken permission to offer them the gifts I'd made; my mother and nieces were allowed to come in and we spent another twenty minutes with each other here. The best and most memorable feature of this meeting was that I was able to shake hands with them, and also to embrace them. When the door was opened for them to leave, I tried to shake hands with my sister too but the security guard shouted at me saying that despite being a high risk prisoner, how dare I cross the threshold? 'Go back in; don't you know that it is a crime to come out of this door when you are anyway involved in such a big case?' I quickly handed over the gifts to my family and got inside when the guard pushed the door hard and locked it; the entire staff at the deorhi had now been put on alert. I was perhaps so engrossed in meeting my family, particularly my mother that I had not paid much attention when the staff had yelled at me to return inside. A complaint was soon registered against me that 'the high risk prisoner, Anjum, had crossed the door'. And so I had to appear before the jail authorities. In this way, with court dates, mulaqats, jail humiliations, another year passed. I had now become used to tolerating these difficulties. Even the 'home food' did not suit me anymore as I had become so accustomed to eating the tasteless dal and roti in jail; in fact, 'home food' invariably caused me indigestion. I had also become more irritable lately, but that happened to all of us prisoners.

There were heart-rending incidents that occurred in jail every other day with the shadow of death looming over us. Jail offered the worst incidents of violations of prisoners' rights and their inhuman treatment. I thought, not months but years had gone by tolerating these and the boundaries of my existence were becoming more circumscribed each day. All the prisoners were helpless and they had no rights in front of the jail authorities, they had to bear the burden of so many difficulties and do so with patience and fortitude. Each day was a test: we had to re-generate the strength of forbearance but at times, this strength gave way to a sense of despair. At such times, God was our only support. The high walls of the jail appeared taller now and one had constantly to guard against becoming a victim of mental illness behind the narrow confines of the dark cell; I too tried my best to keep myself busy in some manner or another.

One day, Gopali Ma, an aged prisoner from ward 2, died. She had been ill for many days; she had returned from parole after two months but her health had begun to deteriorate since then. She was admitted to Deen Dayal hospital – a prisoner was sent to an outside hospital only when chances of her survival were low, or let us say that a prisoner was sent to an outside hospital only to breathe her last.

Days were turning into weeks, weeks into months and months into years; I kept waiting for the moment of my release and this is how year 2004 also went by.

Year 2005 saw thousands of people killed by the tsunami, many had become homeless while others disappeared; thousands of children were orphaned. A fund-raising programme was organized in jail for those affected by the tsunami and nearly all the women prisoners contributed to the fund; the largest amount was collected from the prostitutes' ward. These are women from the 'red light' area of Delhi and many owned large bungalows and were also a source of income for the jail staff. They were allowed to make outside purchases which was denied to common, ordinary prisoners. I, along with other women from different wards, also contributed; my mother had deposited some money for me just a few days before this appeal for funds was made. I found it encouraging that all of us, who were going through our own upheavals, forgot our dismal fate and willingly came together to help the tsunami affected people. There is one thing that is different in jail compared to the outside world; here a prisoner always strives to lessen and ease another's burden. Whenever I was found crying or in a state of dejection, other inmates would offer kind words of solace and reassurance; they were aware that I was from outside Delhi and also that that Indian government had a different attitude towards Kashmiris. However, inside the jail, all the prisoners are against the Government of India as they believe that it is this government that is responsible for the arrest of many innocent people who are then left to rot in jail.

On 6 January the doors were closed early and everyone thought it was a signal for search operations but we learnt that an officer was going to visit the jail. Whenever a team from the National Human Rights Commission (NHRC) or any other officer, such as Kiran Bedi, or a Member of Parliament visited the jail, we were promptly locked in. The NHRC team had visited on many earlier occasions to find out the status of prisoners here but, as long as I was in jail, they were not allowed to meet any prisoner nor did they bother to inquire. However, after each such visit, the newspapers would falsely report that the NHRC team had met the prisoners and instructed the authorities to make certain facilities available to them. The truth is that the team would come, enjoy tea at the chakkar, prepare a report and submit it to the government. I returned to my cell when the matron said that there wasn't any search operation. During this time, matron Kamlesh came to the ward, calling me loudly and told me that senior madam had summoned me to her office as all the Panchayat members had been called. I told her that I was not even a member but she said that I had to be there nevertheless as I was working on the candle project.

I quickly changed my clothes and left for the chakkar where, in the DS's room, the senior madam, the DS and a few women inmates were present. The senior madam looked anxious. I took permission and sat with the other women; we all looked at each other wondering about the reason for this sombre situation. The DS was not able to say anything despite the senior madam's nod. Ultimately, she broke the silence and declared 'Shabbo has died'. We were stunned, and suddenly there was an eruption of grief in the room; two women fainted while madam tried to console us. She was afraid that the commotion that had followed Zohra's death might be repeated now and had therefore locked up the entire jail. Only a few of us, old prisoners, had been asked to come here for consultations on how to deal with this crisis and how to break the tragic news to Shabbo's mother. Shabbo and her mother had been arrested on murder charges and her brother was also in another jail here. Shabbo and her brother were serving term for the murder of their stepfather; she and her mother were lodged in ward 4. She was often unwell and prior to the arrest, she had been engaged to a boy and the marriage preparations were under way but before the marriage, her alcoholic stepfather had committed suicide and although his brothers testified in their favour, she and her mother and brother were arrested and the case was still proceeding against them. Shabbo was a favourite of DS madam and, on most days, was found outside her office. She had been admitted to DD hospital two days ago and had died due to lack of blood in her body. The women who were present complained to madam that many women prisoners suffered from anemia but the senior madam ignored their complaints and asked us to only think of the present and how to break the news to Shabbo's mother. 'Only you people can control the situation now,' she said. What difference does a prisoner's death make to the jail staff? All that mattered to them was that no unpleasant incident had taken place during their service tenure; this was clearly apparent in her attitude. Whether a prisoner lives or dies, the service record of the staff must not be affected. The jail authorities had become alert after former DG Ajay Aggarwal's record had been spoilt at the time of his retirement due to Zohra's death. The matron was sent to bring Shabbo's mother. She immediately sensed that something was wrong when she saw all of us gathered in the office. She began to cry as soon as she entered; women were now beating their chests and wailing, we moved and sat on the ground outside while she kept sobbing, 'My daughter wanted to become a bride and reminded me every day that her marriage should be arranged as soon as we were released.' While we grieved for Shabbo, news came from ward 6 that a prisoner's brother had also died and she was also brought out of the ward; the entire jail turned into a scene of mourning. Senior madam sent someone to bring Shabbo's brother from the other jail but the paperwork took quite a while during which time the mother remained distraught. It is difficult to describe that moment when she met her son and the magnitude of their grief; all the women started crying with them. The brother was brought for only ten minutes after which he was sent out on parole to perform the last rites of his sister and the next day, on 7 January, senior madam arranged for Shabbo's mother's parole too and sent her home.

I had never imagined that there would be such a despairing moment in my life, a moment when our thoughts too could be controlled. I thought, one can apply an ointment on physical wounds but mental scars are too deep to heal even after one is released from prison.

On my next court date in January the judge was again absent – this time he was on leave. Abidji was talking to a policeman on the stairs when I reached the judge's room; I was able to speak a few words with him while the date warrant was being prepared. There were many other POTA prisoners who had come for hearings from different jails and were waiting for their turn, as all POTA cases were heard by the same judge. Since the judge had not arrived, all of us were taken down to SN Dhingra's courtroom where the next day was given as the collective date after which we were taken back to the lockup which was, as always, very cold and the women prisoners were shivering as there was no arrangement for heating. We were bundled into the prison van at 5.30 and taken back to Tihar. I had to again return to the court the next day and was produced before the judge at 10.30. Although the judge was present in court today, no proceedings were held and we had to return disappointed, with another date posted for yet another day.

Abidji came to visit me; I asked him about the status of my case and he said, trying to reassure me, that the POTA Review Committee still had to deliver its judgment and Insha'Allah, it would be in our favour. I was not satisfied with his assurance but there was no option except to be patient and wait. In jail, only those prisoners are able to adjust who are either cunning or sharp-minded but I am neither. I do not know any hypocrisy; I always say what is in my heart. I cannot smile at someone while at the same time holding a grudge against her/him. But it is essential to possess this skill to be able to survive in this world where I have been forced to spend the best years of my life; in this ugly, detestable environment. Things are not simple or straight for me. There is an examination, a test at every step.

Today, the cell had to be cleaned; I removed the bags, blankets etc., put them outside and began to clean. One had to rush through the cleaning as the belongings had to be brought back into the cell before the doors closed but alas, this couldn't be managed and I had to bring everything and put it on the wet floor; no option but to be locked inside the wet cell. I had to appear for a hearing at Tis Hazari court in relation with the jail case on 16 January. Abidji had come with my lawyer but even here, the judge was on leave and we were then taken to another judge but he was also not present in court. Now, we were produced before yet another judge, Sanjeev Yadav who posted 21 January as the next date. The police had a tough time transporting me from one courtroom to another. Being in the category of a high risk prisoner, first, a wireless message had to be sent after which another posse of policemen would arrive, form a cordon around me and only then was I produced in court with my hand firmly in the grip of a woman constable. This was the day of the judges – they had the advantage over me – but I know that the doors of Ka'ba (Mecca) are always open and some day, certainly, my one prayer, one plea will be heard and bear fruit. May God have mercy upon me, Amen.

The Shahi Imam has announced the sighting of the new moon and fixed the date for Eid-ul Zuha. I got busy making Eid cards and spent the entire night doing so. The AS, Dinesh madam came on a round of the wards and, finding me awake, asked me what I was doing. She was often on a round when

I was either painting or writing; I showed her the cards I was making and she expressed her happiness and encouraged me to continue. It took me three days to make these cards; for my mother, Khalidji, Shabbo Rani and Shahi.

On 21 January, I went to court for a hearing in the jail case, along with Tahera and Rehmana. Santosh and Bobby did not come as their date warrant was not ready. Siddiqa was on parole and came to the court from outside. We were produced at 2.45 pm. My lawyer was there and I told him to appeal to the judge not to give an appearance date; this date was presented before the judge in the Prison Headquarters of Tihar jail where we had to wait from morning till evening. The judge accepted our plea and gave 3 February as the next date. Later, we were taken back to Tihar at 6.30 but it was only after 7 that we were able to enter our cell as we were frisked on our return from the court.

By this time I was in no mood to celebrate Eid. Both the weather and my mood were equally bad and I decided to remain inside the cell the entire day. Many women inmates wore new clothes, trying to drown their sorrows in celebrations. But I stayed by myself.

Tihar Jail 6 is reserved for women and the canteen here has many make-up items that they can buy. Even in this difficult hour, women were able to use make-up and also liked to dress in their best, as it is their nature. On any Sunday, many women could be seen with henna in their hair. The beauty parlour in the jail – a fairly well equipped one run by the jail authorities which employs women inmates who are trained in beauty treatment – also had hair colour, but it was expensive and only rich women could afford it.

For Hindu festivals, all these things were made available in plenty and at times, fabric sellers were brought to the jail for women to make their purchases but the clothes were only as good as the 'jail standard' and yet cost much more than outside. Whenever any fabric was brought to jail, women would rush to the chakkar in large numbers and in a few days, you could see many prisoners wearing identical suits as there wasn't much choice in the selection. During festivals, a photographer was also arranged by the staff and women felt happy to pose and be photographed; this was another way to forget their sorrows, even if momentarily. These minor sources of entertainment carried much meaning and significance in jail.

I received a money order from my mother through Shabbo from Jammu. My family sent me a money order at the beginning of each month as well as on festive occasions like Eid. There was also a letter and greeting card but it hadn't yet reached my hands as it was delayed at the censors; my letters were censored more carefully and strictly for which the jail staff had to find a prisoner who was well versed in Urdu. It was mainly for this reason that my letters got delayed causing me great anxiety and restlessness. I had to wait patiently for each letter and this wait was agonizing.

As usual, my cell was searched on 25 January, the day before Republic Day. All my belongings were pulled out and scattered along with my shoes, the ward was also searched but more as a formality. A day prior to both 26 January (Republic Day) and 15 August (Independence Day), my cell was searched as though there was a hidden bomb inside; the belongings of the other two cell-mates were not even touched during the search. Later I would spend hours putting everything back in place. During the search, if the policewomen found anything worthwhile, particularly body lotions or expensive medicines from outside, they would simply take them away and they knew that I would not be able to complain as prisoners were not allowed to get these things from outside the jail.

On 26 January, it was mandatory for us to congregate outside, in the ground, and remain there for the entire programme. However, it ended on a good note for me as I received Khalidji's greeting card and Baji's letter. She had written down an ode 'Anjum Zaman' as Eid offering for me that I really appreciated;

she was also glad that I had started working in jail. I was doing it especially for her as she wanted the jail authorities to write favourable remarks in my case register. It was not easy for me to win the jail authorities' goodwill as the environment itself was hostile to me. Being detained in an Indian jail was a relatively greater challenge for a Kashmiri Muslim, particularly under POTA. However, I was working hard and was also succeeding to some extent, by the grace of God. I was not only working on the candle project but had now been made in-charge of it and this was no mean achievement for me as it is not easy for high risk prisoners to find work or be given such a responsibility. Any officer or an NGO that visited the jail would first be brought to see this candle project. Once, Kiran Bedi also visited, she was accompanied by an INGO team and she appreciated my work when she saw the candles I had made; she asked me to consider working with her on my release. She shook my hand and said, 'Very creative' to which SI madam responded by praising me in front of her. During her tenure at Tihar, Kiran Bedi had introduced many welfare programmes of which only a few were functioning now. Her NGO, Indian Vision Foundation, was running a crèche and carpet centre here where many women were given training and employment; her objective was to ensure that women did not fall prey to exploitation on their release and were equipped to find some employment opportunity. The welfare of women prisoners was the central concern in all the projects that Kiran Bedi initiated in jail, including the IGNOU (the Indira Gandhi National Open University) study programme. However, with 99 per cent of the women being illiterate there were not many who could take advantage of the study programme. There were regular literacy classes every day from 9-11 am which were mandatory; women took the notebooks and pencils gladly but did not put them to proper use. The stock of books, pencils etc., also had a share for the jail staff and it was not uncommon for the matron to secretly carry this home for her own children.

It is known that in the men's jail, many prisoners received education through IGNOU but the trend was not the same in the women's jail. Out of 500, only 6 women prisoners were receiving such education while one was doing 10+2. There was a crèche in jail where their children were looked after and taught, and after completing 6 years of age, they were sent to a hostel (run by Kiran Bedi) through an arrangement with the jail authorities. The children were brought to meet their mothers in jail after every three months in a parent-child meeting. This was always a very emotional scene in jail. These children were quite cheerful and smart and took part in every function by presenting at least one item on stage. The jail authorities provided them with fruit, biscuits and sweets, along with books, school bags etc. They were well looked after with all their needs being provided for. The crèche prepared separate food for them, including porridge. Vaccination was given at regular intervals and picnics and excursion trips were also organized for them. Their mothers would not have been able to provide them with all these facilities in the outside world as they came from a socially and economically impoverished background. However, it was found that once released, the mothers took their children out of the hostel.

On 27 January Tasleem came for mulaqat. My date in the High Court was only a few days away and my family wanted it postponed because my case was in the final stage of hearing with the POTA Review Committee and my family had this firm belief that their judgment would be in my favour. But I was tired of the repeated change of dates in court. I did not ask her too many questions regarding the case as she did not know much about it; she gave me some fruit that she had brought for me and left. I returned to work even when I did not feel up to it as madam came for inspection every evening and I had to make sure that everything was in order; I had to also get the hall cleaned and fetch the material (for candle making) that was lying at the deorhi. After I completed all this work, madam called me over as some candles had to be packed both as gifts for the DG and for a function where madam had been invited.

3 February was to be my court date after a whole month. It

was a strange predicament for me because it was on this date in 2003 that I was arrested. I was feeling disturbed with memories of that day, yet a little hopeful that something good might happen in court but all I got was another date, 4 March. The judge told me, 'Your (case) file is in the High Court because of which I cannot do anything except to give another date.' During this time, Abidji asked the lawyer to write an appeal for 'jama-e-talashi' (personal search and seizure of items found on person). After posting the date, the judge sent me back to the lockup but Abidji requested that I be allowed to remain in the judge's room a little longer as the lawyer was expected to return any moment with the jama-e-talshi appeal. The judge asked him to bring the appeal within five minutes and instructed the policewoman to let me remain in the courtroom for five more minutes and then to escort me back to the lock-up. She made me sit there while Abidji went to the lawyer but as soon as he left, the policewoman made me stand up and took me outside; as we came down the stairs, I saw Abidji approaching with the lawyer from the opposite direction. He requested the policewoman to kindly bring me back to the judge's room so that we could get back the items seized during the search, now that we had got permission to do so, but she refused and got angry when the lawyer repeated the same request. She also refused to let Abidji get my signatures on the paper and when I tried to talk to my lawyer, she got angry and prevented me. I too appealed to her but she began to drag me towards the lock-up. These women cops, responsible for producing us in court, were always in a hurry because of their duty timings. At such times, when every minute was crucial for a prisoner, these women cops were devoid of any sensitivity and did not care at all for even the basic human decency. The only means left for a prisoner to secure some time was to offer them a bribe; it could ensure hours of 'talk-time'. After I had waited for some time in the lockup, Abidji came to talk to me but once in court, we had only a few minutes to talk. I told him that I did not know anything regarding the progress in my case to which he replied that the Review Committee's decision was awaited and if nothing materialized by 7 March 2005, my bail application would be filed in the High Court. Saying this, he left as our time was over and I was back in the lockup, agonizing over the prospects of my case. The long gap between the dates led to prolonged mental stress and a sense of demoralization. That day was also the court date for Farooq Khan and many other Kashmiri men whom I was able to greet, but they met with the same fate; another date of hearing.

I was tired now; the case was not progressing and remained where it was last year. I was not even able to speak to my lawyer and Abidji was not forthright about developments either. What was I to do? Who should I ask? Allah, please have mercy upon me, release me from this burden of worries and from this hell that is consuming my body and soul, Amen. I have given myself up to God and always try to lighten my burden by reposing my deepest faith in Him.

> *Karein zulmatein kya qaid zehen ko us ke*
> *Dimagh jis ka munnawar ho ek qamar ki tarah (Unknown)*

> Oppression cannot arrest the thoughts of one
> Whose mind has the brightness of the moon

I was confident that there would be an end to this dark night and Insha'Allah; it will be the beginning of a beautiful, new dawn. I have bid farewell to a life that is devoid of an intimacy with God, discarding it at the doorstep of the prison. Here in jail, it was the beginning of a new life although this too was full of anguish and suffocation. In the largest prison of this alien city, where beasts lived behind human faces, I tried to confront and surmount all the difficulties with a firm belief in God's omnipresent grace and gradually, I befriended them. I found a couple of friends and well wishers from among these 500 prisoners but they were fortunate to be released sooner and I did not envy them. In the words of Maulana Abul Kalam Azad, 'Even in a jail, the sun sets and rises, even here the stars shine, a dawn tears through the night and brings light. Even in jail, there is spring after autumn, the birds chirp but the meaning and essence of all this remains different from the outside, free world.' Here, one noticed all these miracles of nature, every moment had its own importance and counting each moment until release was an innate human tendency. However, many a spring went by while keeping alive the hope of spring and this hope never died. I too was waiting with eagerness.

On 27 February, a friend of mine came to visit me, she had been released recently. She was a good friend who was there for me during any crisis. Being a child psychologist, she had been given charge of the crèche in jail. We worked on the same projects. When I completed my term at the library after 2-3 months, she was given the same responsibility and when I was moved to the candle project after helping in the legal cell, she took my place. Since the staff was not well educated, some of us educated prisoners were given these responsibilities and this is how we remained in contact with each other.

While I was talking to my friend, Tasleem arrived, looking nervous. She said she had to leave soon as the police had confiscated her driving license (as proof of identity) and told her that an IB inquiry was on. I told her not to worry and spend the time that was allocated because every visitor for me had to go through this harrowing routine. I called the matron and asked her why Tasleem was being harassed in this manner but she said that she had asked her for an ID card and was going to return it after scrutiny but perhaps, she got nervous and left early. My friend had brought some things that I needed; having served two years here, she knew about things that were most needed in jail. I had advised her not to visit me as I knew that the IB would then follow her, as they did with each visitor, and I did not wish her to face any difficulty on my account. Although I liked meeting her, I was also envious of her freedom. The world of imagination is promising in this dark and claustrophobic environment; to imagine oneself 'free' even if for a few moments, makes the soul happy, but then, the familiar voice of another prisoner close by, shatters this magical spell. Opening the shutters of memory, I would recall pleasant events from my past and thereby try to add a bouquet of beautiful colours to my dull life; crossing the distance of many years within a few minutes, only to return and contend with the daily grind of prison. At this very moment, with a newspaper in front of my eyes, I was lost in a world where I was busy making an imaginary snowman, there was a news report of a fresh snowfall in Kashmir and how it had thrown daily life into disarray. Little did the news reporters know that we Kashmiris are used to these winter peculiarities; there may not be any electricity for a month but the joy of a snowfall is unique.

I had joined the candle project in an attempt to forget the searing wounds that this jail had inflicted upon me. Making colourful candles helped me deal with my colourless existence here. The absence of colour cast a lasting shadow on my life even as I tried to entertain myself with fake, artificial means of happiness. I had perhaps not learnt the art of remaining happy under any circumstances but I am determined to do so now and have already made a beginning. It was enough for me that I was still alive; a miracle considering the kind of conspiracy that was hatched against me; very few women go through such an ordeal.

> *Magar mujhe phir bhi yaqeen tha*
> *Raat jitni bhi sangeen hogi*
> *Subah utni hi rangeen hogi*
> *Ghum na kar gar hai badal ghanera*
> *Kis ke roke ruka hai savera*
> *Raat bhar ka mehman hai andhera (Sahir Ludhianvi)*

However sombre the night, I still knew that
The morning will be radiant
Do not lament the dark clouds, dawn is inevitable
Darkness is but a mere companion of night

It was difficult for me to maintain my physical health or mental balance given the inhuman situation around me. God had perhaps ordained for me to arrive at milestones that could either turn me against Him or help me to emerge spiritually stronger. But I only extended my hand of friendship towards my dear God with my heart full of faith in Him. He will one day lift the burden of hardship from my frail shoulders and provide me with some relief and it was with this hope alone that I spent the best years of my life in this prison. I had fastened this hope in my heart as I truly believed that 'hopelessness is *kufr*'. Jail had snatched away my freedom and restricted my movements; it had shrunk my universe to a mere half kilometre. The jail staff, along with some old prisoners always looked for ways to break my heart and persisted in causing grievous hurt to my basic sense of dignity, although the WO had advised me in the beginning itself that I should forget all about dignity or self respect here. There is no one with dignity or indignity here, she had said.

There was a report in the newspaper today that Sheikh Abdul Aziz had been arrested and in this context, my name was mentioned: 'two years ago, Anjum Zamarud Habib was also arrested in a similar case under POTA'. This news left me more anxious.

One morning in February I woke up early, still trembling with fear from the nightmare I had just had; I offered namaz and prayed to God for mercy. I had a court date in early March but as soon I was produced before the judge, another date, a month later, was posted and the policewoman escorted me back to the lockup. However, I was able to speak to my lawyer, Ohri Sahib in the court and he told me that the proceedings could not be undertaken as my file was still in the High Court although he had, in principle, won the case in legal terms. He tried to assure me that even the POTA Review Committee's judgment would be in our favour. I listened to him in silence since all we had got, once again, was another date. There were 5-6 dates given in one year and this is how this entire year was spent.

'Life is what happens to you while you are busy making other plans.' A person may make any number of plans to give shape and substance to life but God has other plans. A woman may think of the worst but never consider the prospect of a life in jail.

I wanted to work for the social and human rights of women and thereby serve my poor community. I had made elaborate plans for the welfare of my mothers and sisters but all these responsibilities, this work remained unfinished with my sudden arrest and imprisonment. There is no room for regret in the path that I chose. To alter the essence of one's nature and temperament is not an easy task and only the one who travels this dark passage of life knows the truth. I could not bear my own burden whereas I had decided to ease the burden of widows and orphans of my community. The loneliness of incarceration brought within its fold another significant aspect of existence:

> *Hum ahle qafas tanha bhi nahin har roz naseem subah e watan*
> *Yadon se mua'ttir aati hai ashkon se munnawar jati hai (Faiz)*

> We prisoners are not lonely as the morning breeze of our country
> Comes each day laden with fragrant memories, leaves bright with our tears.

Over time, a few of my 'prisoner friends' got separated from me. I did not regret their departure as they had gained freedom from this cage and were breathing freely in the outside world. They had found an escape from this hell but for me, the pain of their absence, the loss of their companionship, was profound. But life goes on and I thought I had better leave these dark thoughts behind. I was feeling tired after returning from the court and since tea was served only at 3.30, I went to the canteen and fetched a cup of tea for myself but I could not drink it as it had too much sugar and I gave it to another inmate in the cell. Whenever a prisoner returned from a court date, her cell mates would ask her about all the details regarding the hearing; that night my cell mates asked me eagerly but all

I could tell them was that I had got another DATE! The cells had been changed for all of us. According to jail rules, once every week or once a month, cells, barracks and prisoners were exchanged or shifted. All of us had to go through this and because of this rule, everything would be in a mess, all our belongings scattered around, everything upside down. This is done to prevent prisoners from getting too close or coming together to form an association. After cleaning and tidying, there would be a list from the chakkar according to which cells and barracks were allotted and prisoners shifted. But even in this exercise, the foreign prisoners made their own choice of cells or whether to shift at all. It either depended on their mood or the size of their belongings – they had many more things than other prisoners did. While other prisoners were not permitted to keep more than three sets of clothes, these women had dozens of them. Some NGOs would distribute clothes with western designs as charity and it was the foreign women prisoners who got the largest share of these. The cell I was shifted to already had a British woman prisoner who was serving term for the last six years in a case of financial fraud. Until I was shifted there, she was the only one in the cell. It was the filthiest cell I had ever seen. It took more than a week of regular cleaning for it to become habitable. This white Englishwoman, Clair Mathew, did not like to speak to anyone. She had requested the jail authorities to be allowed to stay alone in the cell because she was a heavy smoker and did not want any complaints from other cellmates. Elizabeth was another one who preferred to stay alone in a cell as she had too many belongings. She was also very quarrelsome, so no other prisoner was willing to share the cell with her and neither did she try to accommodate anyone else. Jail authorities were well aware of her temperament and did not wish to risk 'putting their hand in a snake pit'. Unlike us, foreign prisoners had a plentiful supply of dry fruit, cornflakes, butter and milk apart from other goods that their respective embassies sent them. I spoke with Clair occasionally, but only with her. The habshi women were poor in

English and I always felt nervous talking to them as what I said could be easily misconstrued because of the language barrier and I could not afford to take any risks. Their friendship was as dangerous as their enmity. They were known for their dadagiri, their bullying tactics, and whenever they wanted something from an inmate after her mulaqat, they made sure they got it. They also remained outside their cells even after closing time and many of these foreign women prisoners worked somewhere or the other in jail – in the crèche, the carpet centre, at the tea vending machine or in the MIR. No prisoner was foolish enough to register a complaint against these women. Unlike us, European inmates in jail were considered valuable citizens of their respective countries, their health and well being were a matter of concern to their embassies. Even if their crime was established and they were legally convicted, representatives of their embassy would visit them on a regular basis to personally assess their well being in prison and also bring them whatever they needed. The jail authorities could not be strict with them for fear that they would have to answer to the embassy in case of any complaint from these foreign inmates.

Abidji came to meet me on 10 March. He was agitated and angry and I listened to his outburst silently as I knew that he was getting tired of the repeated rounds of the courts and jail which also meant frequent travel. Being unemployed further took a toll on his patience and endurance and I well understood the financial burden that my case had imposed on him and other family members. Since I was not feeling well I went to the MIR after meeting him. The doctor prescribed a three month course of 'conjugated estrogen' due to the hormonal imbalance I was suffering from. These medicines were available only outside and I waited for a week before I got them.

Abidji visited me again on 28 March and I saw how embarrassed he was feeling because of his angry outburst during his previous visit. To make up for it, he brought a set of pink nightclothes for me. He was leaving for Kashmir shortly afterwards but promised to meet me soon again.

31 March was my date in the jail case. Abidji came with the lawyer and we hoped that the charges would be framed on that day so that the case could progress further rather than be again delayed. Rehmana could not be present in court because she was not well and, frustratingly, we had to once again return with another date. Abidji was, as usual, consoling me that I would soon be released.

I woke up early and stepped out of the ward after offering namaz. It was a Saturday and 'internal mulaqat' day, the newspapers were late and as I went out to check, I saw the matron who was on postal duty. She informed me that there was a letter for me but she could not yet give it to me as she had duty at ward 8 until noon. I was still waiting outside until the doors were closed and the matron returned to deliver letters at 1 pm. My eyes lit up every time I saw this matron with the letters as I felt that she had personally visited my family, met them and carried their letters for me. Postal communication in jail was an emotional experience; sending a letter and receiving one held a different meaning here. I quickly tore open the envelope and found a card from Shabbo Rani that she had posted from Jammu on 14 March but I received it after 14 days! However late, this was no less than a precious gift for me.

My next court date was again cancelled because of a lawyers' strike. In any case, there had been no progress in my case for the whole year. I was produced before the judge at 10.30 in the morning. Abidji was present in the courtroom with a junior lawyer and had already submitted an appeal for 'jama talashi' (personal search and seizure) and the items were handed over to me in front of the judge although I did not get my passport back. I gave these things to Abidji and was escorted back to the lockup. I met him again as he was getting back the bail bond money (which he had earlier submitted for the jail case). The POTA Review Committee had still not come to a decision as there was a stay order from the Supreme Court and the matter could take much longer. I lay down in the lockup for some time and then saw that someone was standing at the door asking for me. I stood up and saw that it was a Kashmiri man who introduced himself as Mohiuddin and after greeting me, he conveyed greetings on behalf of Farooq Khan and many other Kashmiri brothers in jail. He told me that he had contacted an organization to provide me with newspapers and journals and that I should respond if I received any communication from them. He then said 'All of us Kashmiri brothers are with you and know that you are a victim of a conspiracy but we have decided, and promise you that we will unravel this conspiracy. We have managed to convey this to the Hurriyat.' He was about to say something more when the police dragged him away so I quickly told him that my prayers were with him and all other Kashmiri men who were engaged in a life and death struggle in various jails and that I hoped they would be released soon.

On 5 April, I received a letter from Sheikh Abdul Aziz that he sent through Rehmana. It read 'Like you, I am also innocent and we have been implicated by our enemies.' Some days later, I received another letter, this time from Ahsan Untoo. This way, I secretly received letters from my Kashmiri brothers from different jails in Tihar.

A few days later, when Rehmana came back from court she told me that according to the lawyer, Siddiqa and Tahera were ready to accept the charges against them in the jail case following which they might be released but this could be a setback for the rest of the accused in the case. When I spoke to Tahera regarding this I learnt that Siddiqa had already informed her and her family. I felt quite hurt at this and asked her why she had kept this a secret from us. When this case was filed against the six of us, the other inmates had assured us of their unflinching support but now, if there was no unity even among the six accused women in the case, the proceedings could go against us. There are many ways in which a person's true character is reflected inside the jail.

> *Nakurda gunahon ki bhi hasrat ki mile daad*
> *Ya rab! Agar in kurda gunahon ki sazaa hai* (Ghalib)

'Give me credit oh lord for the sins not committed
If I am to be punished for the ones I have.'

No one is able to bring the sense of comfort or the means of comfort from outside. For this, a prisoner has to search her own heart to try and establish a relationship with her life in jail.

Years were passing by. The third year of my imprisonment had begun. Now I was able to recognize the prison walls, the iron fence and the guards. Not only that but I was beginning to befriend them. I was still deeply sad about the separation from my family but gradually the memories were getting blurred. However, there were moments when this cloud disappeared and memories of my loved ones rushed in with such force and intensity that I wanted to scale the prison walls and run back to Kashmir. I was counting each day. Every prisoner remembers the date of her arrest, the number of court dates, what transpired on each date, the number of times that the judge was absent, on which day and date. A prisoner keeps count of all these details however incompetent she may be in her arithmetic. I also kept count of each month through the changing seasons. Many of the prisoners were not familiar with the English calendar and kept count of their imprisonment by recalling the different seasons at the time of their arrest – I was arrested during spring one would say while another remembered phagun and yet another, autumn or summer.

A prisoner named Arti, who has been serving term for the past nine years, was now a Munshi at the day langar. She once told me 'It was during the monsoon, the rainy season that I was arrested. I have spent eight monsoons in jail but I will be released during the mango season when mangoes flood the market.' Similarly, Misri Devi said to me 'We, meaning I and my daughter-in-law, were arrested during winter and this is our sixth winter here.' Her daughter-in-law was however released on parole during the spring. An old woman named Krishna said, 'It was during the wedding season that I was arrested. There were many weddings then among my relatives and in my mohalla. But I could not witness my own niece's wedding.' Each prisoner kept a count of each passing week, month, year and each season but this count was getting longer for most of them but for some others, it was simply a formality as they were released even before the turn of a particular season. Not all prisoners are so fortunate to be released without going through at least one season inside the jail.

We were in the month of April. My head had been throbbing with pain ever since I woke up in the morning. I'd been really unwell the past few days. I received a letter during internal mulaqat from a fellow Kashmiri prisoner who'd been lodged in jail 2 for the last three months. He said he had been arrested from Srinagar because another prisoner, a Kashmiri, also serving term in Tihar, had named him during his interrogation. He said, 'We can now very well understand your difficulties and hardship in prison since we ourselves have landed in jail. I salute your fortitude and patience...' I am thankful to God for providing me the strength of forbearance. I too was put through so much humiliation and torture during interrogation but I did not disclose any single name to those tyrants. In spite of this, the enemies, in the garb of friends betrayed me. In such a situation, I was serving my time in jail only with God's support.

It was getting warmer each day as summer was almost at its peak. I prayed to God for the strength to help me bear this summer heat. On Sunday, we were locked in for nearly the entire day. The matron, in a hurry to go home, did not care that the ones she was locking up for the day were also human beings. She herded us like animals into the barracks and cells and left after depositing the keys at the chakkar. If during this time a prisoner fell ill, she had to clap her hands to be heard by another matron on duty but since it was a cumbersome procedure to 'unlock' a prisoner before time, most of the staff preferred to ignore her plea. There was an emergency bell but only in one particular cell in the ward. To use it, a prisoner in another cell had to raise a din until the other prisoner got the message to ring the emergency bell on her behalf, but to draw the matron's attention; the bell had to be pressed repeatedly. Loud cursing and abuse heralded the matron's arrival on the scene, 'what's going on? Why are you creating such a racket? Has someone died that you're making this din?' After Zohra's death, an emergency bell had been installed in each cell but unfortunately it was switched off at night except in one cell. The emergency bell was 'controlled' from outside but the matron on duty, for her own comfort at night, did not think twice about the prisoners' welfare or plight before switching it off. If there was an emergency, the prisoners were reduced to clapping their hands or banging steel tumblers against the cell's iron bars to draw her attention so she could then either bring medicine from the MIR or a doctor if things were more serious. However, what usually happened was that when a prisoner did manage to get heard, the matron would throw the medicine pouch from outside the fence and go away, without touching or talking to the ailing prisoner. Doctors were not available on a holiday except in jail 7 and were brought from there only if there was a medical crisis here. Though doctors were on duty on other days, they hesitated to visit the barracks at night.

On 25 April Tasleem came to visit me as Abidji was away in Kashmir and expected to return by May 16. When I was returning after the visit, I met Jyothi madam (AS) at the chakkar and she informed me that an ICRC team was coming to meet me the next day. This team had visited me on an earlier occasion too as it was their mandate to meet prisoners from conflict zones. The team visited Kashmiri prisoners once every year. Although meeting them did not benefit a prisoner in any concrete way, their visit carried prestige in jail as I was the only one (from the women's jail) on their list on account of being a Kashmiri. Since the majority of the team members were white and ICRC was of international repute, the jail authorities respected them more than other visiting teams.

Some material had arrived for the candle project which was lying at the deorhi and after mulaqat; I went to collect it and, with the help of other inmates arranged the material properly. At the time, I saw that many women inmates had gathered at the chakkar and there was loud noise and commotion inside the MIR. We learnt that a prisoner from ward 4 had consumed some medicines in an attempt to commit suicide. The doors were abruptly closed and all the wards and cells were searched and any medicines found inside were confiscated by the authorities. In jail vocabulary, a 'brain doctor' actually gave sedatives in place of medicine and many women prisoners were now addicted to these. These sedatives could be bought from any prisoner who was under the brain doctor's treatment as well as from the Munshi and helper at the MIR. Each tablet cost Rs 10 (coupon) and some women prisoners thus collected 7-8 tablets and consumed them to commit suicide. On a previous occasion, an under-trial prisoner had consumed a bottle of phenyl in a similar attempt after which all phenyl and acid bottles were removed from the wards. These two items were not allowed to be kept in the barracks or cells. The ward Munshi, on cleaning duty on Sundays, distributed these under her supervision and the rest was returned to the store but this prisoner had managed to sneak a bottle of phenyl that she later consumed which led to the Munshi being summoned for questioning.

As usual, I woke up early and offered namaz and stepped out for a walk after the locks were opened. I returned to the cell at 7 for tea and lay down to rest. At 8, I took a bath and recited the Quran for some time and felt comforted. I came out at 10 as I had to get a letter posted and I looked for the matron on duty but she was nowhere to be seen. I returned to the cell, put the letter in a bag there and left for the candle project with Shabana who was then working with me. I left her there and went to the store to take stock of the material that had arrived yesterday and returned to the cell after securing it inside a cupboard. It was nearly one o'clock and as I sat down for lunch, a helper from the chakkar came and told me that Jyothi madam had called me there. She was in her office and asked me to come in and sit while she went to the deorhi to receive and bring the ICRC team. She returned with a lady representative whom I recognized as she had come twice earlier with other team members. She greeted me warmly and I shook hands with her and expressed my own happiness at meeting her. ICRC was the only team that visited the jail regularly to meet me. For a prisoner, this was no less than an act of mercy that someone important had come to personally assess a prisoner's well being and also provide her with an opportunity to talk openly and without any fear. It may be a routine matter for those in the 'outside world' but only a prisoner knew the significance of such a meeting. Jyothi madam had the DS's room opened for us to meet but the lady representative, Sandra Wirth expressed her desire to talk to me in my cell to which madam responded positively. We then walked together towards my ward where we began to talk. When I asked her about the other team members' absence she said that they had gone to another jail to meet other prisoners. We sat in the cell for some time but I sensed that Sandra was not comfortable in the presence of my cellmate and asked me if we could sit outside and talk. I readily agreed as it was not every day that one could sit outside even when the ginthi was closed. She asked me if I faced any problems here and simply to unburden my heart, I told her all that I had to even though I knew that it was not in her hands to do anything to resolve these problems. She had met the SI madam earlier and was pleased to see the candles I had made in her office. She told me that the SI held a good opinion of me. We chatted until three o'clock after which she left and I returned to my cell.

At 6 in the evening, there was major commotion at the chakkar where a prisoner, Neelofar [name changed], serving term for the past ten years, was arguing with the AS over something. This is what we heard: She had been feeling quite unwell for the past few days and when she visited the doctor she refused to examine or treat her as her duty was over and she was leaving for home. The argument with the AS was regarding the doctor's negligence but Neelofar was also anxious as the High Court had recently rejected her bail plea. This is her story: She was from Hyderabad where her parents had married her off to an Afghan national who was much older in age. Neelofcr's sister had eloped with a man and married him secretly which enraged her parents who, in retaliation and to prevent her from doing the same, married Neelofar off to this old man while she was still a minor. This is how she described her situation: 'When I saw this man on the first night of our wedding, I was dumbfounded. He was as old as my grandfather. I was inconsolable and felt as though snakes were slithering all over my young body. My parents punished me for my sister's mistakes and I will never forgive them for it. He took me away to Afghanistan after marriage and kept me locked inside the house and did not permit me to meet or talk to anyone. He was afraid that being young I could be exploited or even abducted by other men. Although his own family members were sympathetic to me, he did not care. He was the only uncivilized and tyrannical one in his family and terrorized me with his shameful behaviour. Materially there was everything in the house but my heart remained empty. He would send me to India once every 2-3 months with large suitcases and instructions to deliver these to a certain friend in a certain hotel. Glad and relieved to be visiting my own country, I never questioned him regarding the contents in the suitcase and quietly did what I was told to do. This continued for many years; I had become a mother of two children in the meantime while expecting my third. But he continued to send me from Afghanistan to India in this state; one child in my lap, one holding my hand and the third in my belly. Once when he was making preparations for me to leave again, I chanced upon a sight from my room that took my breath away – this husband of mine was stashing packets of heroin, cocaine, opium and brown sugar in the suitcases that I was supposed to carry. I confronted him saying, "What do you think you are doing?" He threatened me with dire consequences and told me to shut up: "This lavish life that you lead does not come for free, it requires hard work and you have to pay a price too." I was unhappy, nervous and afraid to go to my own country this time. But strangely, this sense of fear in fact made me bolder. I thought that I was the one making all this money for all these years and yet I was made to live in the shadow of fear and torture. I decided that now I will start my own 'business/trade' to earn money for myself and branch out on my own. I already had the contacts that are needed for this trade, though I was ignorant then. The 'friends' that I met to deliver the suitcases respected me as I had never questioned or harassed them in any manner. I rented a place in Delhi through my own contacts that also helped me initially and this is how I took my first steps towards my own freedom but one day, the Afghani arrived suddenly in Delhi. He asked me to return to Afghanistan with him but I refused; I was not a minor anymore and was also a lot smarter now. Since I had refused to go back with him, he decided to stay with me in my house in Delhi, eating free meals but shamelessly imposing himself upon me. When he saw how much money I was earning he also began to spend a little. He employed a young man, Akram as a driver who was sympathetic to me and over a period of time it turned into mutual love between us and a new relationship began. This infuriated the Afghan and he began to torment me in different ways. I decided to leave him as well as Akram and live separately, on my own. When I did this, he had three attempts made on Akram's life but Akram survived. I reacted stubbornly by meeting Akram again and he began to escort me whenever I went out on work. He supported me greatly. The day I was arrested, there was no maal with me but my only mistake was that I had forgotten to grease the palms of the policemen by doling out a share to them. In this trade, you have to earn for the policemen more than for yourself. Even if one tried to give up this dhanda the policemen would never let you get out of it as it was a source of lucrative income for them. My three small children were present in court the day I was awarded a 15 year jail sentence. The judge remained unmoved despite my cries and my children's pleas.

It was Akram alone who visited me in jail and also filed applications for my bail in the High Court. My older son inherited his father's temperament although he was not happy with him. He did not approve of my relationship with Akram but was also not able to forget his father terrorising me. My other two sons were small yet deprived of their mother's care; their father had kept them with him. He later took them to Afghanistan but since the children could not adjust there, he brought them back to their nanihal (natal family) in Hyderabad. They got refugee status, admission in school and a home there. My sister occasionally brought them with her to meet me. My own family had accepted Akram as they knew how much I had suffered at the hands of the Afghani who had also dragged them to court for my children's custody.'

The atmosphere in jail is enough to turn any prisoner into a quarrelsome and short tempered being. This is what happened to Neelofar too – she would argue loudly with jail staff even for a minor reason. The soaring summer temperature added to our woes. The impression in the outside world regarding Tihar jail is that 'it is a reformative institution' but in reality it is a full fledged jail like any other where fear and terror stalk the prisoners. Within this atmosphere, prisoners lived through the kinds of experiences that cannot be had or even imagined in the outside world.

At my next court date in May we were once again taken to the Patiala House court lockup. The usual dal and roti in polythene bags was handed to us. The roti was still soft and at eleven o'clock I decided to have it with a portion of dal. At 11.45, the policewoman and her escort team produced me in court where I met a woman lawyer who asked my name and introduced herself as Ohri's junior lawyer. She told me that 13 July was posted as the next date which was nearly two and a half months away; I felt disappointed as I had been waiting impatiently for the court hearing but, as usual, we got nothing out of the court except another date. Looking out of the caged window of the prison van, I could see that the 'free world outside' was moving on whereas mine had come to a standstill. But it always sparked a strange kind of hope in my heart when I saw, from these small meshed windows, how people walked freely without their hands being held, how the cars sped toward a destination, how busy the streets were. This would remind me that I too was a free being once, one who tried to match each step with this fast moving free world but suddenly my life had stopped, stagnated. The journey from Tihar jail to the Court and back lasted one hour during which I enjoyed the sights and smells of the free world but soon returned to the grim reality on reaching the entrance of Tihar jail. I then envied this free world and its free citizens. Alas! Where has my own freedom gone?

I wrote a card to Abidji informing him about the next date and told him that he need not rush back as we had two and half months before the next appearance. At the time, I was alone in the cell as the other women inmates had been shifted to the barrack. I was thinking that it might be good for me to stay alone in the cell from now on as it always took time and effort to adjust to new women inmates whenever they were shifted. I was mentally exhausted after the court visit and I wanted to lie down quietly but late at night, two new inmates were brought to the cell and lodged with me. The women appeared neat and clean which was a relief to me as I have had to tolerate and adjust with dirty, uncivilized and unclean women but do I or any other prisoner have any option but to tolerate?

I did not feel like getting up in the morning as I had spent the night staring at the ceiling and it had also become terribly hot now and this kind of unbearable summer drove me crazy. I fell ill often during this time with fever, malaria and prickly heat.

An NGO was visiting the candle project along with ZEE TV network. The television team wanted to interview me to know the entire 'process' and also film it. I gave them all the details but requested that my face not be shown on TV. From here, they went on to visit the crèche and sewing center which they also wanted to film.

NGOs visited the jail regularly as did students who came here for research on the living and working conditions of prisoners. This was quite common. But their research did not in any manner benefit the prisoners. The research scholars looked for 'subjects' and there were plenty of them here along with many 'stories'. Many women prisoners shared their stories with an open heart, perhaps with a hope that this exposure would help them out of this hell. Many believed that the NGOs would help the women in their release while others felt that their plea would reach the corridors of power. But none of this happened. Students/scholars certainly managed to publish their thesis or reports but forgot about us, their subjects.

There were occasions in jail when song and dance programmes were also organized and the women prisoners could enjoy themselves for an hour or so. There were complaint boxes in every ward but no prisoner dared to put in any complaint. Every day a matron made the rounds with such a box asking prisoners "if you have any complaints, write a chit and put it in this box!" The box would then be taken each Friday to the DG's office where it was unsealed. Many women believed that the box was opened at the deorhi before sending it on its journey to the DG's office and therefore the complaints, if any, never reached the DG. Kiran Bedi had initiated this practice but after she left, it lost its purpose. The NHRC (National Human Rights Commission) had also arranged for a complaint box at the chakkar along with a writing pad, but till date no prisoner had made use of it fearing that the jail authorities would read it and this could lead to more problems for the prisoners. Once, a prisoner had dropped a complaint in the box after which the jail authorities had sought each prisoner's signature to match the one in the box. Some prisoner had written a complaint against DS madam to the DG (in English) and DS Meena madam suspected me of writing the complaint and got a sample of my signature through an informer but the signature did not match. The SI had warned her that 'Anjum would not do something like this,' which Meena madam misrepresented to the DG saying that the 'the SI was siding with a Kashmiri terrorist prisoner'.

❦

Summer days were particularly difficult to bear as the taps went dry which created a furore and a lot of friction in jail. There was a pervasive stench as toilets overflowed but there was no water available to clean them. Water tankers were brought in every morning and evening and depending on a ward's turn, prisoners had to wait with buckets and earthen pots to collect water but if the ginthi closed during this time, we were deprived of even a drop of water. The tankers delivered water at the langar first and women working there stood a better chance of getting it. The water pump in the jail frequently stopped functioning due to the heavy load on it and its repair took at least a couple of days each time. The fans being old and rickety also did not function properly and threw out hot air at night. There was an abundance of mosquitoes in summer and all kinds of insects could be seen in the cell, particularly in the earthen pots and in the food. All of us were permanently soaked in sweat as though buckets of water had been poured over us. The spray that was used against mosquitoes and insects led to allergies among the inmates. Despite complaints of insects breeding in the water tanks, these were not cleaned. When prisoners raised such things with the staff – for example mentioning that the food was also contaminated by insects, we were told 'this is after all a jail, this happens in summer elsewhere too.' During summer, most prisoners lost their appetite for food. What we really needed was a glass of sharbat but there was none available in the canteen although we have heard that cold sharbat is available in the men's jail. Women prisoners sent an appeal to the SI regarding this but no action has yet been taken.

I went to the candle project at 10 but it was equally hot here. There were air coolers in the crèche, carpet and sewing centres as teachers from outside were invited to work here. Kiran Bedi had got the cooler installed for children in the crèche. We had to use a gel in the candle project due to which the room got full of smoke whenever we burnt it on the gas, and this led to frequent headaches and allergies. However, I tolerated all this simply because I was determined to keep myself busy rather than waste my time brooding inside the cell. One had to labour hard here – and I had never done this kind of hard work before.

Abidji came to visit me on 19 May. He had received a letter from the POTA Review Committee. Their judgment was not in my favour. I was heartbroken and deeply disappointed. Inside me, I was screaming with the pain of disappointment but only I could hear my own screams. It is as painful to write about the disappointments and hardships in jail as it is to endure them. Life had given me desires and aspirations and somehow I wished I could replace the burden of sorrow with forbearance because at that moment, it was crucial somehow to preserve life and sanity. At night when we were locked inside the cell, I offered namaz and lay down and tried to close my eyes but sleep had vanished. The sharp edge of sorrow was piercing my body. I waited for dawn but the morning light seemed to have somehow bypassed the ventilator in the cell as it was way too high and almost hidden from us. For me, the ginthi was like a clock; 'the door has opened so it must be 5.30 in the morning'. The nature and dimension of time had totally altered since I had been in jail. It was a particularly bad day for me, everything went wrong. I bent down to pick up the utensils and sprained my back. The pain was excruciating, I could not walk, sit or even stand. I needed support even to visit the toilet. My cell mate Darshana looked after me and helped me. I got some emergency medication including an injection.

A few days later, I was sent to DD hospital. The lady doctor here advised me to immediately discontinue the hormonal treatment I had been undergoing for the past few months as according to her it could result in cancer. I was sent for a thorough medical check-up including an ultrasound. She also advised me to drink a lot of water before the ultrasound and I had four bottles!

There was one room reserved in the hospital (this was the Deen Dayal Hospital) for prisoners which was surrounded by a posse of policemen. On one side of the room was a large, life sized cage for male prisoners who remained locked inside. To visit the doctor, each prisoner patient was physically escorted by policemen and this was such a humiliating scene. Others around the corridor would cringe and move back as the prisoner passed by them, staring at him with indignation and contempt. A woman prisoner patient was much more of a spectacle, as though she had dropped from the sky or was an alien from another world. In this room at the hospital, prisoner patients often stole a few words with each other by dodging the police glare. Looking at each other here caused much pain.

Once back in jail, I visited the jail doctor but she prescribed the same old medicines that had failed to relieve me of the severe backache earlier. At noon when the ward matron Nirmala came to close the ginthi, she saw me writhing in pain and said 'I also had similar pain but it eased after a massage. If I remember, I will bring the same medicine for you to massage with.' Since I was not being able to sit on the floor, I went to the DS and requested her to permit me to use a stool in the cell. She asked me to submit an application to her for approval. At 4, I took Darshana's support to go to the chakkar where I gave in my application to the DS madam who signed it. Just as I left her room she called me back and suggested that I lie down for her to massage my back, assuring me that it would help. At the time, Kiran Pratap was also present there and madam sent her to fetch some mustard oil from the langar after which she guided her to do the massage which provided me some relief and relaxation. I thanked madam profusely and returned to my cell. At night Kiran delivered the stool for me to sit in the cell. Prisoners are otherwise not permitted to sit on this or a chair.

I was once again taken to DD hospital for an ultrasound which was normal but my backache persisted. When I came back from the hospital, there was a letter from Baji. It made me cry – she reassured me that I would be released soon although I knew how disappointed she herself must have been with the POTA Review Committee judgment. My illness was a result of this judgment but in my letters I did not mention anything about it to my family. Whenever I fell ill I received letters from home because of the strong telepathy between us – they knew I was ill even though I did not inform them.

A few days after this I received a letter from Ghulam Nabi Nijar from jail 2. I had met a Sikh boy in DD hospital and had told him to convey my greetings to any Kashmiri prisoner that he may meet. He informed me that Dar Sahib from Kashmir was with him and it was through this Sikh boy that he had come to know of my illness and sent me a letter. Reading the letter I felt that there were at least some well wishers around who cared for me. It was not easy to exchange letters when each one was silently suffering their own ordeal in jail. It meant a lot to receive a letter from a fellow Kashmiri prisoner when one is away from the family, particularly during illness as these letters had a healing quality about them. Later I also received letters from my mother Boba and my sister Neel. Boba had also sent a money order of Rs 2000 so that I could purchase water from the canteen.

In the next few days the weather became hotter and hotter and I found no respite anywhere, not even at night when sleep escaped me. There was a real danger of going insane as a result of this searing heat. I began to have fainting spells. One evening I went to meet the visiting jail lawyer. She said something unpleasant about my lawyer Ohri Sahib which left me pretty disturbed. I wondered whether to write to my family about this or to my lawyer but later, I decided to write directly to my lawyer.

On Sunday 10 July I woke up early and offered namaz. Since I had not slept at all the entire night, I lay down again to rest and was able to breathe air once the cell was unlocked.

> *Jail ki zeher bhari chor sadayen jageen*
> *Door darwaza khula koi, koi bandh hua*
> *Door machli koi zanjeer machal ke roi*
> *Door utra kisi taley ke jigar mein khanjar*
> *(Faiz)*

> *Mere bekar shab o roz ki nazuk pariyan.*
> *Apne shehpur ki rah dekh rahi hain yeh aseer*

Jis ke tarkash mein hain umeed ke jalte hue teer'
(Faiz)

The bitter, secret sounds of the jail awakened
A door opened at a distance, another was shut
Far away as a chain rattled and cried
A key pierced the heart of a lock far away.

My idle nights and days my delicate fairies
Are waiting for their prince to arrive
Bearing a quiver brimming with hope.

I stayed inside the cell the whole day as it was unbearably hot outside, I rested, had tea and read the newspaper and went to the canteen in the evening. My body was covered in prickly heat and I wanted to buy some talcum powder. I also had to pick up other necessities.

I received a letter from Ahsan Untoo in jail 2 which described the miserable condition he was in. How could I help when I myself was in jail, caught in a web of my own worries? I could only pray for him and others. We could not help each other even if we wished.

After a month and a half of waiting, I finally had a court date, but this time, there were no proceedings as the judge had retired. As legal power had yet to be delegated to the new judge, there would be further delay in my case. When I was produced in court I saw that Ohri Sahib had sent his junior. I requested her to ask Ohri Sahib to come and meet me at the 'legal mulaqat' here and she left the courtroom. There were policemen from the Delhi Police Special Cell sitting on a bench behind me and one of them commented 'Your people have managed to get Shabbir Dar released but succeeded in implicating you.' I did not give any reply as I had none. The policewoman held my hand and began to escort me back to the lockup when I met the junior lawyer who instructed the policewoman to bring me back to court for 'legal mulaqat'. When I explained to her that this mulaqat took place in the lockup she proceeded to get the judge's signature and told me that Ohri Sahib was in High Court and would meet me after half an hour. I often got to meet other Kashmiri prisoners in court; I mustn't call it mulaqat as it was only an opportunity to acknowledge each other through greetings or simply a wave of one's hand. I waited for an hour in the lockup before the policewoman returned to escort me to the mulaqat jangla to meet my lawyer. As we walked, I heard loud and enthusiastic greetings from the male lockup where other Kashmiri prisoners were waiting. Before I could return their greetings, the policewoman pulled me away and hurriedly took me to the jangla. I told Ohri Sahib 'I have full faith in your ability as a lawyer and I am confident that you will win this case for me but you had assured me last year that I'd be released within 4-5 days. These four days do not seem to end as I am still languishing in jail.' He replied, 'I am telling you with utmost belief that I have won this case but since your file has been moving between the Review Committee to the High Court, I have been unable to do anything. Please stop worrying as this case is 100 per cent in our favour. I can understand your being anxious and I am also aware how the jail authorities continue to harass you. I could have filed a case against them as well but I certainly do not want you to get caught in other problems because of this.' My eyes filled up as I told him that he was not only my lawyer but also a brother to me. He reassured me that I'd be released in the near future. Even as we exchanged these few words, the policewoman kept yelling that the time was over and apart from losing concentration it also filled me with anger; she led me back to the 7×9 lockup where I kept pacing, unable to think of anything other than the hurdles in my case. Today, while returning from the court, immersed in deep thought, I felt that the fast-moving-outside-world had also come to a halt. The thread of illusion snapped on reaching the prison door.

I felt very anxious in those days, I did not even feel like talking to anyone, nor was I interested in any activity. I hadn't heard from home for many days. On 15 July, Friday, I bowed my head in obeisance in Allah's court and pleaded for my early release.

On the next day of mulaqat no one came to visit me although I waited impatiently. I was disappointed to see the mulaqat ka parcha. When I went to the chakkar at 10, I saw that a woman prisoner had been caught with tobacco and was being led to the DS's office. Nearly 70 per cent of the women in jail were addicted to tobacco.

Dr Kiran Bedi treated the jail as an institution where prisoners could be reformed but her efforts went to waste as soon as she was transferred. It would have been more meaningful to initiate reforms for the jail staff instead for in many cases they were the source of these ills; the tobacco was also procured through them. They had no hesitation in looting the rich prisoners; even visiting their homes to demand money which the family members gave willingly hoping that this would provide certain facilities to their loved ones in jail, but this never happened.

Jail was known for destroying noble thoughts and pure sentiments. The matron, for example, pilfered oil, sugar and tea meant for prisoners which she took home with her without any qualms even though it meant that prisoners suffered due to this. Whether these items were supplied by an NGO or a government department, the matron had to have her share. Since the matron, more than other jail staff, was in close proximity to the prisoners, no one dared complain against her, for fear of being harassed.

There were preparations under way in jail for a Parliamentarian's visit. The jail was also being decorated to welcome the incumbent DG. Since I had done a course in painting, I was deputed to paint the walls surrounding the fountains in the front lawn along with four other women inmates. I always earnestly carried out any work that was given to me in jail. When I was asked to do this, despite being ill, I worked without any complaint until six o'clock. As instructed, I brought a few colourful candles that I had made and placed them at the fountain. These candles were used for decoration at every function after which I had to collect them and put them back in place. This was not an easy task and keeping them safe was even tougher; I was held accountable if even one candle went missing. Gel candles were in glass containers and since glass is a prohibited item in jail, one had to be extra cautious for its safety and against any pilferage.

Whenever there was a programme in jail, women prisoners were called to serve the guests. They were given white clothes to wear although convicted prisoners had to wear the brown khadi that was provided by the jail. Prisoners were also provided with soap, oil, towels and slippers once every two months and in winter they got a pair of flat shoes as well. Vim and Surf were provided for cleaning the barracks and wards. Nearly all the women worked very hard but the sweeper women's job was tougher and more hectic. Every morning, they picked up garbage from the wards in a cart and dumped it in the large garbage bin which was cleared by the same women once a fortnight when the garbage truck came. On this day, the entire area would stink but the women had to anyhow slog through the stench. In jail parlance, the van that carried the garbage from the wards was known as 'Maruti'. Two new Marutis had been added to the fleet and plying these was less cumbersome than the old carts as there were wheels that made it easier to turn them in any direction. During programmes, the women prisoners with cleaning duty had to bear a heavy burden of work and similarly on days when any visitor came to the jail.

At the next mulaqat too no one visited me. I began to wonder if my family had forgotten me as there was not even a letter from them. I thought, I hope it is not the case of 'out of mind-out of sight'.

Tasleem came to visit me on 28 July but she had no news of my family as they had not called her up. I had started gaining weight due to the hormonal treatment and today I was also running a fever. I was feeling quite restless due to this and felt very low that there was no progress in my case. Apart from this, there were many other worries but I still felt happy to see

Tasleem who was unwell too had not been able to visit me more often as she could not get leave from work.

As I was returning to the cell, the SI madam asked me to come to her office where the DG had sent a box of floating candles that I was asked to fill with gel and pack in gift wrappings. It was an urgent task so I put away the packet of fruit that Tasleem had brought for me and immediately got down to work; it took an entire day with no time to even eat lunch. When I returned to the cell in the evening tea had already been distributed and I missed the much needed cup. My cell mate Darshana had however kept aside my lunch (dal, roti) but since it had turned cold and the dal was tasteless, I decided to eat fruit instead. I started painting and kept busy until past midnight. I could not sleep due to the intense heat till I decided to pour some water on myself, which gave me some relief, but soon; a cat strayed into the cell and chasing her out took away the rest of the night!

I received a letter from Engineer Farooq Ahmed one day. He'd been behind bars for the past 11 years. He sent a piece of Kashmiri 'wudd' (a thick round tablet made of Kashmiri red chillies and other spices). He is from Islamabad, like me. I also received letters occasionally from many other Kashmiri brothers languishing in jail.

During summer, I soaked cotton sheets as well as the durri to use at night; I placed my feet on the wet durri and covered myself with the wet sheet. Many other women inmates also slept in a similar way. The respite was momentary as the heat enveloped us as soon as the sheets dried up. Inside the cells there was no difference in temperature between nights and days. At such times I truly missed the snow-capped mountains of Kashmir, its green fields, lakes and water streams.

Abidji's visit and the news of my family's welfare brought me some relief. He informed me that the hearing for my bail was scheduled for 16 August in the High Court and once again expressed confidence that the bail plea would be accepted but I was not able to share his confidence; my intuition prodded me to believe otherwise; that there was to be no escape from this cage anytime soon. I wondered if we should change the lawyer but my family was against it. I was dependent on them in every way but they knew better what was good for me. There was no room for argument about this but since I was the one enduring this never-ending ordeal, I felt that the case should proceed according to my wishes and what seemed appropriate to me. Anyhow, what I needed most right now was some oxygen for my dehydrated soul and this meeting provided me with it along with the strength to cope with the daily grind.

There was a quarrel one day between two habshi women prisoners. Elizabeth beat up Joy brutally but no one dared to intervene until a small group of other habshi women came and rescued Joy who was wailing inconsolably.

What led to the fight was that Elizabeth, who took care of Joy's 4-year old son, heard a rumor that Joy had told her son not to meet her as she was reportedly having a negative influence on the young one. This enraged Elizabeth enough to beat Joy to a pulp despite her repeated pleas that she had not said this. Joy's two sons were born inside the jail but one of them had died due to AIDS that Joy too suffered from. Joy had become a mental wreck after her son's death and was unable to take proper care of her other young son, Peter as she spent most of her time weeping in a corner of her cell. Since there was unity and solidarity among the habshi women prisoners, Elizabeth had taken the responsibility of bringing up Peter. It was due to some misunderstanding and rumour mongering that a fight erupted between them but as I had mentioned earlier, Elizabeth was an uncouth, uncivilized woman who was ever ready to beat up anyone at the slightest pretext. However, she and the other habshi women managed to take good care of Peter.

Among the women prisoners, there were seven or eight AIDS patients in jail and some fifteen or twenty patients suffering from tuberculosis. Among the AIDS patients, four were Indian while the rest were foreigners, mainly habshi women. Earlier, a woman prisoner who was released on parole and returned after a few weeks was informed (when no one came to visit her) that her husband had died due to AIDS. While this news broke her down emotionally, she also began to suspect that she too could be suffering from the disease and it was her misfortune that the medical tests confirmed her worst fears. She was earlier deployed at the langar but removed from duty after being diagnosed. Now she remained confined to her cell, shedding tears constantly, in silence. When women are incarcerated for prolonged periods their men visit other women, throwing precaution and morals to the wind to satisfy their own needs. If they ended up with AIDS their women too had to pay a heavy price. This widow prisoner, an AIDS patient, has been serving term for the past ten years. Her two children, a son and daughter, were enrolled in Kiran Bedi's school. Being a Muslim, she offered namaz five times a day and to some extent, she was also pleasant in her manner. I use the phrase 'to some extent' because most women prisoners, having spent several years in jail, lose the ability for polite behaviour; they are 'bought' by the jail authorities as slaves and this is enough to strip them of any humaneness as they are the first ones on whom the authorities experimented with their various methods of control.

Although AIDS patients did not face any discrimination in jail they were looked upon with fear and contempt by others. The jail authorities procured medicines for them from outside and also offered them fruit along with a special diet.

The 'old' women convicts, over a period of time, also turned into rough bullies and considered themselves no less than the staff in terms of the power and authority they wielded over 'new' inmates. The Munshi in every ward was invariably drawn from among them. They took the responsibility, quite proudly, of supplying jail ka samaan, helping the matron receive a bribe, demanding from a new prisoner goods they wished to have and of course, being ready to beat up another prisoner. It was also some of these women who served as helpers to the DS and SI. Whenever a new prisoner had a visitor, these women would take away the fruit or any other items that were brought for her from home and at the time of a prisoner's release, they managed to snatch away the coupons from her. It was the same group of women who were also in charge of the canteen. This is how they developed so much clout and bossed over the new prisoners without any concern for them. In fact, they openly expressed their desire that a new prisoner, an under-trial should get convicted or punished rather than being released. However, they were glad when anyone from their own lot was released. Having experienced and endured the bitterest reality in jail, they wanted that others should also suffer in the same way. Jail alters people's psyche in peculiar ways that is then reflected in their everyday behaviour. The best years of their life (10, 12, 14 years) are spent in confinement in the worst possible conditions, scarring their soul and saturating their existence with sheer bitterness. The number of convicted prisoners in jail was 200.

Jail 6 in Tihar had the capacity of accommodating 250 prisoners whereas there were 550 women lodged here. The barracks had rows of mats, without any space, for women to sleep and the cells had three prisoners each instead of one. The Mulaheza (where new prisoners/convicts are first brought) ward was in such a terrible condition that the toilets were worse than the sarkari ones found at bus stops or railway stations.

My cell was again searched on 14 August, a day prior to Independence Day. While everything was scattered on the floor, the search party took away the nail cutter I had recently purchased from the canteen, and the sewing needles and the medicine for back ache that the matron had given me. The earthen pot of water was also emptied and searched. On other days, the same staff would be cordial with me but as 'search party' their behaviour changed completely, becoming rude and stern.

On 15 August, all the women prisoners were asked to congregate at the ground and despite the intense summer heat they were instructed not to move from their place until the programme ended. As prisoners we had no choice except to bear the heat and stand upright, our rights having been snatched from us the moment we entered the jail. The matron and Munshi ensured that each prisoner was led out of the cell after which the wards and barracks were locked from outside to prevent anyone from returning from the programme until it was over and the locks opened. I ran to the cell as soon as the programme ended, soaked a cotton sheet in water and lay down on it. The ginthi remained open today (we were not locked in) but it was no use as the temperature outside was soaring and it was better to remain inside the cell and protect oneself from the heat that could burn our flesh.

There was hardly a woman prisoner in jail who was aware of my case. To most of them I was known either as a Pakistani, a terrorist or an anti-national person. However, they knew of my friendly nature as I had always tried to help other prisoners in need because I believe that only a helpless woman is able to understand the pain of another. There were also 'professional criminals' among the women and it was not only difficult, but impossible, to reform them. Once inside the jail they spent their time thinking of ways in which to commit more crimes as well as how to protect themselves from being arrested again! One woman, who was jailed under Section 420, had duped innocent people in her neighbourhood and had amassed two and a half crore rupees by floating a 'chit fund committee'. She was awarded a three year jail term but was released on bail after only seven months.

My next hearing in the jail case was on 17 August and as usual, at 8 o'clock I was taken in a prison van to Rohini Court. At 11.30 two policemen came to the lockup asking for me. I stood up to talk to them when they asked me if there were any other 'high risk' prisoners with me. I told them that there were none here as I otherwise appeared in Patiala House court for a POTA case. I further added that I was here regarding the jail case in which five other women had also been charged along with me for destruction of jail property and the hunger strike that we observed following Zohra's death. They asked the lockup in-charge, lady SI why I had not been produced in court at the scheduled time of 11.30. Since I was a high risk prisoner, she told him that she had to wait for additional police staff to escort me there. The staff arrived 15 minutes later and I was taken to court where Abidji was already waiting. We gestured greetings to each other as talking was not allowed in this court. However, we managed to exchange a few words as I was being led back to the lockup after a fresh date had been posted. Abidji informed me that the bail plea had not been accepted in the High Court. He visited me the next day in jail and talking to him further I realized that my worst fear had come true; Salman Khurshid had failed yet again in getting me bail. Abidji told me that my file was now going back to the Sessions Court from the High Court (HC) which had passed an order that the case should be finalized within the next three months.

There was not much argument in the HC but the judge, in all respect to Salman Khurshid, observed that the case was in its final stages and if the bail plea is rejected here, the Sessions Court would be more stringent in passing its own judgment. He also wondered why there was no intervention in my case when 'they' (Hurriyat) had intervened to get Shabbir Dar (arrested under the same case) released. However cordially the judge may have addressed Salman Khurshid but the fact remains that the judge rejected his plea for bail. I was unnerved with this rejection and felt more strongly that unless we changed the lawyer there would not be any positive outcome but my family thought differently and continued to repose their faith in him.

Perhaps this long delay was God's will and for my own good in some way but it was beyond my comprehension at present. The status of my case was now different as the POTA Review Committee's judgment was also against me and this was going to influence the decision of the Sessions Court. When I next went to court for my POTA case hearing I learnt that the judge was on leave and I had to be produced before another judge. There were two Kashmiri boys also with me and we greeted each other on our way to the court. From this judge all we got was another collective date. Another day went by without any concrete result and I suffered another day of severe heat in the lockup.

I went to court again a few days later but nothing came out of it even on that day except that 29 September was posted as the next date of hearing; it seemed to me that all these years were a mere offering at the altar of the repeated dates. I returned from the court in a state of mental and emotional exhaustion and when I lay down in my cell, tears began to flow from my eyes as though I had no control over them.

One day, I fell asleep as soon as I lay down. I dreamt that I was sitting in front of myself with a radiant, beautiful and healthy face. I am asking Mahruq Javat (my friend from Bombay, who later died) if she could also see herself in her own dream as I was doing now. I tell her 'look, that woman sitting opposite me, smiling, is none other than me.' I found this to be a strange dream as I have never had one like this before.

A woman prisoner who worked in the pickle unit received summons from the jail authorities as she had secretly made pickles at the langar and given them to the DS and the matron. She was caught because the material she had used belonged to the pickle unit and an 'informer' leaked the news to the SI madam. Perhaps this was done to belittle Meena madam (DS) who was seen as "over smart" in her treatment of prisoners. The woman prisoner was removed from duty for misconduct and suffered great ignominy.

The pickle unit buzzed with activity as pickles of all varieties were prepared there and also supplied to other jails in town. It involved a lot of hard work by prisoners under the supervision of the senior madam who was also particular about maintaining cleanliness and hygiene in the unit. The pickle unit and the candle unit where I worked were located in two separate rooms, both adjacent to the SI's office.

6 September, the first day of the month preceding Ramadaan. I felt sick all night and by morning, my legs were lifeless. Constant illness had rendered me weak. The Hurriyat Conference had a meeting with the Prime Minister of India with an agenda regarding release of Kashmiri political prisoners and a time bound release of those arrested under POTA and PSA (Public

Safety Act). I was not certain if this would yield any positive result as nothing had come out of several such meetings that had been held earlier.

At my next court date the judge was on leave. Ohri Sahib's junior lady lawyer was in court and later he also arrived. He congratulated me saying that my file had gone for 'case withdrawal' (sent by Hurriyat to the GoI). I could not believe my ears but my eyes filled up with relief on hearing this. The '*naib* court' posted the next date and when I arrived there on the scheduled date, the judge was present in court but not my lawyer. The judge asked me 'where is your lawyer?' after which he turned to the public prosecutor for details of the case and its progress. He replied 'the case is at an advanced stage and since we do not have any information regarding the "case withdrawal" I appeal that the case proceeds further. The High Court has also issued an order that the case must be finalized within three months.' The judge picked up his pen and posted 3rd October as the next date of hearing. This is how a tiny ray of hope that I was nurturing also faded. At each court date and appearance I anticipated that perhaps this would be the day of my release but the 'court journey' was turning out to be much longer than I had anticipated. Instead of 'freedom', all I received in court were dates and more dates.

Abidji came on 19 September after a gap of nearly one month. He had met members of the Hurriyat Conference before coming to meet me and assured me that they would raise the question of my release with the GoI in their forthcoming meeting. But it did not make any sense to me as I had heard the public prosecutor say in court that he had no information regarding my 'case withdrawal'. In fact the Hurriyat had had many rounds of talks with the GoI and only those Kashmiri prisoners were released whose names they had submitted to the government. I was not interested anymore in the Hurriyat's efforts because I knew that they never raised my name with the GoI nor would they do so in future. If they had approached the matter with a view to my being a founding member of the

Hurriyat and one who valued the movement, I would not have had to spend so many years in prison.

About a week later, Parvez Ahmed Dar of Peoples League came to meet me as he was visiting another Kashmiri prisoner brother. He conveyed the Hurriyat leader, Abdul Ghani Bhat's message to me, 'Tell Zamarud that she will be released soon.' I found this to be a crude joke. I mentioned this to Abidji when he visited me later and he too was not impressed as he now knew the Hurriyat and its politics better than me. He believed in his own hard work and my elder brother's efforts relating to my case and most of all, in God's support and mercy.

My constant anxiety and my state of helplessness had no meaning for the jail authorities who called me over to say that there was a large order for candles and I should be ready with it in two days time. I set everything aside and immersed myself in this work. Jail is a graveyard of desires and wishes; all I wished to do now was to sit alone in my cell and reflect over my destiny and unburden my heart by shedding tears but the sudden work commitment prevented me from doing so. I had even lost the right or my choice to mourn over the travails and misfortunes of my life. My heart was heavy with a strange kind of burden that I wanted to ease. The NHRC team was visiting and as happens with such visits, all the prisoners were locked in and the door was closed. I failed to understand the purpose of this team's visit when none of the prisoners was allowed to meet them although some of the women were called on duty to serve them refreshments in white starched clothes, but their movement was restricted to only this, serving the team, which the women did as mute slaves. It was only after the team's departure from jail that other prisoners got to know of their visit. For the jail authorities it was enough that the team was well fed and left without registering a single complaint from any prisoner. There were several prisoners who were so poor that despite getting bail they remained in jail as they could not afford to pay the bail amount. Many prisoners continued to languish in jail for petty crimes that did not warrant such prolonged imprisonment while others were serving extended terms for committing thefts of Rs 4-500 but the NHRC team was not concerned or bothered about them.

When I glanced at the newspaper on the morning of 1 October I felt the ground beneath my feet slipping away; I could not believe the unfortunate news that leapt out of the newspaper concerning my elder brother Doctor Sahib.* I cried. I was troubled. Why is this happening to my family members? Why had this sudden bolt of lightning fallen upon us? The whole day went by; I felt there was no sky above me or ground beneath. I kept awake all night. I fell ill the next day because I was so worried about my brother. I prayed to God to help him pass through this test successfully; I prayed that he be released from this moment of difficulty, Amen. What could I do? Who could I turn to at this hour? Oh God, give me strength to deal with this difficult moment. I did not have either a friend or a companion or a well wisher in jail. Who could I share my grief with, how could I lighten this heavy burden that was bearing me down, except to bow my head to God and weep? I decided to pick up my pen and write a letter to my brother.

At my next court date I could barely sit in the lockup and kept pestering the policewoman to produce me in court soon; I wasn't so impatient about my own case. I was just anxious to meet someone from my family so that I could share my sorrow. I was produced at 11.30. Abidji was present but looked anxious too. I started crying when I saw him but he consoled me saying that Doctor Sahib's problem would soon be resolved. I did not know what to tell him as I had this nagging feeling that all this was happening to my family due to me. I gathered courage and told him to stop worrying about me and work hard for my brother's welfare. I was convinced that he was suffering this

---

* A government employee, Doctor Sahib was arrested on charges of corruption but released after a week as the charges could not be proved.

humiliation because of my case; I am the sinner, I thought. We got another date in November but I did not feel either sad or disappointed today.

> *Ranj se khugar hua insaan toh mit jata hai ranj*
> *Mushkilein itni padhi mujh per ke aasan ho gayeen'(Ghalib)*

> Sorrow disappears when one is inured to it
> I have confronted so many difficulties that they became easy.

Inside the lockup I tried to console myself until 5.30 when the prison van took me back on my journey to Tihar. Strangely enough, everyone I saw outside through my window seemed equally worried.

The holy month of Ramadan began on 16 October. I raised my arms and prayed to God to forgive me for my sins and not to punish my family on my account.

Constant illness had made my health worse. I wondered about the well-being of my brother, there were daily reports in the newspaper regarding him. As I lay down in my cell at 10, I felt tremors that shook my body and strangely, I read in the newspaper the next morning that Kashmir had been repeatedly rocked by high intensity tremors the previous night leading to an earthquake. The news deepened my sense of helplessness.

The jail authorities were short on religious tolerance. I used to receive religious and literary books and journals from AR Ansari of Iqra Library in Uttar Pradesh (UP). Due to the censorship procedure in jail it took considerable time for these to reach me as the number of such magazines were far more in Urdu language than in English and the censors took a while to read them. Urdu magazines were stopped altogether after some time, including the ones that had Quranic prescriptions. I appealed to SI madam to let me have access to these magazines but she directed me to seek permission from DS Raman madam who rejected my request on the ground that the senior madam had not given such permission. When I went back to her she refused on the plea that the DG had not given permission. In this manner I was denied access to these magazines whereas there was a regular supply of Hindi and English newspapers/magazines for which the prisoners paid from their own pocket. There was however not a single newspaper in Urdu. Jail authorities associated Urdu with the Muslim community whereas there were many non-Muslim prisoners too who had expressed their desire to read Urdu newspapers. The number of convicted prisoners in jail was far less than the ones under trial. In the entire jail numbers 1, 3, 6, 7 and 8 were reserved for under-trial prisoners whereas jail numbers 2 and 5 were meant for convicts. Caught in the prolonged legal procedures, many under-trial prisoners even completed their entire sentence while waiting to be tried! The legal system was so inefficient and slow that hearings for even the innocent ones were unnecessarily extended due to repeated dates spread over months during which they simply languished in jail. A case that should have been completed in one year often took up to five years. Whoever got lodged in jail once for whatever reason, his/her name was struck off the list of human beings. The slow pace of justice reduced them to a non-being. 'Justice delayed is justice denied.' Ninety per cent prisoners in Tihar were under-trials, the majority of them charged for petty offences and they spent years waiting for justice.

If a male or female prisoner was caught fighting in jail or found with tobacco h/she was lodged in a solitary cell for seven days where even the food and tea was given to them from outside without unlocking the cell. Many prisoners are known to have attempted suicide in solitary. As punishment, they were made to clean the khata, the largest garbage bin in jail, or trim the grass in parks.

Bhaagu Ma was an old prisoner serving a life term of fourteen years but even on completion of her term she was not released as there was a peculiar complication in her case – there was no mention or evidence of two years of her term in jail records. She made many rounds of the UT/CT offices but to no avail.

She was the oldest prisoner in the langar. She was constantly abusing the jail authorities and judges. Having spent a lifetime in jail, she even dared to complain about the staff to their face. She also used to sit on a chair, a luxury that is denied to other prisoners.

During the festive season, Delhi was gripped by fear and insecurity due to some serial blasts. Whenever an incident like this occurred, Kashmiri prisoners faced further restrictions and harassment and the finger of suspicion pointed at them, even if they were inside the jail. I was also beginning to feel insecure inside the jail. Jail authorities, staff and prisoners who considered themselves as patriotic beings, trained their gaze on me in a peculiar manner and passed sarcastic comments as though I had gone out of jail and personally conducted these blasts. They looked at me with suspicion, hatred and contempt even though I do believe that a terrorist has no religion and Islam is categorical in its rejection of such inhuman acts but unfortunately, every terrorist attack was being associated with Muslims. It was natural for me to feel anxious as these blasts could have an adverse impact on my case.

I received letters from home at regular intervals including from Neelji who had also sent me a money order. Apart from news of the family, the letters were full of prayers for my early release. Baji's letter carried a message of courage, consolation as well as details of a particular prayer for me to offer. Abidji came to visit me on 31 October and informed me that Daood, my nephew, would also be visiting me soon. He came shortly after and apologized for not coming earlier as there were restrictions on visitors after the Delhi blasts. He told me 'Our house is lonely without you. Time has stopped at year 2003 at home because nobody has changed the calendar. We still have the same calendar that you had put up on the wall with your own hands. Whatever you had placed in the house remains untouched. Boba does not allow anyone to touch your belongings and we feel your presence amidst us because of your things lying around at home. At times it feels as though you are entering the kitchen, humming your favourite tune and at other times that you are coming down the stairs. The shadow of your presence resides in each corner of the house and I am finding it increasingly difficult to live there. Even Boba suffers from bouts of irritation and depression and says that she finds her daughter's reflection in everything and how your presence brightened our home.'

I was spending lonely days in jail, away from my sisters and brothers, my mother and other members of my family. Sleeping on a bare floor without a mattress or a pillow, without any other comfort, I tolerated all the hardships and humiliations. I had no complaint against God. I only prayed that Eid brings the gift of progress, success and Azadi to the followers of Islam and the people of Kashmir. May it bring the message of peace and happiness for my mother, sisters and brothers. Amen. For me it was like any other day and went by as such.

On 5 November in the early evening, madam invited the Muslim women who were fasting and offered them a cup of tea each. Some women also sang songs. The canteen had prepared a special sweet dish – supposedly made with milk and siwwaiyan – on the occasion but there was hardly any milk in it! There was sweet rice too and although quite tasteless, these dishes were sold out quickly as prisoners were tired and bored of eating the same jail food day after each day. Eid also turned out to be a source of income for the jail staff!

Earlier, the canteen was managed by old prisoners but after Sandra left on parole the jail authorities decided to take it over and manage it as Sandra had incurred more losses than profit. Now the matron was in charge of the canteen and she made women prisoners do all the work there but handled the accounts herself. Sandra used to give credit to only those women prisoners who could arrange (from outside) to have money deposited in her PP account. Most of these women were prostitutes who were considered rich – they ate better than other prisoners as they had the means to directly purchase food from the canteen.

On Eid, I received a letter from home and a money order of Rs 2000. I did not have permission to keep a large sum of money in my PP account – the maximum we were allowed was Rs 1500-2000 although some other prisoners had as much as Rs 20,000 in their accounts. I am referring to those prisoners who were convicted and working in the jail. An old woman prisoner who was released recently had Rs 35,000 in her account! Many prisoners had their money deposited in an outside account by jail authorities and at the time of release an FD (fixed deposit) certificate of the equivalent amount was handed over to them. A few prisoners saved and deposited their money for their own bail bond while others also sent money home and some managed to pay their lawyer's fee from their own savings.

In jail, legal assistance was only in name. The visiting jail lawyers, in the name of free legal aid, looted prisoners and usually it was the most incapable lawyer who was appointed in jail. I am referring to jail 6 and maybe this is not the case in the men's jail but such was the norm in Tihar jails. The jail lawyers would visit at 4 and leave after having refreshments and taking the thumb impressions of women prisoners in a register as though their job was done. On my next court date (7 November) as was usual, we were stuffed in the small prison van and taken to court. As I have mentioned earlier, it was not easy to find a place to sit in the small van and the situation in the lockup was no different. However, it was the dominance of habshi women that ruled the day and every other prisoner appearing in court would fervently wish for a date that did not coincide with that of these women. On that day two foreign women prisoners also had their court dates but as my name was first on the list I got space in the van but not in the lockup as women had hurriedly entered and grabbed whatever space they could find inside. A prisoner from my ward had found a little space which she was willing to share with me. I was taken to the judge's room at 10 and was kept waiting there until 11 o'clock as my lawyer had still not arrived and another case was going on. Abidji was present in court and had brought a pair of shoes for me which turned out to be one size too small. He said that in the eventuality of my case being further delayed, the Hurriyat's talks with GoI during this period would make my release a possibility. I found that difficult to believe, instead I felt quite bitter about this banter. The GoI had earlier rejected the Hurriyat's plea that Kashmiri political prisoners be released. Why would the same government agree this time? Moreover, the possibility of talks between Hurriyat and GoI seemed bleak at present but I was not aware of what if anything, had transpired between my family and the Hurriyat leadership that they displayed such confidence in them. My faith, on the contrary, rested in God's generosity, my lawyer's ability and his hard work. My lawyer Ohri had made me believe that he would win the case.

I was produced before the judge who enquired about my lawyer, I told him he was not available today but his junior was present in court. The judge told me that he was giving me a date after three months. Even though the High Court had already passed an order that my case should be wrapped up within three months, I continued to get such long duration dates. In the court that day LN Rao, DCP of Special Cell was meant to give his witness account in my case but he was not present in court although my file had already been brought by the Tihar police official to place before the judge. The public prosecutor then asked him to take it back as my lawyer was also not present in court. As the police official left with the file I signaled to Abidji to follow and see what was written in the file. In the meantime the policewoman got my date warrant and led me back to the lockup. Abidji returned for a meeting and the policewoman then led me by hand from the lockup to the meeting place. He told me that he had spoken to the jail police official who said 'There is nothing to worry about in relation to the file jottings. The jail authorities want the best for each prisoner and wish for their early release. We do not write anything against a prisoner, and in any case Anjum's record in jail is good and the file carries the same.' Abidji left after assuring me that he would return next week, perhaps with Boba.

I got a cup of tea at 12 noon and although it had far too much sugar, it tasted better than Tihar tea. Women prisoners enjoyed 4-5 cups of tea in the lockup as they waited for their turn to be produced in court but I could not have more than one. At 5.30 we were herded into the van and transported back to Tihar. I was feeling tired having spent nearly the whole day in the lockup.

Pottery work had begun in jail but more than pottery it was POP (Plaster of Paris) that was used to design utensils and decorate them with different colours. I had enrolled my name for this earlier on as there was not much work in the candle project anymore. Although we had worked hard in the candle project the jail staff could not find proper marketing outlets for the candles. Had it been a private project, the same jail staff would have made it sustainable and financially viable but being a sarkari project its status remained as such; sarkari. A teacher from outside had been arranged for pottery classes. We were a group of ten women prisoners and this project too was under the direct supervision of SI madam and located in the same room where the candle project was. On the first day, a puja was conducted where the DIG was a guest of honour, and she also performed the ritual of breaking a coconut on the occasion. Work on the project began the next day, Wednesday. SI madam asked me to take responsibility for this project which I agreed to readily as I found it very interesting. The earthen utensils were made in a factory inside the jail. Then we got large ply wood boards with imprints of flowers, birds, other images of modern art that were then cut out and filled with colour and placed on the utensils. Other materials included POP, chalk powder, adhesives and colours. It was nice work but many women prisoners who had earlier worked in the candle project had not been paid and they'd left. The same thing had happened to me but I preferred to continue to work rather than sit idle or spend time with quarrelsome women inmates.

As in the candle project, sales were initially swift in pottery too and women worked with great interest as long as the teacher was present; she taught new designs each day and also different methods of decoration and creating patterns. Our clothes got soiled here but it did not matter as we enjoyed the time we spent there.

Many personal habits had to be given up in jail but one that I continued to maintain was to bathe every morning, wear a set of clean clothes and leave for work although this was a fairly neglected practice in jail. It was this habit that became a source of strength and consolation for me as I carried a mountain of hardship in my heart and had buried any desire or aspiration for my early release. Although jail authorities called me a strong woman, I was a broken woman inside. Since childhood, it was my habit not to share my worries with others or narrate my woes to anyone. In this regard I am an introvert. When Advocate Miyan Qayyum visited me in jail some time earlier, I was in a troubled state of mind but refrained from expressing it to him; rather I spoke to him smilingly but he somehow gathered what was going through my mind. It had to do with how I was lodged in the same cell with professional criminal women and also the constant harassment I faced at the hands of the previous SI Santosh. When Miyan Qayyum returned to Kashmir he wrote and published a detailed report regarding my condition in jail.

A week later, my mother came for mulaqat; she looked frail and her eyesight had weakened. She is a mother, after all. Crying for me had dimmed her eyes. She was also caught in other household worries. I felt dismayed to see her in this condition but what could I do in the helpless state that I was in? I tried to persuade her to get a medical checkup and to be treated in Delhi but she preferred to return to Kashmir. Abidji had taken her to a doctor here who suggested cataract surgery and a month's medication prior to it but she refused.

I spent the next week thinking and worrying about my mother and missed her every minute. I did go to work but my mind was drawn to her eyes that were filled with tears and loneliness as she repeatedly said to me, 'I do not know if I will ever see you free again.' I remember her and the words she spoke in myriad ways. My sisters and Abidji told me at every mulaqat about how much Boba cried for me each day and how she waited for my return. I often cursed myself for having driven my mother to such a miserable state; her sad face haunted me and remained in my eyes. It was rare in Kashmir for a woman to be incarcerated and that too for such a long period. For many years, my mother and I had been living together in our ancestral home in Islamabad and enjoyed such intimacy that without one, the other felt incomplete. After my imprisonment she found it difficult to live in that house and moved, dividing her time between my two sisters who took care of her.

A few weeks later, another ICRC team visited me and after inquiring about my health in detail they said they would come back with a doctor from their own team. They returned the same day at 4 with a German doctor who conducted a thorough medical checkup and said that he would prescribe medicines for me after consulting the lady doctor in jail. According to him, the medicines I was having in jail carried the risk of harmful side effects. I told the ICRC team that I had stopped visiting the MIR as the doctor there did not let me come and the jail doctor too was quite hostile to me. She is known to have said that being a convicted prisoner under POTA; I should not be permitted to visit the MIR without a police team to accompany me. It was not possible for a policewoman to accompany me each time and this led to friction between me and the doctor at MIR who was rude to me. The German doctor advised me that whatever the problem I should continue to go to MIR for treatment to prevent my health from deteriorating further. He said that he could only offer medical advice but not any treatment as it was not in the ICRC's mandate although he did mention a few medicines that could help in my recovery. However, I knew that jail authorities would not offer these medicines to me as they only relied on medicines that were available in the MIR. The German doctor was pleasant in his manner and also aware that the medicines available in jail were of a substandard quality. Before leaving he advised me to keep myself as busy as possible. Kiran Bedi has written extensively in her book regarding jail reforms but the truth is that the jail doctors consider us to be criminals more than patients.

The ICRC team later met the SI madam but I did not know what they discussed. However, on the third day of their visit, the jail Medical Officer (MO) who was a Kashmiri Pundit called me for a medical checkup after which she prescribed the same old medicines to me.

> *Na kisi pe zakhm ayan koi*
> *Na kisi ko fikr rafu ki (Faiz)*
>
> The wound is not apparent to anyone
> Nor is anyone bothered about its healing.

On 7 December, at 7.30 in the morning undertrial women prisoners were brought together at the deorhi to go for a court hearing. Among them were six of us who had to appear in the jail case. Rehmana was not with us as she was very ill. She was however brought in a wheel chair from the ward to the deorhi but when the DS saw her, he called up SI madam to inform her of Rehmana's state and also sought permission that she be exempted from going to court. We waited till the permission was granted and left for the court as soon as she was taken back to the ward. Rehmana had been arrested in connection with the shoot-out at Red Fort and had recently been convicted and awarded a seven-year jail term with rigorous imprisonment. Her health has since been affected.

Some of the jail staff were present in court as witnesses in the jail case including AS Kiran madam, AS Suman madam and DS Ved Prakash Sir. Kiran madam was the first to give her witness account which was against us but the lawyer of the co-accused argued in such a way that it weakened Kiran madam's statement. Ved Prakash did not give any statement against us. As we stepped outside the courtroom after the proceedings, Bobby (name changed) and Santosh (co-accused) got into an argument with Kiran madam.

The lockup was full of women and as they used the toilet frequently it became difficult to breathe because of the pervasive stench. There was no container or mug in the toilet and the plastic bottle that we had earlier placed had disappeared too. There was not even a mat to spread on the floor nor was there any utensil for drinking water. We had to in any case wait until 5.30 when the prison van came and took us back to Tihar. Male prisoners were transported back to Tihar immediately after the hearing but women had to wait until evening as there was only one bus reserved for them. Although we had registered a complaint with the jail authorities they did not do anything about this and as long I was in Tihar I had to tolerate this inconvenience. Only once, returning from the Rohini court I found a seat in the bus as it was larger than the one that took us to Patiala House court.

8 December is the day of the year which neither I nor my family can ever forget. This was the day a major tragedy struck our family when our happiness was suddenly snatched away from us. It was this day when my dearest sister departed from this world. She left this world but not our hearts which are still filled with grief.

> Ya Allah, grant my sister a place in heaven, Amen.
> Ya Allah, help her with a glimpse of the Prophet, Amen
> May Hazrat Hajera take her in her fold and give her shelter
> Ya Allah, help my sister to cross the bridge, Amen
> Ya Allah, keep my sister from the torment of the grave, Amen'.
> May she attain heaven each time she turns her side.
> Ya Allah, may her grave be an enlightened abode.
> Ya Allah, accept all my prayers for my sister, Amen.

Inside the jail each prisoner's mind and heart is caught in the vicissitudes of misfortune. The sun shines in jail too. There is moonlight at night and the stars also glitter but all of life's brightness has dimmed and my world is ruined. There is a world of difference in how a prisoner perceives the sun, moon and stars and how a free person sees them. Those who belong to the 'outside' world – those who are beyond our view – cannot imagine that there can be a smiling face in jail but jail has offered a mighty lesson that one's face should not reflect the contours of one's sorrow. Thus, every time I met my family, it was with an artificial smile on my face yet with deep anguish in my heart. I saw 500 live faces in jail on a daily basis but they were lacking in any passion for life; every face seemed to hide a lifeless being behind it. They walked and talked but...

8 December was also my court date but the judge was on leave while Abidji was waiting for me. Because the judge was not there, Abidji could not submit an appeal for mulaqat so he spoke to the court registrar and offered him some cash so that we could meet in the courtroom. The policewoman, dragging me by my hand, saw the 'money transaction' and expressed her strong displeasure; mainly because it was the registrar who got the money and not she. She refused to allow me to talk to my nephew despite our repeated pleas. As she continued to drag me away Abidji asked her why she was dragging me in this manner, why could she not just take me away. As we reached the lockup, she complained to the in-charge 'Anjum's relative paid money to the court registrar and forced me to let them talk to each other. When I refused, he behaved rudely with me.' I tried to intervene but the in-charge asked me to keep quiet and instructed the policewoman to register the complaint in the logbook and send a copy to the concerned jail authority.

Policewomen at the lockup were rude and arrogant. They were partial to those prisoners who paid them enough money to allow them extra meeting time with relatives but for us unfortunate ones, there was no consideration at all. Many under trial prisoners had complained about their arbitrary and authoritarian behaviour but nobody really bothered about their complaints.

I was missing my family members terribly, particularly my mother about whom I also remained anxious. Life had come to a standstill in jail. The 'high risk' ward was under construction these days; it was in an isolated area surrounded by high walls. Large mesh walls were also being erected between the different wards. Now life would stretch only as far as the wards.

Abidji came to visit me on 15 December en-route to Dubai to look for employment. He had handed over all the case related work to a junior lawyer Ajay Sinha whom he also took to meet my lawyer Ohri Sahib. I suggested to Abidji that a close friend of mine, Mahruq, had recently been released from jail here and could help them with my case as she was familiar with both the jail and court routine. He rejected my suggestion outright saying that we must not trust anybody; our lawyer is competent and the junior has already been paid a fee. In the next two days the prisoners were shifted around in the wards.

We heard a piercing siren a few days later and immediately the doors were closed for the entire jail. We later learnt that a new prisoner had tried to escape from the inspection ward. The walls around jail 6 had the delivery vans bringing goods for jail and it was known as 'court morcha'. Going out from here was not only difficult but impossible as this led straight to the deorhi. The prisoner was trying to climb the gate at the court morcha when the TSP on duty caught sight of her and informed the authorities through wireless. Soon after, a posse of policewomen surrounded her and beat her up mercilessly after pulling her down from the gate. When the doors were opened all the women prisoners started moving towards jail 8 to get a glimpse of this daring prisoner but she had already been lodged in the 'qusoori' special cell. Another day, a woman drug addict was brought into jail in a terrible state; her clothes were stinking and filthy and she had no physical strength or mental awareness. She was admitted to the MIR but was shifted to a cell in our ward after couple of days; she screamed throughout the night due to which none of the other women could sleep. She was an educated woman who could only speak in English. The entire ward was on tenterhooks because of her presence. Her name was Khumaira and she believed she was a citizen of some Arab country. She was gradually gaining her senses and 'becoming normal' but repeatedly visited the MIR to plead with the doctors there to give her intoxicating drugs or sedatives. It took five days for her to bathe and to change her clothes. During my period of confinement I saw many such women who were arrested and brought to jail. They were known as 'totan' in jail parlance; they did not like to interact with clean women and were in search of women from the slums. A few of them were educated and from a decent family background but their condition was worse than that of a beggar. Indigent women arrested for theft and pilferage continued to carry out their activities, their 'dhanda' in jail too, stealing from other prisoners. Many such women returned to jail after being relased and gladly spent some three or four months in jail before being released again. Most of them were involved in trading in illicit liquor and were not bothered about being arrested or about serving a jail term. In fact, many of them could be seen making purchases at the canteen the day after their arrest!

One night a group of eunuchs, hijras, was arrested from outside a VIP road in Delhi and brought to jail on the charge of creating a public nuisance. It was beyond the jail staff's ability to bring them under control as they continued with the same behaviour inside the jail. There were ten of them and they created such a racket in the ward where they were lodged that other inmates felt harassed until they were bailed after five days. But within this short span they managed to create a flutter in the entire jail as the authorities were not able to lock them in for fear of being abused or cursed by them – eunuchs often use this 'weapon' of casting the evil eye on someone, and this is considered dangerous.

A rumor spread like wildfire in the entire jail that a new prisoner was in possession of a mobile phone, and the doors were closed abruptly and a search operation mounted. The search at ward 8 began at 8 pm. We learnt the next morning that the search for the mobile phone had led to the discovery and confiscation of other forbidden items such as tobacco and other 'outside goods'. The search operation continued for an entire week. SI madam summoned a few old prisoners, Munshis and other women working in different units, including me. She tried to take us into confidence so that we could help her find the mobile phone. There was no dearth of informers in jail where it is an open secret that women prisoners are the ones who lead authorities to the source of tobacco and other illicit items. However, we did not take her initiative seriously as we knew that if at all the phone was discovered it would only be through the help of the jail staff. Why does she not appoint the staff under her command for the task, we wondered? Since she was anxious that the news had now reached the DG, she called an urgent meeting of all the prisoners and instructed them sternly that anyone in possession of a mobile phone should come up to her in the office and deposit it with her and she said she assured them that she would not disclose the prisoner's identity. She warned us that if we did not comply a team from outside would come to jail for proper investigation. After this meeting, every corner of the entire jail including the toilets and all the different centres was searched again with metal detectors but the mobile phone remained untraced.

One day, DS Ashwini madam who was deployed at jail 6 was caught in a bribery case, arrested and brought to our jail. A TV channel Aaj Tak had conducted a sting operation and caught her 'red handed'. The news quickly spread in jail and while women prisoners were happy with this new development, the staff looked wary. This incident did not prevent the staff from taking bribes but made them cautious while doing so. Ashwini madam spent 15 days in jail but with all facilities provided to her; she was given a cell in the Vipasana ward with a Dunlop mattress and a set of clean sheets, food was brought to her from the langar in separate utensils and the door was not closed for her the entire day except late at night. Other women prisoners objected strongly to the authorities that while serving her term in jail, she should be treated like any other prisoner rather than as DS but it made no difference.

Later, matron Sunita, who was involved in the case of Zohra's death, was also arrested and brought to our jail. She approached us (six other women charged in the case) in a friendly manner, sweet talking us, thinking that we would refrain from giving our witness account in court against her. None of the inmates had any sympathy for her. Of the six of us, three were eye-witnesses to Zohra's death. Like other prisoners, Sunita madam was lodged in a cell with two other inmates in it. She was released on bail after serving only three months in jail. With these two women from the staff experiencing a jail term each, we thought that the rest of the staff would perhaps appreciate our difficulties better but… As Zohra had ultimately died of medical negligence we felt that Dr Kakkar should also have been in jail with Sunita madam and the rumor was that she too might be arrested and brought here. But as long as I was in jail, she was not arrested while we continued to attend court in the same case.

This year too was coming to an end and I felt I was still being tested. My fourth year had begun in jail. God willing, the New Year may arrive with a message of my release. The fourth year started on 2 January 2006. Last year too when I began jottings in my diary it was the Hajj season. All the doors of Mecca are open today. I pray to God that Eid this year brings the message of my freedom. I am in prayer to Him to forgive me all my sins and guide me on the proper path.

On my next mulaqat my dear friend Mahruq came to meet me although I had asked her not to do so because of the IB inquiry that would follow. She was in jail with me for a year during which we had become close friends. She treated and loved me like her younger sister. The IB had anyhow asked her about how she knew me and why she had come to meet me, advising her not to come again. Mahruq showed them her ID card and said 'I have known Anjum from the time I was in jail, until I was released recently.' When she told me all this I requested her not to come to meet me in future as it caused her so much trouble but she refused, 'you are my younger sister,' she said and added that because she was older, she wanted to ensure that I was released soon and in this regard she had also met my lawyer Ohri Sahib. When she expressed a sense of urgency regarding my release to him, he apparently told her, 'Put some weight in my hands. I will talk with you only if you are accompanied by a member from Anjum's family.' I informed Mahruq that my family had already paid 75 per cent of his fee and the remaining 25 per cent was to be paid on completion of the case. She wondered why the case was dragging for so long despite the lawyer's previous assurance that it would be over in a year's time. She suggested that I should change my lawyer but I told her I had full faith in him. After she left, I wrote a letter to Neelji telling her all that had transpired between Mahruq and me.

Soon it was winter. One morning, as usual, I offered prayers early and then had a cup of tea at 8. Poonam, my cell mate, had gone to the langar to fetch some hot water which isn't easy to get. As the days got colder I had a written prescription from the jail doctor for some hot water to bathe. Though cold in jail, the winter there was nothing compared to the winter in Kashmir. I read in the newspaper daily about the snowfall there.

Early in January we had a hearing in the jail case and so at 7.30 in the morning, we were brought to the deorhi. We got into the van more than an hour later as Rehmana was unwell and this caused some delay. She could not walk without support and the staff was trying to arrange for someone to accompany her after the doctor refused to give a letter of exemption for the court. A matron was finally sent with her to court. The lockup was freezing but we had to wait until being produced before the judge at 11.30 where the old SI and two ASs had come as witnesses. However, there was a lawyers' strike and none of our lawyers was present in court. Suman madam had given her witness account and then we were given a date for the next hearing.

The courts were now being shifted to Rohini so my next hearing would take place there. The lawyers at Tis Hazari had been agitating for three months against this and this led to undue delay in court hearings as well as other legal proceedings. The lockup was so cold that my legs were numb despite the jacket and shawl I wore. The cup of tea on offer was also cold. We suffered until 5 when we were transported back to Tihar in the prison van. It was late evening by the time we reached and since tea had last been served at 3, I went to the canteen to fetch a cup which too was cold. After the doors closed I offered namaz and sat down to eat dal and roti. The dal container was wrapped in cloth (by a cell mate) and hadn't turned cold. I ate one roti and started to read a newspaper.

The next day I found it difficult to wake up. Going back and forth to court and having to wait long hours there had tired me out. I also could not sleep most nights. The nights were long and sleep intermittent. I had tea at 8 and after a bath at 10, I went to the chakkar to pick up a newspaper and since the door was not closed in the morning because it was winter, I stepped out of the cell and sat in the sun. After tea in the afternoon I went to the canteen to buy some things that I needed but saw Bholi, a mentally unstable woman prisoner, standing outside and asking for a few things from the canteen. I bought her these and returned to the cell. Many women who were brought to jail had lost their mental equilibrium and it became worse here due to lack of proper and timely treatment. Had they been taken to a mental asylum, would their treatment have been better?

On the way back I collected my mail – there were letters from my sister and nieces. Baji wrote that she had not received any letter from me in recent weeks and that I should be more regular. I had somehow become irregular in sending letters to them, perhaps because it did not really help anymore in easing my worry or the burden I carried in my heart although this is the only means a prisoner has to remain connected to those in the outside world. I had become more anxious since the time my bail had been rejected. However, the very next day I bought a few postcards from the canteen and mailed them to my family with brief messages. One day I dreamt that I wanted to buy a new mobile phone for which I open my cupboard at home for money. As I pull out my purse I see my deceased father Thattji who is accompanied by an old woman. He is holding some parts of the mobile phone and asking me for one piece that could be used to create a new phone along with some money. I hand over Rs 1000 to him. Earlier I had dreamt of my deceased aunt Kaka Didi (Khadija) to whom I give my mobile number in response to her calling out to me. I wonder about the possible interpretation of these dreams.

Eid-ul-Zuha: The day passed like any other. Hindu and Christian festivals are celebrated with enthusiasm in jail but one does not even realize when a Muslim festival comes and goes. On Christmas day Christian visitors would come with gifts for the prisoners with an offering of special prayers. A priest also came from the church and distributed sweets, garments and shawls to them.

A few nights later I had another dream. In this, I was walking on a street between Greenland Bank and Mughal Darbar hotel towards a shop. I enter and buy myself a pair of red trousers that fit me well. As I move forward there is sudden firing in the air followed by a frantic rush of people trying to climb the stairs. I also start climbing with them when I realize that I have been shot in my left arm from where marrow is oozing from my bone. I tell a woman close by to help me but she tells me that the bullet was not in my arm but elsewhere in the body. I now begin to think that I will go to Islamabad hospital but I am unable to board the government bus when the firing begins. I woke up with my heart pounding – what a strange dream!

At the next date for my jail case, the court as well as the judge had changed; now we had to go to Rohini but the previous judge was better. Today Suman madam and Neetu madam had come to give evidence but due to the lawyers' strike there were no proceedings and we only got another date two and a half months later. The bus had brought some other prisoners from Tis Hazari court and also took some of us (who had a hearing at this court) to Tihar. This made the journey even longer and more tiresome. There were only two buses in the women's jail because of which women had to put up with a lot of hardship. When I returned I found letters from home that lifted my tiredness away and for the first time my sister's letter made me laugh with joy. She wrote 'You are very clever to send gifts for us that you have made in jail with your own hands. In your absence we find these gifts to be unique as they enhance your stature with their uniqueness.'

On 19 January, a delegation of the Srinagar Bar Association (SBA) visited me in jail. We talked at length and they offered me words of encouragement and moral support. They stressed that I needed to be independent as the Hurriyat leadership had failed to do anything for me. 'None of the organizations that value the movement have done anything for you whereas we, the SBA have organized several protests in which we used large banners with your name boldly inscribed on them, demanding your early release. We approached the Hurriyat asking them to intervene on your behalf as they had earlier done in the case of Shabbir Ahmed Dar. Since you are a woman they should have raised your name first.' They said that in their view I would emerge a big leader in Kashmir politics. They took down details of my case to enable them to meet my lawyer while assuring me that I would be released from the court itself which, they said, would be a matter of pride. Once you win the case you will be respected more, they said. According to them the Hurriyat leadership had become very 'karobari', there was likely to be a meeting between them and GoI but given the political climate they thought this might not happen, although they said the GoI was simultaneously engaging in dialogue with other political leaders to prove that the Hurriyat was not the sole representative of the Kashmiris.

The delegation expressed concern regarding my health. I told them how I had been falling ill in jail frequently and also about the bouts of depression and anguish I suffered. The head of the delegation said that while they could well imagine my predicament, they appreciated my patience and that I should have faith in God; the one who is truthful will remain so under any circumstances. 'You have supported truth and Insha'Allah you will emerge successful. We pray that you win the case with honour and are released by the court. We will continue to raise our voice for you at every forum. When one is forced into the confines of a jail, only God is her protector and what matters is the role played by her family. You have undertaken this hardship and sacrifice not for yourself but for the community. Abdul Ghani Bhat got Shabbir Ahmed out of jail and he is now busy in his own work rather than being part of the peace process. We understand all this and extend our moral support to you which is all we can do.' I thanked them and then they left to meet other Kashmiri prisoners in Tihar for whom I conveyed my regards through the delegation.

After my arrest, when my family members went to meet the then chairperson of the Hurriyat, Abdul Ghani Bhat, this is what he said to my mother: 'Zamarud is a very brave woman. She will endure the hardship and it will not take more than five years.' This is how the 'game' of my entry into jail was already fixed for five years. My family went to meet him despite my repeated pleas that they should not do so as they believed that since the Hurriyat had helped in Shabbir's release it would perhaps intervene on behalf of their daughter too but this was not to be the case. The five-year jail term was already written in my destiny but my innocent family failed to understand this. Such a great conspiracy had been hatched against me and my arrest was the reward for my being a brave woman!

The Hurriyat had split into two factions but Geelani Sahib occasionally raised the issue of my arrest in some public meetings, perhaps due to the fact that the united Hurriyat had failed to do so. However, even he did not raise it emphatically enough. I am not complaining against the Hurriyat. In the first press conference after my arrest Abdul Ghani Bhat had claimed that he did not even know who I was even though I am a founding member of Hurriyat Conference and have been associated with it for eleven years, since 1989. Their true face had emerged now. Through their talks with GoI only those people were released from jail who later became famous for corruption, involvement in the 'sex scandal' case, and who also participated in elections.

Therefore, why would I complain against them? What I understood was that I was being punished in return for the deep love and affection for my community that was an integral part of my struggle and my being. My sin was to have raised my voice against those who claimed to represent democracy but under whom many a Kashmiri youth was languishing in jail.

On 24 January the ginthi remained closed for the entire day; none of us women knew the reason for it. We were not permitted to step out although habshi women were not locked in. I received a letter from Ghulam Nabi Nijar of jail 2 who had written to me earlier too but this letter came after a fairly long time. Letters from other prisoners did not come by post but through other prisoners who carried them during the internal mulaqat on Saturdays.

As usual, a search operation was conducted on 25 January, a day prior to Republic Day but while it was more like a formality for the rest of the prisoners, my cell was searched thoroughly as always. The next day we had to congregate at the ground where SI madam took the salute after raising the Indian flag. On this occasion, announcements were also made for those whose jail terms had been reduced. Prisoners were then served sweet rice and puri. It was also an occasion when some patriotic women inmates took part in the function with great enthusiasm while glowering at me with sarcasm as they considered me to be a terrorist and an enemy of the community. Amidst all this, patriotic songs played on loudspeakers throughout the day.

On 30 January I was produced at 11.30. Mahruq was present. My lawyer and his junior also arrived a little later. After he greeted me I told my lawyer 'You do not care for me. I have repeatedly told you about my condition in jail and that you should submit an appeal in this regard to the judge but you have refused each time saying that I should first be released from the big case rather than get worried over petty cases. But only I know what

I have to endure each day in jail. You are not helping the case progress at all.' He replied 'You would have been released last year but your family had conveyed Salman Khurshid's advice that I should stagger the case a little as they believed that GoI would probably withdraw the case against you. Due to this endless wait, I am applying for your bail today and hopefully you will get it.' When I asked him how long the bail procedure could take, he said 'one month'. His junior came with the wakalatnama (power of attorney) and took my signature on it. At this moment lady judge Ravinder Kaur entered the court room; she had recently been transferred to this court but special powers had not yet been conferred on her. I had already received a warrant for the next date on 10 February by which time the judge would have special powers. Since I did not feel confident about the Hurriyat I thought the decision to apply for my bail was a sound one.

My lawyer did not mention anything regarding his fee and I wondered if my sister had spoken to him about it as I had asked her to do in my previous letter. After the date was posted the policewoman led me back to the lockup where two other women prisoners were present. The atmosphere in the otherwise gloomy lockup was quite jovial as two prisoners had got bail due to which their faces looked bright and radiant. I too felt good for them. In the lockup one only saw sad and withered faces. It is in each other's happiness that a prisoner looks for her own with the hope that one day her face too will light up with similar happiness. A tea vendor came with hot tea and passed a cup to each one of us through the iron bars of the lockup; this was a welcome treat considering how cold it was inside. At 5.30 we were on our return journey to Tihar in the caged prison van.

Dr Kiran Bedi was expected to visit our pottery class due to which I was busy since morning cleaning up the place along with other women. She arrived with a team at 12.30. She had a characteristic way of appreciating each prisoner's work with keen interest and encouraging her individually too. She met each one of us with an open heart and mind. She and her team members interacted with us and asked many questions regarding the project. For a prisoner it was a matter of esteem that a senior officer like Kiran Bedi came personally and expressed her appreciation of our work but the credit also goes to SI madam who took interest in our work and brought every visiting NGO or team to see these projects and meet the prisoners.

Abidji visited me today after nearly two months. I informed him about the next date as well the fact that we had submitted my bail plea without consulting the family but he was supportive of it. On my next court date I was so sleepy that as soon as we were sent into the lockup I spread a sheet and slept as I had stayed awake and anxious through the night. I woke up at 11 when a policewoman called out my name and produced me in court. The judge was not present although Abidji was waiting for me. When the policewoman asked me to sit down I took a chair next to him and exchanged a few words. Ohri's junior lawyer came up to me to inform me that 10 May had been posted as the next date. I felt utterly dismayed; why so long, I asked. He replied that Abidji had advised him to do so. I got angry with him and demanded to know why he had done this and how it would be beneficial to me. Three months is a long time for a prisoner I told him and asked him to appeal for an earlier date but it was not possible to change it once a warrant had already been issued, he said. As I was being led back to the lockup he informed me that my sister would be coming to visit me in a few days but I was so disturbed that I told him that I did not wish to meet anyone and he should tell the family not to come to Tihar anymore.

The next few days were terrible for me. For an under-trial prisoner, going to court always kindles the hope that there is a possibility, however bleak, that the outcome will be positive but now I would have to wait hopelessly for three months. My family perhaps did not understand the significance of a court date for which each prisoner waited impatiently, counting each day. Now I started working long hours at the pottery project in an attempt to keep myself busy but I did not even feel like talking to anyone; I carried the burden in my heart quietly.

On 13 February I woke up early and went out for a walk after a cup of tea. I was feeling exhausted. Since it was my 'rehnumai' court (a court set up within the jail premises where only dates for hearing are posted without any proceedings. It is done mainly to prevent overcrowding of the main courts) today, I took a bath and got ready. The mulaqat parcha had reached by then and I saw my name listed in the fifth one and when I went to the jangla I saw that Neel, Bashu and Daood were standing there. We spoke for three minutes from a distance. I told them 'Today is my rehnumai for which I have to go now. I will return in half an hour and meet you.' When I was getting into the van to go to court I requested the matron to call my family members waiting at the jangla; it was for the first time that I was able to embrace them a step outside the jail. When I returned from court they were still waiting for me. I got out of the van and told them to wait for me at the jangla – I went there and was able to spend some time with them. I felt comforted talking to my sister; it was strange that as much as I discouraged them from coming to meet me I also waited for them eagerly. I gave them some of the pottery items I had made as small gifts to take home with them. After mulaqat I returned to the cell, ate a roti with dal and subzi and went to the pottery unit where the teacher taught us a new design.

A few days later, Mahruq came with Abidji to meet me. They had earlier gone to meet my lawyer to enquire about the progress in my case but since the judge had still not been conferred with special powers, he told them to wait for further developments.

I had another dream. This time, I was crying loudly. I was screaming at my sister's in-laws, saying that they were the ones who had killed her. I was shouting and screaming but they did not seem to hear me, not even when I was crying myself hoarse. When I opened my eyes from this terrible dream I found myself actually crying and my throat was hurting badly. Such dreams inside the jail troubled me greatly. I also dreamt that my deceased father was taking me and my sister to meet his relatives. It was a strange place near Pantha Chowk where his relatives lived, they were all dark skinned. In the dream my father told them that he now wished to live there as well and wanted his share of the land and property but they turned him down saying that he had left from here a long time ago, and therefore had no claim on the property

During this time, I found myself in a strange situation, with a sense of nagging restlessness that stayed with me all the time. I felt a great sorrow weighing on my heart, as though a slab of stone had been placed on it.

It was the day of mulaqat on 23 February. I offered early morning prayers, got ready and waited for the mulaqat parcha which fortunately had my name in it. When I reached the jangla, I saw Mahruq and Tasleem. I soon sensed that they wanted to tell me something but were not being able to do so. I shared with them my own sense of foreboding that had been nagging me for the past few days, urging them to tell me whatever they had in their hearts. It was then that they gave me the news that my younger brother had had an accident. I was stunned. My head was spinning; there was no ground beneath my feet. I could not follow another word of what they said. I rushed from the jangla but do not have any recollection of how I reached the ward; my tears wouldn't stop. The word 'accident' shook me to the core as my sister had earlier died of a road accident too. I kept roaming around in the ward like an insane person until I went to meet the DS in the evening and requested her to call up my family to find out about my brother's condition. She tried to comfort me and said that she would do so as soon as she went out and send a message to me by night time.

I remained standing in the cell, holding the iron bars and waiting for the promised message from the DS. At 11.45 Renuka madam came and stood opposite me briefly and told me that my brother was all right and I need not worry. My cell mates tried to console me as I was still not satisfied with what I had just heard. I was afraid to fall asleep as strange images crossed my mind as soon as I shut my eyes. I offered prayers in the morning and started making repeated rounds of the chakkar to meet the DS. When I met her at 10.30, she looked at me and asked, 'What has happened to you? I had already sent you a message last night. I called your family as soon as I left and urged them to tell me the truth regarding your brother's condition. I was told that he was injured in his back and was in hospital and that you should not worry.' I felt a little calmer on hearing this and thanked her before leaving. I had a premonition that something terrible was going to happen. Is this why I had those weird dreams? What about the heaviness in my heart?

Abidji had gone back to Kashmir immediately after the news and came to meet me a few weeks later. After the DS called my family on my behalf, they realized how anxious I was and therefore sent him back to meet and reassure me regarding my brother. He had received a spinal injury when he was driving from Islamabad to Srinagar in his car which had skidded due to heavy rain. I told Abidji to go back to Kashmir and said I would let him know if there was any news about my bail. At times of such crisis in the family, it becomes even more difficult for a prisoner to bear the pain of separation and yet cope with the daily grind of jail. I saw the image of my brother lying in a hospital bed each time I shut my eyes.

To maintain my mental equilibrium, I had decided soon after landing in jail that I would join any class or project that was initiated by an NGO or the jail authorities. An NGO called Divya Jyothi had started music lessons in jail for which I promptly registered. The organization also conducted satsangs – prayer meetings – twice a week for prisoners as well as classes in the art of mehndi (henna) application which were joined in large numbers by those women inmates who had attended satsang. The music classes also had a few Muslim inmates.

On 20 March Abidji informed me that my bail application had been rejected by the court. This unfortunate news felt like a stab in my heart. He told me not to cry but I was not even aware that I was crying; my tears seemed to have matured in their defiance of me. Had I lost control over my emotions? I went to the pottery class after mulaqat, trying desperately to keep myself busy. I returned to the cell at 2 and forced myself to eat the lunch that my cellmate had saved for me. After namaz, I lay down and stared at the ceiling. My cellmate had gone to the barrack to watch TV and the other one was at the Supply Centre. Being alone was a boon; I needed to think, to understand the trajectory of recent events and how my own life was caught in them. My concentration was suddenly broken as the chakkar Munshi called me out as a new music teacher had arrived. I had forgotten that I had to be in class. The Munshi unlocked the cell door and I stepped out and walked towards the class. I returned in the evening, had a glass of tea that my cellmate had wrapped in a towel to retain whatever warmth she could. I offered namaz after tea. There was a report today in the *Kashmir News Bulletin* that 40 Kashmiri political prisoners had been released but these belonged to jails in J&K. I felt happy for them.

Those days the BJP (Bhartiya Janata Party) was running a 'jail bharo' campaign against the demolition of 'unauthorized' commercial establishments as well as certain slum sectors in Delhi and many of the Party women workers were coming into jail every day as part of the campaign. Today, its leader Sushma Swaraj had arrived in jail and elaborate arrangements had been made for her. She was sitting at the chakkar with SI madam and I got an opportunity to meet her. It was for the first time today that I got such an opportunity to meet a woman political leader inside the jail and talk to her. Their campaign had been going on for the past ten days when batches of 10-20 women landed in jail on a daily basis but were released within three days. Ward 8 had been reserved for them where clean sheets had been spread and a few women prisoners had been appointed to serve them food and water. These Party workers shouted slogans inside the jail and their doors remained open throughout the day. Nearly all the women prisoners approached Sushma Swaraj with an appeal hoping that she would help in their release. She too was keen to meet the women inmates and for the three days that she spent in jail, she was surrounded by them. Many of the Party councillors gave me their visiting cards and asked me to contact them on my release. They wanted me to join their Party and treated me respectfully despite knowing about my sentiment for Azadi. They told me they felt proud that a fearless woman leader like me was representing the Kashmiri cause. Sushma Swaraj remarked that she would be glad if I joined her Party for the Kashmiri cause but I refused flatly. She had this conviction that her Party would solve the Kashmir problem and wanted that women like me should support them in this endeavour.

One day, I had a lovely surprise. My elder brother Dr Hamidulla came with Abidji to meet me. I could not believe that he was standing in front of me. My eyes filled with tears when I heard his voice. He said 'Why have you lost courage when we are still with you? You must remain strong.' After giving me details of the case, he said, 'I am trying every possible means to ensure that you are released with honour. There is no reason for you to worry. Everyone in the family is well and happy except you. Please take care of yourself.'

I felt encouraged and comforted by his words and his visit. Recently, Yoga classes had commenced in jail and I decided to join the course even though it was for a brief period of one week but I had heard that Yoga helped in easing mental stress and pressure.

A Hurriyat delegation was going to meet the Prime Minister on 3 May. This time it was possible that they would raise the issue of the release of Kashmiri political prisoners. However, for the past few days the media, both print and electronic, had remained focused on the murder of BJP leader Pramod Mahajan. There was no mention anywhere of the Hurriyat meeting with the PM, so I could not find out what had happened.

After a gap of three months, I had another court hearing but as usual, all I got was another date. Abidji was waiting for me in court but the policewoman got the date warrant and dragged me by hand to the lockup. I remained upset throughout the day. I had thought that there'd be some progress in my case after three months but had to return disappointed. Summer was at its peak and this added to my woes. There was no place to sit inside the lockup and the toilet was in a shambles. We had made an appeal to the lockup in-charge that the toilet should be repaired but our plea was ignored. The policemen around the lockup ogled the women prisoners which caused us great embarrassment. However, some women prisoners eyed the policemen to fulfil their need for tobacco. The lockup in-charge was aware of all this but did not do anything to stop this nuisance. The policemen felt free to crack cheap jokes with the women but thank God, none of them dared to behave in this lowly manner with me and even the other women prisoners' maintained caution with me during a court date as they were well aware of my nature. But many others openly talked to the policemen and made gestures. On a couple of occasions I had raised this matter with the jail in-charge as well as the jail SI who managed to control this impolite behaviour of women but only temporarily.

For a long time I had been feeling depressed and aggrieved. I have been in an environment where it was not possible to even breathe freely. I often felt I would choke because of my inner suffocation. At times I felt like crying aloud. Life had brought me to a new world where darkness stretched all around me. There was no respite or sense of comfort anywhere. All one saw were iron bars, metal chains and imposing high walls. The light and joy of the outside world was beyond us and the sounds of happiness were totally lost. Problems regarding food, the lack of physical comfort, and long period of separation from the loved ones, searing heat and ill health had ruined my world. I could compare this confinement of life inside the jail to a sort of death.

In the four years of life here, the small plants had grown into tall trees whose branches were now being trimmed and trained. When I entered the jail, these were tiny shrubs that had now grown big enough to provide shelter. They provided an ideal place for prisoners to sit in their shade even though a warm wind blew from the branches – perhaps the trees had also become familiar with the reality of jail existence. As I mentioned earlier, high walls were being constructed around the wards; prior to this women prisoners could be seen sitting and sharing their troubles but now we were expected to pay a fine of Rs 250 (in coupons) for trespassing here and also face a beating at the hands of the policewomen on duty. There was a rumor doing the rounds at the time that hidden cameras were also being installed in jail which created fear among the women. Stringent rules and restrictions imposed with the aim of keeping a strict control on prisoners in an already restricted area is the true character of a jail, a fact that people in the free world are not able to comprehend.

I had complained to my lawyer about the restrictions imposed upon me by jail authorities as well as the harassment from other women prisoners but he believed that once I was released from POTA, all these troubles would automatically come to an end and this is how I continued to tolerate whatever hardships I faced. Since I had also been implicated in the jail case, my family was worried that the jail authorities would never let me out. If a prisoner took the problems in jail seriously enough, I can say with conviction that many cases would be filed against the authorities. But how can a prisoner do this when she is burdened by her own case and secondly, if you're living in a pond, how can you nurture any enmity with the crocodile? A prisoner ages much before her time with the daily struggle of shuttling between the courts and coping with the dismal conditions in jail. The large gates at the jail opened and shut so many times in a day either to let a prisoner free or to bring one into captivity. They had shut on me long ago to seal my freedom. Now I waited for them to open for my release but the wait was turning out to be much longer than I had anticipated. My eyes were turning into stone waiting for these gates to open for me.

We heard the roar of airplanes flying above the prison every day. Perhaps there was an airport close by. Watching a plane high in the air, prisoners wished and prayed for it to fly them away from these confines. There's a large hall in jail called Vipasana which has a wooden floor and many prisoners believed that there was a treasure trove of weapons underneath and that whenever a prisoner was given a death sentence the hanging took place there in the dungeon. Vipasana reminded me of our martyr Maqbool Bhat who was given the death sentence and was perhaps hanged here. During the day prisoners went in and out of it as many programmes were held there but Vipasana took on a terrifying aspect at night when prisoners were afraid to go there.

One day Medha Patkar, who worked for human rights in Madhya Pradesh was arrested and brought to jail. She appeared to be a very simple and good natured woman. She was in prison for ten days prior to her release while her NBA (Narmada Bachao Andolan) comrades were staging a dharna in front of Parliament. At night, fire broke out due to a gas leak in the langar but Kiran Pratap (langar Munshi) did something brave by turning off the main supply switch and thereby saved many lives. Women prisoners working at the langar believed that they would not have survived this fire had it not been for Kiran madam who did not even care about the leaping flames around her. The next day, SI madam gave her an award of Rs 250.

The night langar was adjacent to ward 5 and women who worked at the langar were from this ward. The majority of them were convicted prisoners. The food that was delivered to prisoners during their court date was prepared at the langar. The van would come at 6.30 and women would load the food that they packed in polythene containers, separate ones for dal and roti and subzi.

Superstitious beliefs thrived in jail. If a lizard fell on someone it was considered a good omen. Women inmates revered a tree trunk opposite ward 8 and called it 'pir baba' – both Muslim and Hindu women offered prayers there and could be seen prostrating themselves. It is said that the tree was felled after a woman prisoner climbed it to escape and succeeded in her attempt. She had a suckling infant and was driven by her motherly instinct to reach the baby as she could not bear the forced separation from him. She is believed to have gone home straight from jail and when the authorities went to arrest her again, she was found suckling the infant and returned to the jail with the policemen without offering any resistance. It is also said that she was released within three days of her re-arrest. It was Kiran Bedi who had initiated the practice where prisoner women could keep their infants with them in jail.

The sacred tree had incense sticks and diyas lit at the base and chadars were also offered by devotees; Muslim women offered namaz at the spot while Hindu women did puja. Everyone took off their footwear out of reverence and remained barefoot in its vicinity. In case there was no single release from a particular ward for long, Hindu women conducted satsang, bhajan and kirtan and if the opposite were true, even then women performed these rituals and hung lemon and chillies at the door; the thread used to string these would have first been tied on the tree for auspicious blessings. I often told the women devotees that a tree that could not protect itself from being felled was hardly going to offer them any protection. There was no dearth of women astrologers in jail; they would predict the duration of sentence for a prisoner by reading her palm but could not do the same for their own sentence. There are also women who offered sacred amulets to other inmates but mostly only Hindu women went to them. Quite often, these women got released much earlier. There were women inmates who were engaged in black magic and who claimed that they could see Mata Devi who empowered them.

Towards the end of May my cell was changed and I was shifted to another one which was so filthy that it took a long time for me to clean it, leaving me totally exhausted. My health suddenly deteriorated. My whole body had swollen up but when I visited the doctor she did not give me any medication but suggested an LFT examination. After the test I was given tablets that would help me pass urine more frequently to help reduce the swelling in the body. Due to the acute heat my blood pressure had also risen. I did not step outside the cell for nearly three days.

A bit of rain one night helped in lowering the temperature during the day. There were clouds in the morning too but the sun later was much stronger due to the rain. Summer – especially the month of June – is the worst experience when the body burns and there is no comfort either in the day or night; even repeated baths fail to help.

At 1.30 in the night there were sounds of women screaming and yelling from ward 6; they were also clapping their hands and banging steel tumblers against the iron bars. A television had caught fire in a barrack in ward 6 and because of the intense heat, the flames fanned rapidly. We at ward 7 were wide-eyed, without a trace of sleep and started clapping and shouting desperately to draw the attention of the staff on duty. The locks at ward 6 were opened at 2.30 and those of the cells 15 minutes later by which time the women were in a terrible condition; crying, screaming and cursing. Once they rushed out the commotion got louder and the cacophony sharper. Prisoner women from wards 7 and 5 also started demanding vociferously that our locks be unfastened as the danger of fire spreading to other wards was now real. We were screaming for help when at 3.30 in the morning the locks were opened at ward 7 but the main door of ward 5 had got jammed and women were rescued from the side of the langar. A fire brigade was called and during this time the SI and DS madam also arrived on the scene. All of us were made to sit outside while the fire was extinguished; it was a miracle that women from this ward saved themselves and came out alive. It is easier to vacate burning buildings outside but within the jail it is not so; the matron has to first establish contact with the SI to get the door opened after permission is granted. This incident created an uproar and a sense of terror amongst the women who continued to cry through the night thinking of the fearful, near-death situation. SI madam had called a special squad that sealed ward 6 at 5.30 and allowed us to enter our ward after it was thoroughly examined but we experienced a sense of strange fear as they entered the ward. As soon as I entered I offered namaz. Many women inmates of ward 6 also came into our ward and according to them, the fire would not have raged so much if the policewoman on duty had responded to our cries and not gone away after seeing that we were trapped because of the locked cells. They described how they nearly suffocated due to the billowing smoke but no one came to help them until much later. Instead, the two policewomen on duty just watched the fire from outside even when we started hurling abuses at them. They did not have the keys they said and we would have to wait until they returned with them. Women said they had lost all hope of survival on seeing them leave; our faces had turned black with layers of soot and our throats were parched due to the suffocating smoke. One prisoner had fainted in the meantime. The locks were opened and we were made to come out in a single file when death was staring us in the face. The same policewomen were given bravery awards the following day.

I felt listless due to the hot wind that slapped my face. My body had erupted in a heat rash and prickly heat as it happened each summer. I was also running a high fever. Fortunately an ICRC team had come to meet me and the doctor in the team examined me in consultation with the jail doctor. I was diagnosed with malaria and sent for a checkup to DD hospital the next day. There is a cooler for the staff in the hospital lockup which was a great relief from the heat in jail and one did not mind waiting here for as long as it took. I met a Kashmiri prisoner here named Javed whom I greeted and also conveyed greetings for other Kashmiri brothers in jail through him.

On 5 July I went to the canteen to make certain purchases and saw Sharda Jain checking the High Court gazette at the chakkar. I glanced at it and saw that my name was also written there as it was my bail date on 4 July but I did not know the outcome yet. I sensed that it was not good news otherwise I would have been informed. I began to wait impatiently for mulaqat so that someone from my family could give me the news, whatever it was. My elder brother Doctor Sahib arrived for mulaqat a few days later and told me that they had withdrawn my bail appeal from High Court but that Insha' Allah I would be released soon. I immediately understood that the bail had been rejected but this was his way of consoling and reassuring me. Perhaps he did not know that I had by now become accustomed to such disappointments and setbacks and these did not affect me as much as before. He gave me coupons for Rs 2500 because he too had figured out that my release would not be any time soon. The electricity had snapped during mulaqat and it disturbed me to see him soaked in sweat but he looked at me with regard and affection. When he left, he turned and looked at me in such a desolate manner as though pitying not just our destiny but his own helplessness in the matter. I returned to the cell and lay down as I was feeling sick and emotionally exhausted.

Joy, a habshi woman was lodged in ward 1 where she got into a physical fight with her cellmate and when the complaint reached SI madam she summoned them both to the chakkar to investigate the matter. The reason for the fight was that she had killed pigeons, cooked them at the langar and eaten them. Being an AIDS patient she was permitted to prepare her own meals but no one knew until then that she was taking undue advantage of the concession that was granted to her. Her cellmate objected when she saw the pigeon in the cell as Joy waited for an opportunity to sneak it to the langar to cook it. The cellmate could not tolerate it as the dead pigeons smelt foul in the cell due to which she felt sick and both of them got into frequent arguments but today the truth was revealed after they fought physically over the same matter. Joy was supported in this sleazy activity by another woman inmate from ward 4.

It was my court date on 7 August and I was made to sit in the van at 7.30. The same van picked up minor girls from Nari Niketan because of which there was some delay as we waited for the other women but the heat was cruel. The court lockup too was so hot that it was impossible to sit down even for a minute. There was only one fan in complete disrepair and women inmates fought over it; each one trying to pull it in her direction. We requested that another fan be provided and the lockup in-charge assured us that a new one would indeed be installed along with an exhaust fan by the next date. I was produced in court at one o'clock but the room was empty; there were no lawyers and no judge. This courtroom is otherwise filled with newspersons and policemen as many high profile cases were heard here including the Nitish Kataria case, other POTA cases as well as those relating to other Kashmiri prisoners. My warrant had already been prepared with 17-18 August as the next dates. The policewoman picked up the warrant, held my hand and led me back to the lockup. I was once again produced in court on 18 August at 1pm but the lawyer had not come and the next date was posted for 27-28 September. Since the judge was a woman I had a flicker of hope that she would help the case to progress from this stalemate. My lawyer came at 4 for legal mulaqat and looking at my pale face he tried to reassure me by saying that the case would definitely be finalized in September. I told him that he disappointed me to a great extent but the meeting time was over within five minutes when I returned to the lockup. I wanted to drink water but it was so warm that my thirst remained unquenched until I asked a cleaner to bring me some water from the cooler outside. I gulped the water while also splashing some on my face as it was burning with heat. I wet my handkerchief and kept patting it on my face.

Preparations were under way at Tihar for Independence Day celebrations on 15 August; walls were being whitewashed and every nook and corner cleaned. Wards were being fumigated because of the mosquitoes as many prisoners had contracted Malaria. The chemicals used for fumigation led to allergies among some prisoners. In short, it was a time of harassment and botheration.

News arrived from the men's jails that many of them had already succumbed to the heat wave; this resulted in a unanimous decision among the authorities that all the fans will be repaired in each cell and in the barracks and exhaust fans installed. The kind of commotion and confusion this effort bred was unimaginable; holes were being drilled into the cell and barrack walls for the exhaust fans but the authorities suddenly got nervous that women might attempt to escape though these holes! Women inmates were thus shifted from one cell to another until the authorities realized that the hole was too small for women to crawl through and escape. As long as I was in jail, the holes remained in place but without an exhaust fan but the insects found a way of invading the cell through these gaping holes in the wall which we had to suffer. We finally had to use newspapers and pieces of cardboard to cover these holes as these had become a thoroughfare for stray cats too.

As usual, my cell was searched on 14 August. I am not writing the details here as I have already mentioned how belongings are searched and scattered during the search. The next day we all had to congregate at the grounds for the function.

During summer I preferred to remain inside the cell as the heat was intolerable for me. This suffocating heat got worse; no less than the torment in hell, whenever the electricity failed. It caused me to fall ill frequently and drained all my energy. Fans had been repaired in most of the cells while new ones installed in a few.

As I had mentioned earlier, there was a large number of women prisoners who used tobacco both as a habit as well as for commercial purposes. There was one Ruby (name changed) who ate it in large quantities and also traded in it, both with a sense of pride. She tried to appear like a decent woman for SI madam but actually spoke against others to her. Initially madam believed her blindly but soon her true character surfaced and along with it the fact that she was making money on the sly. To please madam and win back her trust and confidence, she promised to her that she would give up tobacco and irrigate the barren land behind the MIR to grow vegetables. Ruby was arrested for her involvement in the flesh trade and all the young women who were brought to jail on similar charges became friendly with her. She made good use of it by getting them to help her on the piece of land. She also picked up new women prisoners for different tasks from the inspection ward. She received a stipend for her work from the jail authorities. As long as I was in jail I knew that Ruby had not given up tobacco but she had turned the barren land into a fertile one with a variety of vegetables growing there. She was also good in henna application and earned enough money by applying different designs on the palms of other women inmates; Hindu women came to her at every festival. Inspired by her, other women also tried their hand at it both as a craft as well as to try it for a commercial venture. When SI madam learnt of this she issued instructions that mehndi application could not be done outside the parlour. Ruby was asked to deposit 50 per cent of her earnings into the welfare box. Some women continued the trade but, secretly.

Ruby was upset with jail authorities and spread the word wherever she went that one could never trust them, not even when she had grown vegetables through her sheer hard labour. She had now stopped working on the field but the main reason we heard was that the madam was angry with her as she was making money here too by selling the vegetables on her own whereas these were to be kept in the canteen for sale. Madam rebuked Ruby saying that she had breached jail discipline also because new prisoners were made to work on the field without any remuneration. An additional reason for madam's displeasure was that Ruby was using the vegetable garden to hide tobacco pouches from being confiscated. However, Ruby had inspired many women prisoners who also took the initiative of growing flowers in small patches of land in front of Vipasana. When I first entered the jail, this entire stretch of land was barren with snakes and reptiles thriving there but now it was a riot of colour, a beautiful garden. The prisoner's own lives remained barren but their efforts created these habitats. Women also enjoyed working on this land as the doors remained open during the day due to the nature of their work. Being locked inside a cell resulted in emotional and psychological stress for most of us.

On 21 August Advocate Ajay Sinha came to the jail for legal mulaqat. He was my lawyer's junior and looking after my jail case. We discussed the case details and I gave him Rs 2000 from my PP account. There were many innocent prisoners in Tihar jail who were from impoverished backgrounds. I had spent many months in a cell with Teja and her mother-in-law Misri Devi and was aware of their condition and their innocence. Because they were so poor these women could not apply for bail; I therefore asked Ajay Sinha if he could help secure bail for Teja whose 13 year old daughter was growing up with her alcoholic father and burdened with household responsibilities at this tender age. Teja shared her pain and anguish with me and broke down often while talking about her daughter. Teja worked in the langar and whatever money she earned she gave to her husband whenever he came for mulaqat but when she raised the question of her bail he used his poverty as an excuse. It was for Teja's young daughter's safety that I had asked Ajay Sinha to pursue her bail and thank God, he was successful in doing so and Teja was released.

Clair Mathew was also released on bail one night but she was back in jail the very next morning which created great disappointed not only for her but other prisoners too. She was released after six years and was imprisoned for her involvement in the narcotics trade. Soon after she was set free another branch of NDPS had her arrested again and did not allow any appeal for her bail. I accompanied all the other women prisoners who went to express their sympathy to her. She had distributed whatever belongings she had among fellow women inmates at the time of release and had nothing at all now. She cried so much that it was difficult to recognize her face. Women prisoners serving term under the same Act were a worried lot now as they could face a similar fate.

Baji and Khalidji came for mulaqat in August. My sister found it difficult to remain standing as she had fractured her foot and the other reason was the sweltering heat but I was happy to meet them after so long. She told me that my mother was also keeping ill and this was causing much anxiety to the family. I pray to God to resolve my family's problems. Amen.

They returned for mulaqat a few days later. Since I knew they would come, I had taken permission from the authorities for a little extra time to meet them as they would leave for Kashmir after this; my family stayed for a week in Delhi whenever they came and this is how we were able to meet a few times before they left. Prolonged time was for 40 minutes whereas a regular mulaqat lasted for 20 minutes. How quickly these 40 minutes were over! I was irritated that the Munshi and matron kept interfering during our mulaqat to remind us of the time left; it also led me to forget many of the things I wanted to tell them. But what difference did it make to them that my family came from such a long distance? Before leaving Baji blessed me and told me about certain prayers that I should offer for my peace of mind. I had asked her to bring a few things for those fellow prisoners who were very poor and this way I was able to do something small for them for the period that I stayed in jail. A prisoner's needs are few in jail therefore it is not difficult to fulfil them. I tried very hard to help some women prisoners to give up tobacco and encouraged them to speak truthfully. I also helped some of them by writing different applications or letters on their behalf as many of them were unlettered. However, those who wrote in Hindi on their behalf charged them Rs 10 per letter. Most of these letters were meant for women's male relatives in jail. I did not know what was written in these letters as I could neither read nor write Hindi but recently, I had started attending Hindi classes where I also tried to initiate discussion on the real meaning of 'patriotism' particularly with those women inmates who called me a traitor. Those who suffered from religious prejudice, I addressed them regarding the value of religious tolerance. I found that the majority of Muslim women prisoners did not have a clue regarding Islamic teachings and I tried, in my limited way, to share with them at least the basic tenets and teachings of Islam. By now most of the inmates were familiar with my temperament and my simple way of life and knew that I never spoke against one prisoner to another which was a normal practice in jail. While some women benefited from my efforts others believed that it meant nothing as they had already spent 14 long years here or were expected to do so. Where's the room for reform, they would ask.

Living in this 'different world' gave me the opportunity to meet different kinds of women which would not have been possible in the world I came from. I got a chance to understand their psychological compulsions. There were many 'chandi matas' in jail who tried their best to prove every good word or deed to be wrong and compared any good work to a corrupt and debased activity. They had never learnt anything about truth in their lives and were untouched by even a trace of human friendship. They burnt in the fire of prejudice and only saw which religion another inmate belonged to; if a Muslim spoke anything sensible it was rubbish for them for the same reason. They only saw the worst in everything; at times I felt as though jail was perhaps the best and most appropriate place for them.

It was my court date on 28 September and I was taken under strict security to the courtroom and produced before the judge at 11.30. As I climbed the stairs I was surprised to see Abidji there as I was not expecting anyone from home today. He told me that Baji had also come and the news made me both happy and anxious as it was the month of Ramadan and the heat was severe. I saw Baji pouring water on her face; she could not drink any as she was observing a fast and I could see how the heat was bothering her. The policewoman led me into the courtroom and Baji also followed and stood in a row behind me. As I entered, Judge Ravinder Kaur asked everyone to leave the courtroom including my sister who she spotted later. There was more police with me in the courtroom today as the judge had received threats earlier but she had defiantly told the TV news channels that she was not afraid of such threats, but I could see in this courtroom, in front of me how afraid she was. The arguments continued for nearly an hour along with witness accounts. I was given the following day as the next date of hearing. When I was led outside, I saw my elder brother waiting for me along with my nephew. After greetings, when I was being escorted to the lockup my brother said 'Don't worry', while my nephew handed over some documents to me. Baji was waiting near the stairs. I was brought out of the lockup after 15 minutes to meet my family members. I asked Baji why she had returned so soon during Ramadan to meet me. She told me that she was missing me terribly, specially as it was an auspicious time. I became emotional and kept staring at her without being able to say anything more. Abidji also came but I did not have any time left to talk to him; lockup mulaqat is usually for a mere seven minutes or so. Since I had to return to the court the next day, he said they too would come there. The lockup was not only hot but dark as there was no electricity. We had no option but to wait and suffer until the van took us back to jail.

The then Delhi Police Commissioner, Ujwal Mishra, who was now posted in Goa, came to court on 29 September as a witness, and gave a false account. I was produced before the judge at 11 and I saw that Baji and Abidji were waiting outside. The proceedings had already begun by the time I entered the courtroom. Commissioner Ujwal was recording his statement and my lawyer Ohri Sahib was working hard and using his expertise to counter it. The proceedings continued until 1.30 after which another date was posted and the judge left the courtroom. Ohri Sahib then told me that God willing, we will win the case and by November the judgment will be in our favour. Baji said that she would come to meet me at the jail but I told her to return to Kashmir instead. I was very unhappy at being given such a long next date. While leaving she expressed her confidence in the lawyer and said that she spoke to him on the phone on a regular basis. Yes, the lawyer was doing his job but it is all in the hands of God who alone knows what is best; I could do nothing but pray. Back in the lockup I kept wondering why Ujwal Mishra gave a false witness account. His account really hurt me and I was also surprised that such a senior officer had to take support of lies. If he could speak such untruths one can well imagine the degree of honesty among junior officers.

Ujwal Mishra said in court that Anjum Zamarud Habib had confessed to her guilt in his presence whereas when Shabbir Ahmed Dar and I were produced before him I had not uttered a single word. We were coming from the interrogation centre and I was in such a state that I could not understand anything that was happening to me then. I was in a state of shock, wondering if the situation was real or imaginary. He had not asked me any question and I had not confessed anything. A net had been cast around me and Ujwal Mishra was one link in it.

Since the auspicious month of Ramadan was on, I concentrated on spending as much time in prayer as possible. Due to the severe heat I felt thirsty all the time but could not drink much water after breaking the fast. On 13 October, Afzal Guru was awarded the death sentence and the news was repeatedly being telecast on all the TV channels. There were agitations and protest demonstrations taking place in Kashmir against this judgment. Two days later, I saw on TV that his mother, wife and son were going to meet the President of India to submit a mercy petition. Looking at Afzal's family in Kashmiri clothes brought home the image of my own mother so I pulled out a paper and pen and wrote a letter to her. These days I was missing my family more than ever. Later, I received a letter and money order of Rs 2000 from Abidji.

I was stuck in such an awful place that it is beyond my ability to describe the details in words. There was a large group of Jat women in jail among whom some were convicted prisoners and others, under-trials, and most of them worked at the langar. The convicted ones considered jail to be their permanent residence. Under-trial prisoners who were arrested on murder charges did not think differently either as all these women knew that life imprisonment was inevitable for them. Most of them had been charged with murder and in some cases, more than one murder. This was the reason behind their eagerness to look for work as soon as they were brought to jail and to slowly but certainly establish friendship with old prisoners. They wanted to exercise their dominance over other inmates but I defiantly stayed out of their reach, so they found different ways to harass me. They often used foul language and apart from calling me a terrorist they also abused me. They were full of hatred for Kashmiri prisoners. There may be only a few in India and in Indian jails who did not hate us; we Kashmiris had to tolerate a lot in Indian jails.

I knew that my patience was being tested. I prayed to God not to let go of my hand in this difficult hour and guide me on the right path. Many days went by in this worry but their behaviour did not change and I was now beginning to lose patience. I therefore went to SI madam and registered my complaint against these women. After due consideration, she summoned these scoundrel women who knew instantly that they were in trouble as getting a peshi against their name would be detrimental for them; their character assessment was noted in their nominal rolls which could affect their prospects for parole as well as for a reduced sentence. Madam SI reprimanded them in my presence and told them how insulting it would be if Anjum went back home and said that Indians were not decent. I told her that the matter was more serious as I felt my life was in danger because I had been receiving threats from these Jat women that they have already committed several murders and would not be afraid to kill me too. Madam was outraged on hearing this and gave them a fitting warning to behave in future. I returned to the cell and got busy with iftar preparations. There was no difference in the Jat women's attitude towards me the next day but since it was an auspicious month I did not wish to get into any fights with them but their comments continued to cause me great mental stress and the more I tried to overcome it the more they tried to cause tension. To be rid of this constant friction, I decided to stay inside the cell as much as possible. Another woman inmate under NDPS was contemptuous of me and found any excuse to harass me. I complained to madam against her also but beyond peshi and rebuke, there was not much she could do although she was sympathetic to me and knew that I had no choice but to share space with these women. One day, all of a sudden, this particular prisoner's name was called out for court appearance and when she returned from there she started abusing me as the summons was from the jail judge where my complaint against her had reached but I was not aware of this development. It was madam who had forwarded the complaint. The prisoner told other women inmates, 'I told the judge that if I had been summoned here so should Anjum have been. She is a terrorist and a sycophant of SI madam.' She later learnt that I had not sent any arzi against her to the judge and somehow, towards the end of my sentence she had become a close friend of mine and regretted all that had happened and in fact, supported me against the other Jat women inmates, some of whom also befriended me. Now one group of Jats was on my side and the other against me. I learnt of the many twists and turns that exist in a friendship or an enmity. I pray to God to release me from this prison soon. Amen.

It was the last Friday of Ramadan: This month too passed by; it was filled with prayer. Due to sehri and iftar we got tastier dal roti during this period and an extra cup of tea for those who observed a fast. Since I had not been able to sight the moon I decided to fast for another day. In the morning at 7, a chakkar Munshi called Beena came to inform me that it was Eid today and AS Raman madam had called me to the chakkar. When I went there she greeted me for Eid and asked as to what should be prepared in the canteen on this special occasion. I told her that I as well as all other Muslim inmates were fasting but she said that the Shahi Imam had declared last night that Eid would be celebrated today. I went and informed all other Muslim women and after we greeted each other, we bathed and changed into better clothes and broke our fast together. I did not feel enthused as I was under the impression that today was my 30th fast. However, there were news reports from different cities where Eid was being celebrated including in Delhi. In Kashmir it was celebrated the next day. I was missing my family members on this happy occasion. Sweet rice and vermicelli was prepared in the canteen and distributed to Muslim women inmates.

Having graduated to the status of an old prisoner and one who was educated I was respected accordingly by the staff who sought my opinion in certain matters, particularly relating to those that required educated prisoners. In this manner, a lot of misunderstandings that had crept up between me and the authorities gradually disappeared. They also realized that I was helpful to other women inmates but I decided to ignore those women prisoners who did not wish to overcome their sectarianism and religious prejudice.

A Vipasana meditation programme was starting the next month for which madam had already enrolled my name thinking that it would help me overcome the psychological stress that I was suffering from. I was therefore shifted from ward 7 to a ward that I found calmer than other wards. Here too there were many Jat women but my relations with them remained cordial. Factionalism was a common practice in jail but the surprising element was the involvement in it of some of the staff.

At the next hearing in my case we were taken to the POTA court at Patiala House at 8 in the prison van. It was after two months that I appeared in court. I was produced before the judge at 11.30 but the policewoman escorted me back to the lockup within two minutes as another date for the next day had already been posted. You can well imagine my mental agony that even after two long months I am present in the courtroom for barely two minutes and return without any bit of hope! I always left the jail for court with a hope that perhaps there will be some positive outcome today but all I ended up doing was to cry in the lockup over my fate. In a state of dejection, all I saw was darkness around me. Later I was called for mulaqat and I saw my lawyer and his junior waiting for me at the jangla. When Ohri saw my face he said, 'There was not a single witness today which is why there were no proceedings. We have called them tomorrow and God willing, everything will be all right.' He further told me that he had been to Srinagar the previous week and had met my family. I was now concerned about my mental exhaustion more than the physical. I had to return to court the next day which is tiring but the doubt and uncertainty about my state caused me great mental tension. On the next day in court, my elder brother was seated in a chair and we gestured greetings to each other. There was yet another disappointment today; no witness was present in court and the judge picked up his pen and posted another date. My lawyer appealed for an earlier date but the judge refused on the ground that not a single date was available in the month. I was back in the lockup from where I was returned to Tihar nursing a hurt and damaged soul.

Winter was advancing rapidly. I went and brought a few black blankets from the chakkar and spread them on the floor of my cell. I received a money order from home on 1 December. I stared at the ceiling the whole night.

The sirens wailed throughout the day and therefore the doors were closed for the day. I was still feeling sad and dejected. I wrote a letter home asking for a few warm clothes to be brought at the next mulaqat. Once again it was 8 December. It is nine years today since Behenji (elder sister) separated from us, from this world although I always sensed her presence around me. I woke up early and spent time in prayers as my mood was low and upset.

These days, I spent most of my time lying down in the cell. My elder brother came to visit me. He told me that Geelani Sahib had expressed concern over my deteriorating health in a public meeting. I could see from his face that my brother was anxious and also trying to hide something from me but I could not bring myself to ask him. He deposited Rs 1500 before leaving. At night I dreamt that my mother was looking for me and searching for me everywhere; she appeared to be in a dishevelled state. Suddenly I woke up; I raised my hands to God and kept praying for her well being and to have mercy upon my own state of helplessness. Amen. I had never imagined such a painful day in my life where my powerlessness would be so acute that I would not be with my family despite such intense longing. On the 30th I received a letter and a greeting card from Neelji. I felt somewhat comforted with news from home.

This year too passed away; consumed by court dates and humiliations in jail.

The first day of the next year was Eid-ul-Zuha. My fifth year had begun in jail and this was my fifth Eid in confinement. I pray to God that this Eid and the New Year bring me success, progress and freedom from these confines. Now, each moment in jail was even more burdensome. I was becoming less tolerant and less capable of coping with the daily grind. Four years is a long time. The high walls of jail now seemed to be kissing the skies. I could not keep up my interest in any activity. I did not like anyone's speech or any words. I remained lost within myself. My health continued to deteriorate and one morning I was admitted to the MIR. I stayed there until the next day when Daood came for mulaqat and I reached the jangla. I was carrying the drip that was attached to my hand and when he saw me in this condition he began to weep. I tried to console him despite feeling broken inside. I tried to turn the mulaqat into a pleasant one for both of us but succeeded just a little. From what I had heard, I realized that much had changed in the world outside. I returned to the cell and wept bitterly. My cellmate asked me repeatedly for the reason and started crying with me. When some other inmates from the ward saw us crying they came to our cell and joined us in our tears. We cried together but each one was shedding tears for their own predicament.

> *Jab apne naghmon se aseeron ko rulatha hoon*
> *Dar o deewar aur zanjeerein, kahfas ki sari bunyadein*
> *Hamare sath rothi hain dar zindan larazta hai*

Kabhi sayyad sochtha hoga
Ke yeh shaheen safat bulbul
Bayaban mein hi achha tha (Sahil)

When my songs move the prisoners to tears
The chains, doors and wall shudder
The very foundation of the prison weeps with us
The bird-keeper must wonder
If the eagle-like nightingale was better off in the wilderness.

Yet another court date, yet another ride in the prison van. The glass window was broken, and the strong chilly winds that blew into the van caused me a severe headache. The lockup was also cold. I was produced before the judge at 12 noon but the proceedings had already begun with Commissioner Ujwal giving his witness account. My brother and nephew were present in court. During arguments, my lawyer asked Ujwal Mishra how he was giving his account since he did not have the mandate for POTA confessional recording. Misra replied that he had received orders from the government. When my lawyer sought a copy of the order Mishra kept silent for a few moments and then said that he would need time to furnish it and asked the judge for time. In turn, the judge posted the next date. My lawyer met me after the proceedings and told me not to worry. Abidji got the mulaqat arzi approved by the judge and we came out of the courtroom. I hugged my brother and wept inconsolably. He told me to have strength and it is now only a matter of a few days. We are with you he said, just as the policewoman began to drag me by my hand to the lockup; I found this treatment very humiliating in front of my family. After 15 minutes she led me out for mulaqat where I discussed the details of my case with my nephew.

On 12 January there was the witness procedure as well as arguments in court. My lawyer again submitted my bail application today and the judge directed that arguments for bail be taken up on the 17th. I was kept inside the lockup for the entire day. I heard there was a good argument on my bail plea. The judge had asked for me to be brought before her at 2 pm but I was not taken because she had already left as she did not sit in the courtroom after 2. The policewoman only took my warrant and returned after having got it stamped for the next date. On this day, the case proceedings continued for more than two hours but the judge refused to grant me bail saying that she wanted to complete this case soon. Today, after Inspector Gurcharan Singh's witness account was done, the next date was posted. My lawyer asked him if, at the time of my arrest he had provided me with legal aid including a lawyer to which the Inspector replied 'We had offered to provide a lawyer for her but she refused, saying that being a law graduate she understood law and would therefore represent the case herself.' However, the reality was different; until my challan was produced I did not have any lawyer and this is exactly what I had said when I was produced before judge Dhingra and in response he had promised that his court would make a lawyer available for me. I was also not given any legal assistance or help during interrogation which is my right.

Once one is caught in the police net, all rights are destroyed, including the right to life; not to mention the right to have a lawyer. It is a common practice for the police to treat us as worse than beasts, to look upon us with contempt and to behave in an insulting manner with us – indeed they do their best to destroy our image. To treat us as human beings is completely beyond their consideration; a sense of humanity and a culture of politeness and respect is alien to them. I had not said anything regarding the individual offence and the charges that had been entered against me by the police. I am innocent. At the time, judge Dhingra had said in court gently, 'I do not trust them and Anjum; you will be given an opportunity to prove your innocence.' However, I never got a chance to speak in front of the judge.

Preparations were on in jail for Republic Day celebrations and as usual, my cell was searched· after which I spent the rest of the day collecting and arranging my belongings. This of course meant nothing to the staff. At my next court date I met Abidji outside the court. There was no one present in the courtroom except an individual policeman and a Munshi. The judge was in her room. There was another case of a male prisoner who had been serving term for the past nine years. When he was brought in and did not see the judge in court he started yelling 'Vishal Yadav is a special citizen of India and hearings in his case take place daily whereas I have been in jail for the past nine years but no decision has been taken in my case.' The judge perhaps heard this in her room as she quickly sent a policewoman who took his and my warrant from us and returned with a date for 2 February. When I asked her regarding mulaqat she told me I should meet my nephew here in the courtroom. He pulled a chair and sat down to talk but the policewoman dragged a chair between us and sat there. Abidji told me that though my lawyer had come, the prosecutor was absent because of which there were no proceedings in any of the cases under this judge. I was led back to the lockup after mulaqat.

Because of Republic day this area was closed with restrictions on the entry and exit of vehicles. Those of us under-trial prisoners who had their date today were produced much before 3 after which we were taken to Karkar Duma courts where we were kept in the lockup until 4 pm when other women under-trials returned from their case hearing and all of us were then taken in a bus to Tihar by a different much longer route. I felt exhausted with this journey as I was already tired after the search operation in my cell; my body was hurting with pain and soreness. On 26 January all the women prisoners were brought to the ground where the Republic Day function took place. This time I also took part; mainly to entertain myself.

An old under-trial prisoner who worked in the Mulaheza ward died as she had injured her back after she slipped and fell while cleaning the ward. She was admitted to DD hospital where she breathed her last. A prisoner's death caused fear, terror and helplessness among others as each one prayed that her death take place at her own house, amidst her own family. The cumbersome and harrowing procedure following a death turned it into a painful and agonizing thing; the delay caused by the long drawn-out post mortem ensured that family members did not get the body of their loved one in time to perform the last rites– their suffering was thus prolonged.

My next court date arrived. Investigative Officer DCP LN Rao was giving his witness account. My lawyer had come well prepared and the proceedings continued for two hours with another date being fixed for the next hearing but the judge was on leave on that day and therefore we got yet another date, nearly a month later. However there were no proceedings on this date either. As I was being led from the lockup, my lawyer's junior met me on the way and informed me that all the witnesses had given their account and my statement would be recorded on 20 March. This date too went without any proceedings. The court was busy with the Nitish Katara murder case for which the accused Vikas and Vishal Yadav were in the dock before the judge. The victim's mother Neelam Katara was sitting on a chair in the courtroom. The policewoman made me sit next to her while she took the date warrant to be signed and stamped. I was then escorted back to the lockup.

Compared to previous years I was brought to court more frequently but there was hardly any progress in my case. Since it was in its final stage, I was more anxious than before; only God knew what was due to me. I repeatedly read whatever case related documents I had in my possession and often took advice from the jail lawyer regarding the case. This was simply to give myself some confidence and hope. I also spoke to the new jail lawyer about my case but I never got a satisfactory reply.

Jail lawyers were not a capable lot. Their objective was to spend the day and go back. All they did was to register the prisoner's name, take her signature or thumb impression which they would then show to the jail authorities to prove that they had indeed provided legal aid to the prisoners who sought their advice. The truth is that if the jail lawyer helped any prisoner they expected to receive a monetary compensation for their service although this was meant to be free of cost.

My statement was to be recorded on 10 April. Just as I was brought out of the lockup I saw my elder brother waiting for me and he started talking to me on the way even though the policewoman tried to restrain him. I told her that he was my lawyer and without bothering about the policewoman he told me, 'The case will be over in less than two months and there is 95 per cent hope that the decision of this court will be in our favour. In case it is not, then you will certainly be released by the High Court.' When I entered the courtroom my case proceedings were under way and the junior lawyer was noting down something. As the policewoman sat next to me on a chair clutching my hand, Ohri Sahib took the other chair beside me and said, 'There is no point in arguing about your bail today as the judge is not in a mood to grant bail. She does not want to drag the case any longer and I am quite hopeful that the decision will be in our favour.' The questionnaire was being prepared now and the answers had to be given after lunch. The judge noticed during this time that the pages had no numbers marked on them and declared that the investigative officer (DCP) LN Rao should be produced before her the next day and I should be produced the day after. The policewoman led me back to the lockup and in this manner my statement was not recorded even that day.

I was once again produced before the judge as directed but within five minutes I was led out of the courtroom with another date as there was another case going on in court then. I had to spend the entire day in the lockup. It is demoralizing for a prisoner to come for a court hearing, be lodged in the judicial lockup repeatedly and yet return without anything more concrete than a date. LN Rao's witness account continued for two days and all other witness accounts were completed a few days later with May 1 being reserved for the defense lawyer's arguments.

I was supposed to be produced before the judge on 27 April and since my statement was to be recorded I was feeling tense and nervous. When I entered the courtroom it was empty; the judge was on leave and my warrant had already been signed and kept for another day so even on this day I suffered inside the lockup the entire day. It was hot and humid with frequent power breakdown. The policewoman barely took me inside before I was back in the lockup. Even for the hearing in May the judge was on leave. I was totally exhausted with these repeated dates that resulted in a vacuum. My back hurt badly and it only got worse by travelling in the prison van which was so uncomfortable.

An ICRC team came to visit me once again, asking about my health and consulting with the jail SMO who was a Kashmiri Pundit woman. She was a good doctor but declined to give those medicines that the ICRC team had prescribed for me. Even though she discussed my health status with the team, she insisted on continuing the same treatment that was prescribed by the jail doctor. After their meeting with the SMO the team spent some time with me and I could sense how sympathetic they felt towards me, particularly due to my deteriorating health condition. This time they had brought a couple of books for me, *Long Walk to Freedom* and *Health Guide* along with some other literature. We were served tea at 3 and the team also drank jail tea from steel tumblers with me. Some of my family members had visited the team in Srinagar to express their concern regarding my health and requested them to arrange for certain medical facilities for me.

Daood had come to visit me with news of my family's well being as well as their growing anxiety regarding my failing health. My next hearing also resulted in the same thing and I returned to jail, burdened with exhaustion, my body, mind and soul saturated with tiredness and disappointment.

A 10-day Vipasana meditation course began the next week and it was mandatory for prisoners in ward 1 which was inside Vipasana, to attend the course but since my case was at its final stage and I was getting dates in quick succession, I did not wish to attend as we were not permitted to go to court during the course. I therefore appealed to madam who then shifted me to ward 2 which was a prisoner ward; under-trial prisoners were not shifted here but since the jail was overcrowded and there was no space in other wards, a few under-trial prisoners were shifted here and kept along with the convicted ones. As I carried my bag inside the prisoner ward, I felt a sense of unease, almost like a warning. I tried to rid myself of this unease and accepted the fact that I had to be here for the next ten days – and as it happened these were spent in relative calm. The tiny cell was hotter than the other one but quieter too. With me in the cell was another undertrial prisoner Nina and a convicted prisoner Siddiqa. We talked late into the night and due to the severe heat; sleep had anyhow vanished from our eyes. In the prisoner ward, the locks remained open all day and were closed only late at night.

On my next court date my brother Doctor Sahib was waiting for me. I was produced before the judge at 2.30 and as soon as I entered I was handed the questionnaire sheet. I took it and sat down on a chair to read it. My brother also sat down and read it along with me, later I put my signature and it was given to the court registrar. Due to the severe heat my brother was constantly wiping the sweat from his face and I felt sad to see him in this condition. I was so embarrassed for him, I could not even talk to him. The questionnaire procedure continued the next day too along with the arguments for nearly two hours but before it could be completed, another date was fixed for the next hearing; 15 May. I was again produced in court at 2.30 but the court was busy with another case and after waiting for fifteen minutes the registrar asked the policewoman to take me back to the lockup and produce me again after one hour. The heat inside the lockup made me restless and caused me a severe headache. The dal had spoiled due to the heat and the roti had turned dry; the taps were dry too. Outside, many Kashmiri men prisoners were being brought out of their lockup to board the waiting bus. One of them gestured his greetings to me from a distance. I was led to the courtroom again at 3.30 and the judge entered after a few minutes and ordered the proceedings to begin. When the prosecutor said that he would begin from tomorrow she told him not to delay it any further as she wanted to complete all the POTA cases. The proceedings commenced and continued till 5.15 pm. Doctor Sahib said that our defense witness will be produced within this month. After the proceedings my lawyer suggested the next date to be 28 May but the judge refused saying that so much time had been given today and the case had to be finalized in the next two days. When my lawyer explained to her that the defense witness had to travel from Kashmir, the judge posted 21 May as the next date.

There seemed to be an inverse proportion to the progress in my case and the mental pressure I experienced. Summer too progressed rapidly and threatened to singe our skin; the sky was breathing fire on us. On 21 May, in the thick of this blistering heat, I was taken to the POTA court at Patiala House but the defense witness was not present. I was told to return on 28 May; the next date. My family members had spoken to my lawyer regarding the possibility of producing defense witnesses in my case but he had said 'I will win this case without defense witnesses, so there is no need to produce one.' The judge was on leave on 28 May so once again nothing happened and now the courts were getting ready to close for the long summer break.

Since many prisoners had lost their lives in the men's jail last year, two water coolers had been installed this year for us; one was placed at the mulaqat jangla and the other in the langar. These were old coolers that had been repaired but no sooner were these installed, that women collected there in large numbers; while no one was willing to fill water in these everyone was ready to pick up a fight to get some cold water. Only a few women had access to the one at the langar because with the support of old prisoners, the langar Munshi hid milk pouches inside the cooler for sale along with cold water. Even the langar in-charge matron Nirmala was involved in this secret deal; and the habshi women always had easy access to the water cooler.

It was a bit of a joke that the authorities had installed two old coolers for 500 inmates. Although I was in ward 1 which was closer to the langar and easier for me to reach, I only went to the cooler occasionally to fetch water. One day, I picked up a jug and went to the langar intending to bring back some cold water but as soon as I entered, the langar Munshi shouted at me and said, 'It is not your father who fills water in this cooler that you can just come and take it.' Nirmala madam was also sitting there. She sprang to her feet and addressed the langar Munshi, 'Throw away her jug.' She then turned to me and said 'If you take water from this cooler, my dharma will be ruined.' Without saying a word, I picked up my jug and left but I did register a complaint with the senior madam. She called the matron while asking me to return to my cell but I did not get to know any details of their meeting. However, both the matron and Munshi had to face peshi because of which they turned even more hostile to me. Nirmala matron asked the women inmates working in the langar to carry the cooler and place it outside the langar. The coolers were now placed at the chakkar but they were hardly used then. As in the previous years, we lived through yet another ferocious summer.

> *Zarra zarra hai mere Kashmir ka mehman nawaz*
> *Rah mein pathar ke tukdon ne diya pani mujhe*
> *(Braj Narain Chakbast)*

Every particle of my Kashmir is hospitable
Pieces of stones offered me water on the way

Due to the complaint I had registered against the langar Munshi and the matron, they started an elaborate campaign against me in which they managed to mobilize many other inmates. They found different ways to inflict mental torture on me, they abused and cursed me. When I stepped outside the cell some of them would even spit on me and be sarcastic. I was at the edge of my patience. The langar Munshi's mother was also in jail – she'd been there for the last 13 years and together, they bossed over everyone else; supporting them was one Sharda Jain who had been convicted in the Atma Ram murder case. She considered herself to be a Congress Party Councillor. She was hostile to me the day she set her eyes on me and began to try her best to malign me to other inmates and the staff. She was always in attendance to the staff, being sycophantic to them while the langar Munshi kept the same corrupt staff on her side by secretly supplying them various items from the langar. It therefore did not matter to her that there were any number of complaints against her. In this state of disempowerment, the only option left for me was to write to the NHRC, and I sent a copy of my letter to the State HRC. This led to local newspapers publishing the letter I had sent regarding the mental agony I had to suffer on a daily basis. The chairperson of SHRC sent a communiqué to the DG Prison (Tihar) that the matter should be investigated. As this news spread in jail it brought about some transformation among these foolish women. The DG sent an investigative officer to jail to meet me and record my complaint personally. It was afternoon when the chakkar Munshi came to call me to meet this officer and when I arrived, the senior madam, DS madam and a gentleman were sitting in the DS room. I removed my footwear and asked for permission to enter the room. Senior madam informed me that the DG had sent an investigative officer to talk to me but I could see that she was in a foul mood; none of the staff wanted that any complaint should be registered with higher authorities during their term of employment as it reflected poorly on their own employment record. When the officer asked me about my complaint in front of the DS and SI, I told him in a straightforward manner all that I had to including the fact that head matron Nirmala had sought money from me. My blunt speech did not go down well with madam. She was not able to comprehend the extent of harassment I faced from these women prisoners and the matron and had I taken this step earlier I would have perhaps been spared the kind of humiliation and hardship that I had to bear. The officer wrote down the details of my complaint and assured me that in future I would not be harassed in this manner. Soon after the officer left, the news spread in jail that he had come to meet me personally and record my complaint; it took the wind out of Sharda Jain's sails and those of her group of women inmates. Sharda was wicked and cunning but cowardly. However, there were many other women prisoners who were glad and felt relieved that I had taken such a bold step; they knew it was for the benefit of all those who were victims of such harassment.

I did not wish to take up any quarrel with anyone as my case was in its final stages but some women prisoners were bent on ruining my life. I had earlier tried to resolve things by myself but these women were determined to wield power over me and keep me under their control. Since I avoided interacting with them, this was their way of pulling me down and to show me in a poor light to others. They thought that I perceived myself as Iflatoon, a philosopher, whereas in their view I was a professional terrorist and the distance I maintained from them became a sore point for them. On the contrary, I was only trying to maintain my own peace of mind and dignity but they thought I was trying to be superior. They maintained their enmity with me until the time I was released from jail.

It was a fellow Kashmiri prisoner, Ahsan Untoo in jail 7 who had brought the local dailies back with him from Srinagar (where he was taken for hearing in his own case) in which news reports regarding my condition in jail had been published and the letter to SHRC reproduced. These newspapers had reached the jail authorities including SI madam who was both upset and cautious with me. After this, even the jail staff began to maintain caution with me.

The next day, head matron Nirmala sent another matron to my cell with a request that I should withdraw my complaint. She feared formal proceedings for bribery against her. A couple of days later she came on her own to my cell and started talking to me in an affectionate tone that was new to me, saying we should all live amicably in jail. Was I not a fanatic Muslim terrorist in her eyes anymore, I wondered. A few days later there was a letter against her from Police Headquarters but SI madam rescued her by writing in her favour.

Nirmala matron told me, 'I have a black tongue and whenever I curse someone it comes true.' Unlike me, women prisoners were afraid of this and therefore gave in to her whims because most of them had personally heard how she cursed prisoners for the worst punishment to be imposed upon them. When all her efforts to intimidate me failed she tried to ensure that I became isolated and alone; she urged other women inmates not to talk to me as I was 'an enemy of the nation' and this found a resonance among patriotic women who supported her. I simply ignored them as well as their attempts to discredit me. However, the langar Munshi Raj Rani was removed from langar duty which brought a bad name to her and also impacted her money-making ventures. Most prisoners were untouched by even a thought of self respect; the ones who loudly showcased their supposed patriotism found it turning cold as it was not a genuine sentiment but just a way to denigrate me.

For insensitive people, to maintain a grasp over their dignity is a battle in this war-of-Lanka. Despite many constraints I tried my best not to take favours from anyone which was the direct opposite of the practice in jail. But in return, what did I get? My peace of mind was snatched away from me and it was almost impossible to find a like-minded companion in jail.

Once the court vacations were over, I was produced in court. On the first date, there were no proceedings. I was again produced before the judge on two dates. The case was reaching its final stages and the proceedings continued on a regular basis for nearly two months.

The judge was going to pronounce her decision on 28 September. I had tea at 7 and got ready to go to court. At 7.30 I was taken to the deorhi and boarded the bus for the POTA court at Patiala House. I was produced before the judge around 3 pm. My hands and legs were trembling and each step I took was heavy as lead. With my entry in the courtroom began the shuffling of papers and documents. Doctor Sahib was pacing up and down in a state of nervous restlessness. I was made to stand in the dock at 4 pm when Judge Ravinder Kaur announced her judgment, awarding me a five year jail term while exonerating me from the Terrorist Act. Bells were ringing in my ears. There was so much noise and commotion around me that I felt as though I was inside an iron manufacturing factory; it muffled the voice of the judge, I could not hear her words. I felt that I was orbiting in thin air with my own voice only an echo. I think the judge was telling the policewoman to release my hand from her tight grip; she left my hand. Doctor Sahib was telling me something which I could not follow. I was perhaps telling the judge that I was innocent. She was telling the lawyer something which I could not hear nor comprehend.

My lawyer was arguing while my tears flowed without stopping. The policewoman made me sit on a chair. Doctor Sahib's eyes were moist as he sat beside me and tried to console me. The proceedings ended by 4.30 pm. The policewoman grabbed my hand again and as we climbed down the stairs, there was a tiny room into which she led me; it was here that my hands and feet were dipped in black ink and I was made to hold a black slate with my name written on it. A photographer was taking my pictures and those who were passing by stopped to look at me. At 5, I was made to board a vehicle that took me to Tihar jail. At reaching the deorhi and after the mandatory search I was not allowed to enter but treated like a Mulaheza and made to go through a medical checkup. My name was then entered into a register and I was handed a prisoner card with 100 as my prisoner number (Prisoner number 100) with a list of hard labour written on it. Inside, my cellmates were waiting for me and guessed from the look of my face that the news was contrary to our expectation. Many inmates collected at the cell to give me solace and strength but there was not a single teardrop in my eyes; I had turned to stone by now.

The next day I was lodged in the prisoner ward and given space in a cell with an old prisoner, Shakila Amma. This ward was suffocating as every cell was filled with belongings and odd things. Some prisoners had been languishing in this ward for 8-13 years; their faces were different from others with the bitterness of years etched in them. None of them spoke to the other with any degree of softness or affection; each one more irritable than the other. Each face was dull; this ward belongs to the living dead, I thought. Their day was spent in hard labour, a burden that each one tried to free herself of.

The jail authorities were in a dilemma about what kind of hard labour to allot to me but considering my educational qualifications I was given work related to reading and writing. Jail authorities had a big teaching project from Jamia Milia Islamia University with all the necessary equipment provided to the jail. As usual, the matrons swiped their share from the teaching material too. Although of good quality, the material was not much use as most women prisoners were not inclined to study but I went to class at 9 each morning. Like other prisoners, I was also provided with a jail uniform, oil and soap, a pair of slippers and 250 grams of milk.

The ward was very noisy as every prisoner had a radio and there was a television set in nearly every cell. There were frequent quarrels amongst the prisoners but the staff preferred not to intervene where old prisoners were concerned. All the inmates of this ward were working because of which the locks opened relatively early and shut late. Having spent all day at work, most of the women liked to relax watching TV or listening to the radio. Earlier, the TV had many entertainment and news channels but presently only one news channel was relayed. The women inmates therefore made an appeal to madam to renew the Star channel so they could watch their favourite 'saas-bahu' episodes. My health began to deteriorate soon after I was lodged in this ward, I was rapidly gaining weight and I was not able to sleep without sedatives given by the 'brain doctor'. Raj Rani, her mother and Sharda Jain were also lodged in this ward. They enjoyed standing in front of my cell and laughing loudly at their own jokes (but meant for me) but I had decided not to complain anymore as I was now well aware of their difficulties and their psyche.

MY RELEASE

I CHALLENGED THE Session Court judgment against me in the High Court and it was on 8 December 2007 that I was finally released by the High Court after completing five years in jail as an under-trial. My elder sister had found release from the prison of the world on the very day that I was released from Tihar jail. The 'scene of release' is a mighty emotional one; the years spent in jail with other women prisoners and sharing the collective pain and suffering creates a mutual bond among the prisoners – eating together, quarreling and fighting, nurturing love and friendship and then to suddenly separate from each other forever without the possibility or the desire of meeting again, all these are peculiarities of prison life. Release is effected after 7.30 in the evening when the entire jail is under lock and key; this ensures that one is not able to meet one's comrades at the time of release.

Outside at the gate, my brother Doctor Sahib had come to receive me. He had parked his vehicle at gate 2 of Tihar to avoid the media glare and the police that was deployed to keep the situation under control. When I took my first step outside the gate, my legs gave way, and I could not walk; I had lost the habit of walking without my hand being held. I was exhausted walking from jail 6 to the gate as I had also lost the habit of walking even this much. When Doctor Sahib opened the door, I sat in the vehicle with him and after reaching a certain point, he asked the driver to stop the car as I was feeling dizzy. He got down and asked me to also step out of the car; look at the sky and the stars. Breathe in this open, fresh air, he was telling me. Today, after five years I saw the moon and the stars. I was overwhelmed with a strange sensation, and with a sudden tiredness. My brother took out his mobile phone and made me speak to my mother Boba.

I was bereft of emotion, there was neither happiness nor a sense of sorrow. I seemed to have stepped into a world of its own kind, I was in a state of delusion, not being able to decide if I was still in jail or a free being now.

I am a free person today but the wounds and scars that the jail has inflicted on me are not only difficult but impossible to heal. The jail has left indelible, deep imprints on the core of my being along with several serious, complex questions that echo in my mind and I continue to seek answers to them.

Much has changed in these five years. The political situation in Kashmir was different now. The Hurriyat's unity had scattered, for one. The guides and conductors of the movement have turned into rogues. The sentiment for freedom has metamorphosed into political one-upmanship.

My eyes were searching for those willing to sacrifice their lives for our dear nation. The hard labour of those who had offered many sacrifices in their mission and struggle for Azadi was being waylaid by the looters whose factions had taken root everywhere. The very people who had been willing to make sacrifices for our nation had now turned into its enemies. Their frightening, true faces were now being revealed. In this storm, I was looking for those comrades who believed in the prosperity, success and Azadi of our community. The only ray of hope was to see that hordes of common enthusiastic people (as opposed to leaders) still nursed the sentiment for freedom. It seemed like the movement had taken a new turn; lakhs of unarmed people had come out on the streets demanding Azadi and shouting slogans that reverberated to the skies for days, a non-violent agitation against the mighty Indian state. Holding burning torches in their hands, people walked the streets night after night. However, the GoI remained rigid and brutal in its attitude and behaviour. Hundreds of unarmed people were arrested under the draconian PSA (Public Safety Act) leading to a fresh round of hartals or strikes. Indiscriminate firing by the personnel of the Security Forces on peaceful, unarmed protestors led to the death of many. Indefinite curfew was imposed repeatedly, affecting people's lives and livelihoods. The Security Forces did not spare our women, our daughters either; the sordid tale of their exploitation stretched from Kunan-Poshpora in the past to Shopian in recent times. As for me, I had returned from hell and was ready to join the struggle again.

> *Nisar mein teri galiyon ke aye watan ke jahan*
> *Chali hai rasm ke koi na sar utha ke chale*
> *Jo koi chahne wala tawaf ko nikle*
> *Nazar chura ke chale jism o jan bacha ke chale*
> ----
> *Hai ahle dil ke liye ab yeh nazm bast o kashad*
> *Ke sung o khasht muqeed hain aur sug azad'.* (Faiz)

I am devoted to your lanes oh my country where
It has become a norm to walk without raising your head
When a lover is out to roam the streets
His glance is secret, his body and soul unsafe.

This poem is open and shut for the followers of heart
As the stones and pebbles are locked and the dogs free.

Appendices

These appendices include poems, pieces of writing and letters that the author refers to in her narrative.

1

Some One to Count on, Someone Who Cares

When the world has lost its lustre you never lose your faith
in me and some how through clouds I find my winds....
You are my light in the darkness
Laughter in the night
And all the things that keep me
Going on life's unwinding road
You are a special kind of person
A unique and caring friend
I know I am really lucky
And I wish every one
Could have a sister like you.

(From *The Times of India*)

2
Sister Act

To Baji

A sister is a part of your life that you can never separate from. Whether she's older or younger, through all your formative years, sisters share your pain and sorrow, your happiness and joy even when you're not aware that they're there.

A sister protects you from all harm and is always near when you need her. She's a friend who listens when others turn away. She brings sunshine where there are clouds. She is like a breath of spring through the storms of winter, a guiding star in this darkness of night. She smiles at you when others frown and welcomes you with open arms. She accepts you for who you are and doesn't expect you to be anyone else. She thinks that you are the best, and makes you feel so important that you start to believe it yourself. There is no one like a sister... And there is no sister like you.

Sister Act – II

To Neelji

When things do not go as planned. You're the first one there beside me.

3
A Letter to My Brother

20 October 2005
C/J. Tihar

Respected dear Bhai Lala

Aasalamu-Alikum

I really don't know where to begin this letter and it is with a heavy heart that I am writing today, this being my first communication with you.

The sad calamity that has befallen you has hit me with the same intensity as it has hit you. When I heard this news I was shattered and the whole world stood still for me. After the trauma of Bahanji's passing away this episode is one which will have the worst bearing on all of us in the family.

Deep down in my heart I feel guilty, thinking that may be in some way my situation that has caused this trouble for you. It really pains me but I am helpless.

I pray to Almighty Allah to look after you, shower His blessings and guide you through these difficult times, I am positive and sure that HE will. I am with you mentally and feel every bit of pain that you are going through and regret this distance at a time like this.

There is nothing that I can say to lessen your grief and trauma except pray. Please remember that I am always proud of you and love you dearly. You hold a very special place in my heart.

Love and regards to Jiji. Mosa and Massi.

Yours Loving

(Zama) Anjum Zamarud Habib

4

National Human Rights Commission Faridkot House
Copernicus Marg

New Delhi - 110 091

Dear Sir/Madam

With regards I am submitting this application for sympathetic consideration.

1. I Anjum Zamarud Habib am in Tihar Central Jail No.6 Under POTA from Feb. 14-2003. From day one I have been harassed mentally and tortured by some inmates, backed by some jail staff members.

2. Though I have been booked under POTA, I am not a terrorist but I am constantly being harassed by being called a Kashmiri terrorist, which really hurts. I have tried a lot for the last four years to adjust and to avoid any kind of confrontation but in vain.

3. For the last three years one head Matron Nirmala has made my life hell. She is constantly demanding money which I cannot afford. She is also using some convicts to harass me. Raj Rani and her mother Battu are here in this jail for the last 12 years. They are very arrogant and "dada" type ladies. Raj Rani/Inderjeet is the day Langar Munshi, she has a hold on some immates (CT/UT) working in the langar. Sharda Jain (Ex.Councillor of the Congress Party as she calls herself) is a close friend of Raj Rani. They have been provoking some immates to tease and harass me. (Sharda Jain is in jail in connection with the murder case of M.P. Aatma Ram of the Congress Party).

4. Last week I went to the langar for cold water (for the first time a water cooler had been placed in jail). They did not allow me to have water from that cooler. Raj Rani/Inderjeet shouted at me and used filthy language and said, "This water is not for Kashmiri terrorists" and when I reported this to the In-charge staff member of the langar H.M. Nirmala she also screamed at me and said that if I took water from the same cooler it would harm her religion – "Mera dharam brasht ho jayega."

5. Whenever I come out of my cell these people make rude remarks and pass comments H.M. Nirmala stops other inmates from talking to me. They want me to be confined to my cell.

6. I am in deep depression as they are always ready to have a fight and beat me. I do not know what to do. I feel all alone being the only Kashmiri woman in this jail. I feel insecure and there is a threat to my life.

I am waiting for justice.
Kindly treat this application as very urgent.
Looking for your cooperation.

Thanking you,
Sincerelyn Yours,

Anjum Zamarud Habib
POTA UT (Hawalati)
C-J 6 Tihar New Delhi - 64

Dt. 08-06-2007

Copy to : SHRC (Srinagar)

∞

5

A Letter to My Advocate

To Advocate V.K. Ohri
Patiala House Courts Delhi
Ch. No. 236

Dear Sir,

I trust this letter finds you at your best. As you know, life for me is at its lowest ebb. I am at a loss about what is happening in my case.

My case is being looked after by the best expert in the field. I have vested my trust and faith not only in your expertise but in your person as well. In my mind I know that you will succeed in your endeavour to get me released from this hell (Inshahallah). However the conditions of my life, the stagnation in everything, and the traumas I have to live through are very hard.

I would be most grateful if you could make it a point to finalize my matter favourably, now that my file is in the concerned court. (Patiala House Courts).

I reiterate that I have the highest regards for your capabilities – but like anybody in my situation I am eager to end this torture as soon as possible, which you can do.

With regards,

Sister Anjum Z. Habib
C/J6, Tihar New Delhi 64

Dt. 21-06-2005

6
A Letter to the Prime Minister of India

His Excellency
The Prime Minister of India
Prime Minister's Office
Delhi

Subject : *Participation of Women in Kashmir Talks*

Respected Sir,

I, the undersigned am currently in judicial custody in Tihar Jail since February 2003, and have been booked under POTA. I felt overwhelmed and could not stop myself from writing to you when I learned about your call to the political leadership to think out of the box regarding Kashmir.

In the last three years of judicial custody I have remained always connected to the Kashmir cause for which I had been truly involved at a personal level.

I seek to take your kind self and travel with me down memory lane so that you can see the untold pain and agony of my people in the last two decades.

Women have paid the price in Kashmir as in any conflict area in the world. The crime of a woman Jala Bano was that she tried to stop the army from beating an innocent school-going boy of 14 years for which she was butchered.

The rape of 13-year old girl and an 80-year old woman in Kupwara only points to many more such cases and has been an eye-opener for the world community.

Can any nation expect that an 11-year-old boy, who saw his mother being raped before his eyes by the Indian forces, will feel passionate about being a subject of the Indian State:

I had started working for women – subalterns – very early in my life. I started an awareness campaign regarding dowry and other social evils in Kashmir and got a positive response from all sections of society as the issues were of common concern to all. After militancy erupted in the valley, women were the worst sufferers – they lost husbands, brothers and sons, they were raped and humiliated at the hands of Indian forces, psychological torture was designed to undermine their confidence and psyche. All this compelled me to raise my voice against all these atrocities. I founded the Women's Welfare Association in my home town Islamabad which was later turned into an umbella organization namely Muslim Khawateen Markaz which rendered its services to all irrespective of caste, colour and creed in a purely non-violent mode. Due to its growing popularity Muslim Khawateen Markaz was affiliated to the All Parties Hurriyat Conference as its social and human rights wing, being a founder member and the only one representing women in the conglomerate.

I am individually committed to the cause of upliftment of Kashmiri women. I have been falsely implicated by the police at the behest of some individuals whose objectives were frustrated by my work and the healing touch it provided to the women of Kashmir. There is a long way to go to free women from the clutchjes of suppression, atrocities, crimes and violence committed against them.

There are so many human rights violations in Kashmir that it has become the moral duty of every Kashmiri to raise his or her voice against them. The woman dies in silence. In a religious and conservative society like ours, she is unable to articulate her sufferings and her disgust over the deep humiliation she suffers.

My submission therefore is that a personal effort be made to include women in the dialogue process. I as a woman plead for the voice of women and the participation of women in equal and fair measure. I trust that this submission will be received as a representative voice. I am looking forward to the real meaning of your statement on 18.02.06: 'Our government wants to involve all men and women of goodwill, in a dialogue to end suffering.' I am looking forward to a peaceful solution of the Kashmir problem, a solution that upholds the principles of justice, euqality, freedom and dignity.

My good wishes are with you. May God grant us all peace.
Submitted Respectfully

Anjum Zamarud Habid
Central Jail No.6, Tihar, New Delhi

Dated 23.02.206